THE
JIANGYIN
MISSION
STATION

THE JAMES SPRUNT STUDIES IN

HISTORY AND POLITICAL SCIENCE

PUBLISHED UNDER THE DIRECTION OF

THE DEPARTMENTS OF HISTORY AND

POLITICAL SCIENCE OF THE UNIVERSITY OF

NORTH CAROLINA AT CHAPEL HILL

VOLUME 61

EDITORS

JOEL WILLIAMSON, CHAIRMAN

WILLIAM L. BARNEY

THAD L. BEYLE

MICHAEL R. McVAUGH

RICHARD J. RICHARDSON

LAWRENCE D. KESSLER

THE JIANGYIN MISSION STATION

AN AMERICAN

MISSIONARY

COMMUNITY

IN CHINA,

1895–1951

THE UNIVERSITY OF NORTH CAROLINA PRESS   CHAPEL HILL AND LONDON

Library of Congress Cataloging-in-Publication Data
Kessler, Lawrence D.
The Jiangyin Mission Station : an American missionary community
in China, 1895–1951 / by Lawrence D. Kessler.
p.   cm. — (The James Sprunt studies in history and political
science ; v. 61)
Includes bibliographical references and index.
ISBN 0-8078-5062-4 (pbk. : alk. paper)
1. Presbyterian Church in the U.S. — Missions — China — Chiang-
yin shih — History.   2. Presbyterian Church — Missions —
China — Chiang-yin shih — History.   3. Missions, American —
China — Chiang-yin shih — History.   4. Missionary
settlements — China — Chiang-yin shih — History.   5. Chiang-yin
shih (China) — Church history.   6. First Presbyterian Church
(Wilmington, N.C.) — History.   I. Title.   II. Series.
BV3425.C48K47   1996
266'.5151136 — dc20   95-41591
CIP

00 99 98 97 96   5 4 3 2 1

THIS BOOK WAS DIGITALLY PRINTED.

For Bonnie

CONTENTS

ILLUSTRATIONS

MAPS AND TABLES

ACKNOWLEDGMENTS

Over the many years this study has taken shape, I have discussed my ideas on the American mission movement in China with numerous colleagues whose comments have helped sharpen my focus and argument. Foremost among them are scholars also working in China mission studies, notably Daniel Bays, Li Li, Judith Liu, Kathleen Lodwick, Jessie Lutz, Murray Rubinstein, Tao Feiya, and Peter Chen-main Wang. Others who offered useful critiques, bibliographical suggestions, or research advice include Laura Walters Baskett, David Buck, Paul Howard, Michael Hunt, Irwin Hyatt, Louisa Kilgroe, Terry Lautz, Donald Mathews, John Thomson, Tom Tweed, Grant Wacker, and John Witek. I thank them all and hope they find my study worthy of their efforts.

I am grateful to Ruth Worth and Alex Moffett, both of whom served as missionaries at Jiangyin along with several other members of their families, for willingly sharing their memories and their papers, and to Mrs. Charles Worth for allowing me to peruse her husband's papers about his missionary work in China. I only regret that Ruth, who maintained a constant interest in my research, did not live to see this account of the mission and her family reach print.

At the First Presbyterian Church of Wilmington, North Carolina, the Reverends Robert Hewett and Douglas Vaughan graciously allowed me to pore over church records and poke around church storehouses to uncover many useful materials relating to the China missionaries whom the congregation supported for half a century. Gibbs Willard, the church historian, was most helpful in locating relevant church records and photographs. Connie Evans, the church secretary, deserves special thanks for giving so generously of her time and providing assistance in innumerable ways to facilitate my research and to make my several visits to the church such pleasant experiences.

I also wish to thank two former directors of the Historical Foundation of the Presbyterian and Reformed Churches in Montreat, North Carolina, Kenneth Foreman and Jerrold Brooks, and the former librarian, Mary Lane, for their unfailing courtesy and help in accessing the very rich archival resources of the Southern Presbyterian Church located there. Following the reunion of the Northern and Southern Presbyterian denominations, the archives at Montreat have been reorganized and renamed as the Department of History and Records of the Presbyterian Church (U.S.A.). The current staff, especially Diana Sanderson and William Bynum, were helpful in the finishing stages of bringing this manuscript into print.

I also acknowledge the help of the staffs of the Southern Historical Collection at the University of North Carolina, the Manuscript Collection of Perkins Library at Duke University, the Presbyterian Historical Society in Philadelphia, and Union Theological Seminary in Richmond.

The Research Council of the University of North Carolina provided partial support for research and publication of this project. I gratefully acknowledge the council's generous assistance but bear sole responsibility for all statements, opinions, and conclusions contained in the book. Paula Wald at the University of North Carolina Press skillfully edited the manuscript and saved me from numerous infelicities of expression and argument.

Finally, I extend a special note of appreciation to my good friend and historian of American–East Asian relations, Burton Beers, with whom I have collaborated on a number of projects. His encouragement and advice from the beginning propelled me forward on this project, and his wisdom and good cheer remain a constant source of inspiration.

THE
JIANGYIN
MISSION
STATION

1

RIVERSHADE

INTRODUCTIONS

In April 1925, a group of American Protestant missionaries in China erected a large tent in the middle of the city where they were stationed in preparation for celebrating the thirtieth anniversary of the beginning of their work in that community. The celebration in itself would not be worthy of much comment. This particular station was not a pioneer in the American mission effort in China; it was, in fact, established fairly late in the game. Nor were any of its personnel well-known members of the mission force in China.

What is significant about this event is the participation in the celebration of the city's notables, including the "mayor" and many prominent businessmen and scholars. They presented the missionaries with a number of gifts and lauded their contributions to the welfare of the city. How had these foreigners earned such praise and esteem from their hosts at a time when nationalistic sentiment was running rampant in China?

The tale is a fascinating one and justifies a careful study of the life of this particular mission station in the city of Jiangyin[1] in the eastern coastal province of Jiangsu. But the history of this station provides more than a good story. An in-depth study of this fairly typical American missionary community can reflect more broadly on the nature of American interaction with China during a half-century of momentous change, from the late nineteenth century to the middle of the twentieth century, placing local history in the context of national and international history.

Within the limited scope of this study, my central concern is whether and in what ways this missionary community fit in with the local Chinese society. As the opening account indicates, the Jiangyin missionaries at one point had achieved a measure of integration with their Chinese community. But their success, I will argue, was based on certain secular activities rather than the religious message they sought to spread. One can conclude, therefore, that the Protestant missionary movement in twentieth-century China was most successful when it proved itself useful in secular ways.

This study began as an outgrowth of a public education program I helped organize a number of years ago on North Carolina's historic ties with China. I realized very quickly that significant untapped archival and human resources that would be valuable in examining Sino-American relations were near at hand. Furthermore, many of the participants were advanced in years and failing in health, so the task of preserving their memories and papers was urgent.

I came to concentrate on the Jiangyin mission station because several of its missionaries were still alive, because very detailed documentary records of the station were available in several archives and in private hands, because the station's work had educational and medical as well as evangelical dimensions, and because some possibility existed of examining the station's history from a Chinese as well as an American perspective.

The Jiangyin mission station was maintained by the Southern Presbyterian Church (Presbyterian Church in the United States, or PCUS). Most studies of American missions in China have focused on northern denominations, using materials drawn from the files of the American Board of Commissioners for Foreign Missions. Southern Presbyterians have generally been neglected, but the denomination's rich archival resources as well as personal and institutional resources specific to the Jiangyin Station afford a fairly comprehensive look into the life of that station and its involvement in the dramatic changes China was undergoing at the time of its operation.

The Southern Presbyterian Church broke away from its northern counterpart during the American Civil War to form a separate denomination with its own Board of Foreign Missions. In 1866, the PCUS board sent out its first missionaries to foreign lands, including one to China. The PCUS was one of the smallest of the mainline Protestant churches and one of the last to enter the overseas mission field, but it came to assume a leading role in foreign missions. In 1907, an interdenominational agreement assigned to the Southern Presbyterians responsibility for designated areas in several countries with a combined population of 25 million.[2] Within a decade, among the nine major American Protestant churches, the Southern Presbyterians ranked first, on a per member basis, both in the number of missionaries sent abroad (about 9.5 per 10,000 members) and in the amount of support for foreign missions (about $1.50 per member).[3] Most of the PCUS mission force and investment was in China, where it operated fourteen stations in the lower Yangzi province of Jiangsu. The PCUS divided its China field into two sections, the North Jiangsu Mission and the Mid-China Mission, separated by the Yangzi River. The Jiangyin Station was under the jurisdiction of the latter.

This study will focus on the mission station and its inhabitants, their attitudes, and their relations with the Chinese at certain critical points in modern Chinese history—the anti-Christian riots of the late 1890s, the fall of the empire in 1911, the warlord and revolutionary movements of the mid-1920s, the Japanese invasion of China throughout the 1930s, and the Communist triumph of the late 1940s. The missionaries were on the cutting edge of the penetration of American and Western institutions and values into China, and they consequently were among the first to experience the Chinese (and Japanese) reaction to that penetration.

An account of the Jiangyin Station leads to a consideration of many of the key issues concerning Chinese-American relations, such as Westerners' role as a force for social reform and modernization, the corrosive effect of Christianity on Chinese life, the relationship between Christian missions and Western imperialism, the growth of Chinese anti-Christian and antiforeign sentiments, foreigners' use and abuse of extraterritoriality priv.leges, the devolution of authority from Westerners to the Chinese in social institutions (churches, schools, and hospitals), and the impact of mission work in China on American attitudes and church organization.

How did the Jiangyin missionaries respond to the opportunities and challenges present in twentieth-century China? How was their Christian message received? What was the relationship between their religious and secular work? How did their work change in response to political and social upheavals? What role did they play in the lives of the communities that hosted them? What contribution did they make, along with missions elsewhere in China, to the modernization of that country? What, in the end, did they accomplish?

These questions may seem to be ethnocentric and mission-centric, and until recently, the search for the significance of missions in China has largely been a Western enterprise. But now the Chinese also have begun to consider seriously the nature of the Christian missionary movement in modern China. No longer are they content to dismiss the entire effort as simply a part of Western imperialist aggression. In the openness of the post-Mao era and with attention turned to economic and political development, Chinese scholars are trying to assess the contributions missionaries and Christianity made to the development of modern China.

The story told here is based mainly on missionary sources, including interviews with several of the Jiangyin missionaries, the missionaries' personal papers, station reports published in missionary journals, private letters and the circular letters sent home by all Southern Presbyterian missionaries, and the archives of the denomination's Board of Foreign Missions. But Chinese sources are not lacking. In the past decade, a series of articles published in the Chinese journal *Jiangyin wenshi ziliao*, some by Chinese who had been involved in the mission work, traced the history of the station and its institutions and evaluated its impact. Additional Chinese sources on the Jiangyin Station have been discovered, and they have been used to supplement the very full missionary record. It should be noted that missionaries were probably the most knowledgeable and perceptive foreigners in China. Most of them spoke Chinese well (usually the local dialect), and unlike foreign businessmen or government officials, missionaries were in constant contact with the Chinese in the small towns and villages, not just in the treaty ports. If handled carefully, missionary sources can provide a China researcher with a rich and intimate picture of the social and political conditions within the missionaries' field of operations.

One valuable set of data was found at the First Presbyterian Church of Wilmington, North Carolina, with which the Jiangyin Station had a special relationship throughout its more than fifty years of existence. One of the station's early pioneers, George Worth, was a Wilmington native and the grandson of a governor of the state. James Sprunt, an elder of the church and a prominent textile merchant, was the station's main benefactor. The Woman's Auxiliary of the church, in cooperation with other churches in the Wilmington Presbytery, tirelessly raised the funds needed to build and maintain the mission hospital at Jiangyin. The Wilmington church, in fact, became the first in the Southern Presbyterian denomination to assume responsibility for a specific mission field in China, the Jiangyin Station. The Jiangyin church was considered the "spiritual daughter" of the First Presbyterian Church. Matching the Wilmington church's zeal in supporting the mission effort was its care in preserving all materials relating to that mission, including letters from missionaries recorded in the weekly bulletin and minutes of the Woman's Auxiliary meetings.

The country about which Jiangyin missionaries wrote home and in which they were trying to effect a major ideological and cultural change was beset by enormous problems, many of them caused or exacerbated by the Western penetration of China since about 1800.[4] Under the leadership of the British, Western traders were opening up China and seeking commercial and political advantages there. In their wake came secular and religious missionaries promoting Western values. Also around 1800, China's internal difficulties mounted. Population growth began to outstrip the country's ability to increase agricultural production. Added to this potentially explosive situation were administrative mismanagement and corruption. The Chinese government was now faced with the classic "internal disorder/foreign aggression" combination that had led to the downfall of earlier dynastic regimes. By the mid-nineteenth century, a series of crises confronted China.

Militarily, China suffered the first of many defeats at the hands of outsiders in the Opium War (1839–42), so-called because the British insistence on maintaining their very profitable trade in the drug precipitated a clash with the imperial government. The Taiping revolutionary movement erupted in the 1850s and for over a decade controlled a large part of south China, and smaller rebellions kept the government on edge for some time after that. In time, international incidents provoked other wars with Britain, France, Russia, and Japan. As a result, by the end of the century, foreigners had forced China to its knees and had gained enormous privileges codified in a series of "unequal treaties." These included the right to reside in certain cities, the right to station troops there to protect foreigners' lives and property, exemption from Chinese laws (extraterritoriality), control over the setting of duties on the importation of goods, and the right to propagate Christianity.

Intellectually, some Chinese leaders began to question the value of their traditional way of life and their cultural roots (generally referred to as "Confucian," although other intellectual streams nourished them) and the ability of traditional methods to steer China safely through the storms of the modern world. Disillusioned intellectuals began looking for guidance to Western values that later came to be epitomized as "science and democracy" and to a variety of "isms," such as liberalism, pragmatism, capitalism, individualism, socialism, and Marxism. This iconoclasm became stronger in the twentieth century, reaching an apogee in the New Culture and May Fourth movements of the late 1910s and early 1920s.

Politically, the Chinese (as an ethnic distinction) began to question the legitimacy of their government, some because it was headed by Manchus (who had conquered China and founded the Qing dynasty in 1644), and some because it was an authoritarian anachronism and yet, paradoxically, too weak by the late nineteenth century to defend China and provide effective rule. The strong political and economic development of neighboring Japan, a country the Chinese had long seen as subordinate to and influenced by China, only made matters worse and provided reformers and revolutionaries with a readily available model for change. The culmination of their efforts came in 1911 when the old imperial regime was overthrown and a new-fangled form of government, a republic, was established, founded on "democratic" institutions.

The dawn of this new age, however, was not exactly rosy. Weak republican institutions gave way to militarists ("warlords") who imposed their rule, or rather misrule, on China until they were swept away by revolutionary nationalism. Two revolutionary political organizations emerged in the 1920s:

the Nationalist Party (Guomindang, or GMD) and the Chinese Communist Party (Gongchandang, usually referred to by its English acronym, CCP). These parties competed with each other — sometimes peacefully but for the most part through force of arms — for the next thirty years, each seeking to assume the mantle of nationalism, reunite the country, and restore China's rightful place in the world order as a powerful and respected nation. Chiang Kai-shek (Jiang Jieshi) led the GMD to power in 1928, but he was never able to eliminate the CCP as a political and military threat.

Throughout this period, the foreign presence in China remained strong. Japan enlarged its presence and eventually engulfed China in another war from 1937 to 1945. Merging with the international conflict after Japan's attack on Pearl Harbor in 1941, the Sino-Japanese War devastated China's economy and tore apart its social and political fabric. The postwar years quickly gave way to a renewal of the civil war between the Nationalists and the Communists. Finally, in 1949, the Communist forces overcame their rival. On 1 October, standing on the rostrum of the old imperial palace overlooking Tiananmen Square, Mao Zedong proudly proclaimed the birth of the People's Republic of China and announced that "the Chinese people have stood up" and removed the imperialist powers from their country. Included in the removal was the entire Christian mission force after nearly a century and a half of work.

The geographical setting of our story is the city of Jiangyin on the south bank of the mighty Yangzi River, about 100 miles upriver from Shanghai. The two Chinese characters of the city's name literally mean "river-shade," referring to the city's location on the "yin" side, which in China's traditional yin/yang cosmology means the south or shady side, of the river. Arriving by steamer, passengers were transferred in mid-river to a ferry that took them to a north-side landing, where they then could hire a small boat to cross the river to reach the city. Traveling to Jiangyin became easier after 1926, when a landing was built on the south side of the Yangzi so passengers could alight directly from river steamers. The nearest city of any size was Wuxi to the south, which could be reached by boat along the canals that crisscrossed the area. Jiangyin was also the capital of the county (or district) of the same name. As such, it contained the government office (*yamen*) of the district magistrate (*xianzhi*), whom some foreigners referred to as "mayor." In the early decades of the republic, the county had a population of about 600,000, distributed in about 50 small market towns and 5,000 villages. The city itself contained about 50,000 residents.

Jiangyin County, shaped roughly like a rectangle thirty miles long and fifteen miles wide, was a rich agricultural region, producing rice, soybeans, cotton, and silk. The level fields of the Jiangyin plain were surrounded by

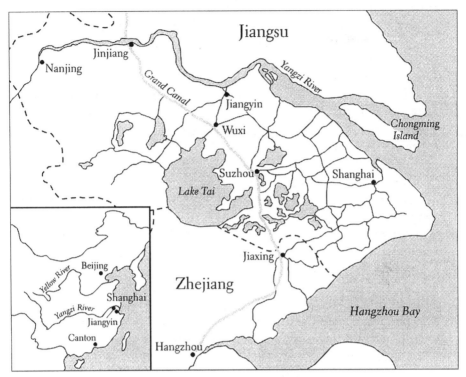

Map 1-1. Jiangyin and the Yangzi Delta Region
Source: Based on map in John Fairbank et al., *East Asia: Tradition and Transformation*
(Boston: Houghton Mifflin, 1973), p. 481.

low mountain ranges that stretched south and east toward Shanghai. One of the missionaries, Virginia Lee, described an imaginary aerial view of the surroundings: "Could you be on the top of either eminence [Flower Mountain or Chicken Mountain], this plain would seem a patchwork of tiny fields of golden rice and emerald mulberry groves [for sericulture], embroidered with blue canals, beautiful to behold."[5] The canals may have been sparkling to the eye from a distance, but they posed constant problems. Fed by the Yangzi, they were often brown and thick with mud. The main canal to Wuxi had to be dredged about every ten years, and the smaller ones about every five years. When water rose quickly in the Yangzi, many canals became so swollen that some villages were inundated and houseboats could not pass under the bridges.[6]

Since the tenth century, Jiangyin has been seen as a strategic point for the defense of the upper reaches of the Yangzi River from naval attack. Although it is some distance from the sea, some have called Jiangyin the "mouth of the Yangzi" because the river first narrows (to about one mile) at this point. In

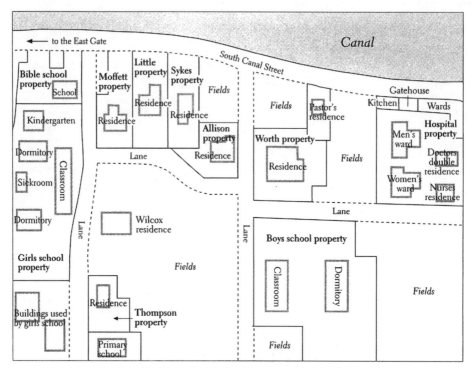

Map 1-2. Jiangyin Mission Station at the East Gate
Source: Based on 1940 map in Lacy I. Moffett Papers, copies in possession of author.

the Ming dynasty (1368–1643), the government strengthened the city walls
and built ramparts along the river. In the 1640s, Ming loyalists in the city re-
lied on these fortifications to launch a furious but ultimately futile resistance
to the advancing Qing armies.[7] The Qing government and successor regimes in the twentieth century further fortified the city, making it the military stronghold of central China. Its walls of brick and stone were thirty feet
high and were supported on the inside by an earthen embankment ten to
twenty-five feet thick. Just north of the city walls, forts were constructed
along the river on low hills that rose abruptly a few hundred feet from the water's edge. The forts were guarded by a garrison of 2,000–3,000 troops and
were equipped with 6-, 8-, and 12-inch cannon trained on the river to command the traffic. These guns also could be, and on occasion were, directed
southward toward the city, thereby holding it hostage to the troops controlling the forts. A number of warships remained anchored in the river at the
foot of the forts. Because of its strategic location, the city has often found itself at the center of fighting between rival combatants in modern Chinese
history.

Founded in 1895, the Jiangyin mission station was located just outside the walled city, near its East Gate. Unlike other stations in which the buildings were all situated behind one big compound wall, in the Jiangyin Station, each building was enclosed by separate walls. The station expanded in size and scope over five decades, halting its work at several junctures due to unsettled political conditions. It finally closed after the establishment of the People's Republic of China in 1949.

In exploring the microcosm of the Jiangyin Station and its relations with the larger Jiangyin community, this study will cast light (and shadows) on the American interlude in China prior to the Communist ascension to power in 1949.

2

CARRIED AWAY

BY A TIGER

OPENING THE

JIANGYIN STATION

The Jiangyin mission station was established during the height of Chinese xenophobia, fanned by decades of increasing foreign invasion in the late nineteenth century. It was a time of violent reaction to Christian missionaries, who were seen as agents of Western cultural penetration into China and also as rivals to the local gentry in offering leadership and protection to the community. The initial years at the Jiangyin Station were, consequently, a harrowing experience for its founders.

For several years, the Southern Presbyterian Mission in China sought to establish a presence in a city north of Wuxi. Three of its missionaries, George Hudson, Hampton DuBose, and John Paxton each had visited Jiangyin (or Kiangyin, as the missionaries transcribed the name) many times before they were finally able in the spring of 1894 to rent a small house for a base of operations. Before any missionary was assigned to the post, however, the station was abandoned due to strong opposition from the local gentry and the district magistrate. The former organized a protest demonstration in June, and the latter proclaimed that although foreigners would be protected, any natives who entered their service would not. Some interest in the mission existed, however, among the inhabitants of Jiangyin, and some of them traveled to nearby Wuxi to visit the missionaries there.[1]

A second attempt in 1895 to open a station at Jiangyin encountered the same determined opposition. Eventually, a larger building was secured, but only after the American consul at Jinjiang, A. C. Jones, intervened. The Reverends Hampton DuBose (who had founded a mission station at Suzhou in 1872)[2] and R. A. Haden (a native of Louisiana who had come to China four years earlier and at this time was stationed at Wuxi) had first presented the Jiangyin magistrate, Liu Yan Kwang, a letter from the consul requesting permission to rent land and open a station. Liu initially dismissed them without a reply. Consul Jones and the two missionaries then approached the Jinjiang *daotai* (circuit intendant) for help. In the conduct of Sino-American relations, U.S. consuls were afforded direct access to customs *daotai, who generally were charged with the supervision of foreign affairs in a given port and its surrounding area. Daotai*, in turn, usually left the actual conduct of foreign affairs to the local prefects and magistrates.[3] In this instance, the Jinjiang *daotai*, surnamed Lü, directed Magistrate Liu to cease his opposition to the missionaries. Finally, in May 1895, Haden rented a building and took possession of it in the company of two native Christians, one an ex-soldier and the other a day school teacher.[4] Reverend DuBose returned to his family and work at Suzhou, leaving the recently widowed Haden to carry on alone.

Haden's first year at Jiangyin was spent repairing the station building, treating patients with simple diseases (reportedly seeing over 700 patients in one month), doing some preaching, and trying to make friends among the populace. A *North China Herald* correspondent visiting Jiangyin in the fall of 1895 reported that the people had a friendly attitude toward the station.[5] In September, the Reverend Lacy Little, a native of North Carolina who had just arrived in China, joined Haden in this fledgling operation. Little spent his early days there tackling the mysteries of the Chinese language with the aid of a local scholar who knew no English. Before the establishment of language schools for missionaries in the large centers of China, private tutoring on the job was the only method of acquiring competency in Chinese. Haden and Little eventually converted the station building into more usable living and working quarters. Under the watchful and curious eyes of neighbors — who Haden was convinced were spies for the local gentry still opposed to their presence — they installed flooring and erected partitions to create five rooms. Each missionary had a room for lodging and study, and the remaining area was converted into a chapel, a supply room, and a kitchen.[6] On occasion, they decorated the house with golden azaleas fetched from nearby Flower Mountain in order to add, as Little wrote, "a touch of brightness to our bachelor quarters."[7]

It was not long before the climate of suspicion and opposition fostered by the local elite produced an ugly confrontation that quickly led to official U.S. intervention.[8] The house used by Little and Haden had been rented in May 1895 for ten years from a landlord, surnamed Shen, who was willing to deal with the "foreign devils" because he was an opium addict and in dire need of cash. Even though the two Americans had paid five years' rent in advance, within the year the landlord sent a representative, Huan Chi-yao, to demand a $100 payment for the doors and windows of the house, which Shen claimed were not included in the original rent. Huan, identified in the sources as a "quack doctor," apparently had acted as the middleman in securing rental property for the missionaries in 1894 and 1895. He also may have been an opium addict because he frequented a little shop in town known to be an opium den. Huan reportedly had sought a loan from the missionaries earlier but had been rebuffed. Now, in late April 1896, Haden and Little refused to satisfy Huan's latest demand as Shen's representative, which they took to be preposterous and extortionate. Quick on the heels of Huan's visit, the landlord himself came to clear up the matter. After some discussion, the missionaries agreed to extend their lease for another year (from ten years to eleven) and to advance one more year's rent. To celebrate the conclusion of this deal, the landlord hosted a feast for Haden and Little and other friends but notably excluded Huan, with whose services he was dissatisfied.[9]

At this point, the two young missionaries may have thought the incident was over and that they could return to their primary task of gaining the trust of the community and attempting to attract its people to the Christian message. But it was not going to be that easy. The presence of foreign missionaries in China's interior towns and villages produced an atmosphere of suspicion, anxiety, and tension. The local elite considered Christian doctrine superstitious and a challenge to the Confucian humanism of which they were the caretakers and beneficiaries. They also resented the missionaries as usurpers of their traditional role as educators of the people and guardians of the community welfare. Within the community, Christian converts were regarded as cultural traitors who had abandoned their Chinese heritage and neglected communal obligations when they conflicted with their new religious beliefs. For example, protected by government decree in 1881, converts frequently refused to contribute money and labor in support of ceremonies honoring deities of local religious cults.[10]

Two very specific causes of friction between missionaries and the local populace are particularly relevant to our story. Property transfers involving foreigners were a constant source of unrest. According to the Berthemy Convention of 1865 between France and China, French missionaries had the right, also claimed by other foreign nationals by virtue of their most-favored nation clauses, to rent and purchase land in the interior in support of their evangelizing work.[11] In 1894 and 1895, French authorities repeatedly pressured the Zongli Yamen, China's foreign office, to reaffirm these rights, and the Chinese government issued several proclamations calling on provincial officials to observe the Berthemy Convention regulations and not to obstruct the purchase of property by missionaries.[12] But local resistance was not so easily assuaged. As Arthur Smith, a senior American Board missionary in China at the turn of the century, noted ruefully, "Whenever there has been friction securing property, which is not unlikely to have been the case whenever any mission has had occasion to buy, there are always old scores which some one is glad to settle by the lurid light of a riot." [13]

Likewise, popular fantasies and rumors about necromantic rituals in the practice of missionary medicine (such as using human eyes and brains to concoct prescriptions) could always be stirred up by those who wished ill of the foreigners. Mary Carleton, who opened a missionary clinic near Fuzhou, Fujian, in 1894, one day faced a mob who shouted, "We know what you are doing! You tear out babies' eyes and boil them up to make your medicines." [14] Haden, as related earlier, had also practiced basic medicine, so the Jiangyin Station was susceptible to charges of this sort. Lacy Little, writing thirty years later, recalled the precariousness of their situation:

> It will be easy for the reader to imagine how inexplicable to the natives of Kiangyin was the presence of two unmarried Americans in their midst. It was altogether "too good" to be told that we were taking up our abode in this city simply to be of some benefit to them. It was much easier to believe . . . that we were the representatives of the American government in disguise, spying out the land, to be followed at no distant day by armed battalions who would seize the country at the point of the bayonet. Such suspicions as these [were] accompanied by rumors that foreign missionaries were known to have used the bodies of little children for the manufacture of medicine. [15]

Despite such a frank admission of the potential dangers facing their mission, when trouble came, Haden and Little professed that it caught them by surprise, "like a clap of thunder from a clear sky." [16] The fateful events unfolded on 12 May 1896, during the height of what the *North China Daily News* of Shanghai dubbed "the riot season" [17] and about a fortnight after landlord Shen had sent Huan Chi-yao to demand additional rent. Huan marched into the chapel that afternoon with "a number of rough characters" and accused the missionaries of mutilating the bodies of children to extract their eyes and brains and then burying them on the station grounds. They demanded entrance into the yard to conduct a search, but Haden stopped them by drawing a pistol and proclaiming that "he would use it on the first man who touched the door." In the meantime, his colleague and a Chinese assistant rushed to find the district magistrate. By the time they returned over an hour later with the magistrate and a dozen runners, a crowd of several hundred people had gathered.

The missionaries invited Magistrate Liu to search the grounds to prove they were innocent of the charges. After nothing was found, the magistrate ordered Huan to substantiate his claims. Huan at first hesitated, then went to a spot near the base of the compound wall and began digging under a pile of rubbish. After some effort, he unearthed a package wrapped in coarse matting. Huan opened it, and to the horror of the Americans, who had watched the proceedings from the back porch of their house, the object proved to be a dead infant about eighteen months old (whose eyes had been gouged out, according to a Chinese account).[18] Haden and Little could offer no explanation for this surprising turn of events to the magistrate, and as the grotesque package was passed through the crowd, a surge of anger swelled. Brandishing poles, knives, hoes, and reaping hooks and yelling "kill the foreign barbarians," the crowd pushed forward. Magistrate Liu and his men, all unarmed, could not, or would not, control the situation. Again drawing his pistol, Haden kept the crowd at bay while Little grabbed a chair and dashed to the back wall. The two men clambered over the wall and took off at full speed, their coattails flying, for the nearby forts at the river's edge. Pursued by the screaming mob, they ran over a mile to the forts, where they were given protection by the imperial military authorities stationed there and their chief foreign instructor, Captain John Jürgens of Germany. Jürgens had befriended the missionaries earlier and had recently promised to help them obtain a concession of land to build a Christian hospital in Jiangyin.[19] Thwarted in their efforts to wreak vengeance on the foreigners, the crowd returned to the missionary compound to loot and destroy the property. The missionaries' Chinese assistant and servants were taken into custody by the magistrate.[20]

Out of immediate danger, Haden and Little contemplated the day's events and considered their next step. Should they abandon the mission post in the face of such obvious anti-Christian agitation? What were Huan's motives, and where had the dead infant come from? Would the Jiangyin magistrate, who had been so hostile to them from the beginning and who had not taken decisive action to prevent the riot from occurring, be willing or able to get to the bottom of this matter? Several puzzling incidents of the past week came back to them. One day, they recalled, the widow next door claimed she had heard noises the night before in the missionaries' yard, but nothing had seemed out of order. The following night, the missionaries' servants surprised a man in the backyard, but he escaped before they could apprehend him.[21] Could there be some connection between these incidents and the discovery of the baby's corpse? They decided to travel to Jinjiang the next day, 13 May, to inform the American consul and seek government aid. Upon hearing their story, Consul Jones promptly contacted the Jinjiang *daotai*, who sent a deputy to Jiangyin to investigate. Jones also notified the American consul-general at Shanghai, T. R. Jernigan, who consulted with the commander of the U.S. cruiser *Boston* about the possibility of sending it upriver to Jiangyin as a show of force (it was not sent, however).[22]

News of the riot spread quickly through American and Chinese channels. Haden, who seems to have been something of a hothead, wrote several articles about the incident. One such account appeared within a week in the *North China Daily News* and was read by Charles Denby, the chargé d'affaires of the U.S. legation in Beijing. On 17 May, the Zongli Yamen informally notified Denby of the Jiangyin disturbance.[23] This news of Jiangyin came at a time when the U.S. government was reevaluating its policy on missions in China. Earlier, it had rejected missionary claims to protection for their work in the interior, but the increasing friction caused by the missionary presence caused American officials in China to shift their stance. By the mid-1890s, according to a noted historian of United States–China relations, "Washington had dramatically broadened its definition of missionary rights and demonstrated its willingness to defend the exercise of those rights, even in the face of undiminished Chinese opposition."[24]

Prompting this change of policy was a series of anti-Christian incidents preceding the one at Jiangyin. Members of the American missionary community in China, for their part, in 1895 drew up a list of demands they urged their government to press on Chinese officials in the wake of these xenophobic outbreaks: an immediate investigation into the incidents; the punishment of wrongdoers regardless of position or status; the punishment or dismissal of local Chinese officials within whose jurisdiction the incidents occurred; the issuance of a statement by the central government recognizing missionaries' rights of residence; the reimbursement of missionaries' losses; and the release of a formal proclamation from local officials welcoming missionaries back to their posts.[25] American missionaries also perceived a reluctance on the part of Great Britain, the dominant Western power in China at that time, to deal effectively with missionary-related incidents. The prominent missionary Arthur Smith decried Britain's "frustrating feeble-forcible policy," which permitted Chinese officials to resist foreign demands to uphold the treaty rights of missionaries.[26]

American diplomats in China, and the secretary of state in Washington, D.C., now saw an opportunity to establish the United States as a major power in Asia by taking a strong stand in support of the missionaries. In June 1895, the American minister in Beijing urged the Chinese government to order officials in the Yangzi area to take precautions to ensure the safety of missionaries there. A few days later, the Zongli Yamen directed all Manchu generals-in-chief, governors-general, and governors across the empire to issue proclamations granting protection to foreign missionaries and their churches.[27] In the following year, American officials pressed additional demands on Beijing: formal recognition of the right of Americans to reside in the interior and to buy land there as stated in the Berthemy Convention and the assigning of responsibility for any attacks on missionaries in their provinces to governors-general and governors, permanently barring them from holding office. Although at this time the Zongli Yamen accepted only the first of these demands, an imperial decree in the *Beijing Gazette* of 17 January 1898 later placed responsibility on high provincial authorities.[28]

In the context of this newly assertive policy, Charles Denby's report of the Jiangyin incident to Washington, D.C., prompted a strong response that largely echoed the missionaries' demands of 1895. The U.S. government officially requested the severe punishment of the Jiangyin magistrate and the local headman (*dibao*) for neglect of duty in not preventing or controlling the riot. Charges against the *dibao* stemmed from a report (which was never confirmed) that an inflammatory placard had been posted in the vicinity of the missionaries' house. The *dibao*, the government reasoned, should have been aware of the potential for violence and notified the magistrate.[29] The United States also insisted that the Jiangsu provincial authorities post proclamations denouncing the riot and explaining why the local officials were being punished.[30] W. W. Rockhill, the acting secretary of state, confided to Denby that the punishment of local officials was more important in this case than any monetary indemnity that might be awarded.[31]

The consular authorities' consideration of the use of a cruiser as a show of force and Rockhill's focus on the punishment of local officials involved in the Jiangyin riot revealed America's new commitment to demanding Chinese adherence to treaty obligations. Some missionaries professed an aversion to relying on this sort of political intervention and protection for their efforts, but Haden and Little, as noted above, were not among them. Little, in fact, became an ardent advocate of consular assistance. Later in 1896, an article in the *Missionary* exhorted missionaries to avoid appeals to consuls and ministers because they "are fraught with failure in establishing the spiritual kingdom." Little, with the Jiangyin riot fresh in mind, replied in the pages of the same journal with arguments justifying the action he and Haden had taken:

When we allow an infuriated mob to come upon the mission premises and destroy our property, without reporting it to the proper authorities, are we not encouraging deeds of violence and robbery? And are we faithful trustees of the property of the church which is placed under our control? . . . I contend that one of the best ways to maintain and advance the eternal principles of right and justice in this land is to hold the Chinese authorities responsible for deeds of violence and bloodshed, by appealing to the proper representatives of our own government, who are placed here for our protection. And, I contend furthermore, that when an individual missionary allows the property of the church to be destroyed by mob violence without demanding reparation for the same, he proves himself unfaithful to the trust committed to him, and thereby makes less secure the lives of all the other men, women, and children who have been sent to bring the light of the gospel into this darkened land.[32]

Back in Jiangyin, the mystery surrounding the riot of 12 May was unraveling. On 13 May, a woman whose child had died in late April went to its grave to burn incense. She found the coffin had been opened and the body removed. Chinese friends of the missionaries, who at this time were in Jinjiang, heard of this incident and convinced the woman to report it to the magistrate.[33] The latter, with the aid of the deputy sent from Jinjiang by the *daotai*, began an investigation into a possible link between the missing body and Huan Chi-yao's activities. Within a few days, the owner of the suspected opium den frequented by Huan, Tsiang Suk-chu, divulged the plot he and Huan had concocted that had led to the riot. Huan, as related earlier, had suffered several setbacks at the hands of the missionaries. He was refused a loan and had "lost face" by being excluded from the landlord's feast concluding the doors-and-windows incident. He therefore was determined to seek revenge and discussed an extortion scheme with Tsiang. They decided to accuse the missionaries of mutilating a child for nefarious medicinal purposes and to demand a payoff to keep quiet. They hired a town loafer, a man named Chen, to dig up a newly deceased infant and bury it in the missionaries' yard. It was Chen who was seen escaping over the back wall just a few nights before the riot. Huan and Tsiang claimed they planned to approach the house with only several other people, but many more showed up as word of the accusation circulated, and the situation got out of control.[34]

The court condemned to death the three principals and dispensed minor punishments to fifteen other people involved in the riot. Huan and Chen were to be decapitated for desecrating a grave, and Tsiang was ordered strangled as an accomplice. Huan and Chen died before their sentences could be carried out, reportedly by taking poison in prison,[35] but Tsiang eventually had his sentence commuted to permanent banishment. His reprieve may have been due to intercession by the missionaries, whom it is said he had befriended when they first arrived in Jiangyin. Haden and Little expressed doubts to Consul-general Jernigan as to Tsiang's guilt and suggested that Huan had implicated him for having divulged the plot. They also believed that his confession in court had been obtained through torture. Consul Jones, who had been present at the formal trial held by the *daotai* at Jinjiang, denied the use of torture, reporting that each defendant had only been forced to kneel on a coil of iron cable to give his testimony. Nevertheless, the American legation in Beijing raised the issue with the Zongli Yamen. The latter reproached the missionaries for questioning the fairness of the trial and indicated that it had instructed provincial authorities to deal severely with this case.[36]

Several months later, in October 1896, while Tsiang's case was under review by the provincial judge in Suzhou, a convention of Presbyterian missionaries in Shanghai again called for diplomatic intervention. Charles Denby once more approached the Zongli Yamen to request a delay of the hearing until Consul-general Jernigan could be present. The Chinese authorities refused on the grounds that the case was not being reinvestigated but merely reviewed according to regular procedures.[37] The final disposition of Tsiang's case, however, may have been affected by the Chinese awareness of American sentiments.

Besides their efforts to help Tsiang in the judicial process, Haden and Little attended to him spiritually. They visited him in jail before his banishment and gave him a Bible and some other Christian literature. The missionaries' efforts on Tsiang's behalf appear to have been effective. In 1906, they heard from a China Inland Mission representative in the northwestern province of Gansu that Tsiang still retained the Bible and was leading a Christian life. Later the exile's sister also became a Christian after being cured of an illness by the missionaries.[38]

The Jiangyin magistrate, Liu Yan Kwang, also suffered for his role in the affair. As Acting Secretary of State Rockhill had instructed from the start, the punishment of local officials was of paramount importance to American policy. Consul Jones demanded that Liu be degraded in rank and dismissed from office for his opposition to the missionary efforts from the outset and more specifically for his failure to afford protection to Haden and Little at the time of the incident. Jones noted that the magistrate had come to the scene of the riot with only unarmed runners and had not sent for soldiers from the nearby forts. The Jinjiang *daotai*, Lü, was cooperative and promised Jones that his demand would be met. But action was deferred for about six months to enable the magistrate to pay the indemnity to the missionaries of about $9,000 (which the *daotai* had advanced) and to arrange for the missionaries to secure title to new property, as Consul Jones also had demanded. Finally, in 1897, the governor of Jiangsu, acting on orders from the Zongli Yamen in response to American pressure, dismissed Magistrate Liu.[39]

The missionaries were completely exonerated of any wrongdoing, and the magistrate posted a proclamation explaining the facts of the case.[40] With their indemnity, Haden and Little began to repair the property, completing the work by the end of 1896, and returned to their evangelical and medical activities. Relations with the native population were still marked by tension and distrust. Some Chinese feared the missionaries would seek revenge, and few people visited the station. Slowly, however, the missionaries made progress in breaking down the barriers through, in Haden's words, "uniform kindness, the practice of medicine, and earnestly following up any who seemed to be in any way interested." [41]

Among the larger Chinese Christian community, the Jiangyin Station was acquiring a heroic reputation. At a Christian conference held in Jiangyin in 1900, one of the Chinese preachers recalled the riot of 1896:

> There is a story I have heard of a child who was snatched and carried away by a tiger. He was recovered, bleeding and with great scratches on his face and forehead. The doctor examined him and said he was not so bad after all, and he would get well. And the little boy's fame began to grow. People from far and near came to see the wonderful child that had been carried away by a tiger and still lived. And he found it was not so bad to be scratched up after all, and he would get well. People would take pride in saying that they were the uncles and cousins of the boy who was borne away by a tiger and lived. He found he had gotten to be quite a somebody.
>
> So it was with Kiangyin. A few years ago we heard of the riot. We did not know much about it, except that we had a special concern because it was our own mission. The tiger had done his work, but now they were back from the clutches of the tiger all right again, and we are glad to claim kin with them. [42]

The tiger in the story, of course, represents the initial opposition to mission work at Jiangyin, and the little boy represents the station. After the station survived the riot, and the Chinese perpetrators were punished, the missionary effort gained an air of legitimacy that enhanced its chances of success.

3

AGGRESSIVE
ALL ALONG
THE LINE

LAYING THE

FOUNDATIONS

OF MISSION WORK

By the end of 1897, the Jiangyin Station did indeed seem to be "back from the clutches of the tiger," and the increased interest shown by the Chinese warranted additions to station personnel and property. At the suggestion of Samuel H. Chester, the visiting secretary of foreign missions of the Southern Presbyterians, the Mid-China Mission decided to abandon the Wuxi Station twenty-five miles to the south, which had also begun operation in 1895, and transfer its missionaries and building funds to Jiangyin to make one strong station.

The Wuxi personnel who came to Jiangyin included Dr. and Mrs. George Worth and three members of the McGinnis family: the Reverend James McGinnis, his widowed sister, Anna Sykes, and their mother, Mary ("Mother McGinnis," as she was affectionately called). The Reverend R. A. Haden, whose first wife had been Julia McGinnis, a sister of Reverend McGinnis, had remarried in 1897. The other pioneer of the Jiangyin Station, Lacy Little, had married Pauline DuBose, daughter of the Reverend Hampton DuBose of Suzhou, in June 1896, but she died in July 1897.

With the additions from Wuxi, the Jiangyin Station flourished. George Worth took over the medical duties, James McGinnis and Little took up itinerating, and Haden was temporarily engaged in constructing additional buildings for the station.[1] The new magistrate, proving to be friendlier to the missionaries than the previous one, facilitated the purchase of desirable property on which to build additional residences.[2]

Before examining the growth of the evangelistic, medical, and, eventually, educational work of the Jiangyin missionaries, it is necessary to delineate the organization of mission fields in China. The control center of a field was the mission station, which was located in a city or town, protected by extraterritoriality, and staffed by several missionaries and a much larger number of Chinese assistants. Typically, the station walls encompassed Western-style residences for the staff, a chapel, a dispensary or hospital, and a school.

One historian has described these stations as "outposts" providing "something like back-home levels of hygiene and comfort, physical security from harassment, and psychological refuge" in an alien environment.[3] Andrew Allison, an educator at Jiangyin, referred to his Chinese surroundings as "a terrible environment to live in just as a part of it, — not largely insulated and isolated as we missionaries and our immediate associates live." Missionary Charles Worth likened his return to the station after an evangelistic swing through the countryside to a "trip from hell to heaven."[4]

If the station was an "outpost," then the street chapels set up in town beyond the missionary compound at strategic gathering places can be seen as "beachheads" where missionaries distributed religious tracts and engaged in informal preaching to attract nonbelievers. Reverend DuBose, a pioneering Southern Presbyterian missionary, described the missionaries' forays into heathen territory:

> The street chapel is the missionary's fort, where he throws hot shot and shell into the enemy's camp; the citadel, where he defends the truth; the school, where he teaches the A.B.C. of heaven; the home, where he loves to dwell; the altar, upon which he is laid a living sacrifice; the church, in which he worships; the throne, on which he rules the minds and hearts of the heathen; the happy land, where he enjoys communion with his Maker; the hill of Zion, where he sings sweet songs; the gate of heaven, where the angels ascend and descend.[5]

The militaristic imagery DuBose employs here was common in mission literature and speeches. A speaker at the first convention of the Student Volunteer Movement for Foreign Missions in 1891 issued a ringing call to arms: "This is a council of war. In the tent of the Commander we are gathered. . . . Here are his subordinates, the heads of departments, the under captains, and here are the volunteers in the army."[6] The most famous expression of this imagery came in 1922 with the publication in China of a study of missionary progress entitled *The Christian Occupation of China*.[7]

Beyond the relative security of the urban stations and street chapels, Western missionaries periodically ventured into the surrounding countryside, where they established branch operations. Here, in the small market towns and villages, grass-root evangelization occurred, and here independent Chinese Christian churches arose. These local Christian congregations were often served by a Chinese pastor, and self-sufficiency was at least an attainable goal since they did not maintain the elaborate and costly institutional work

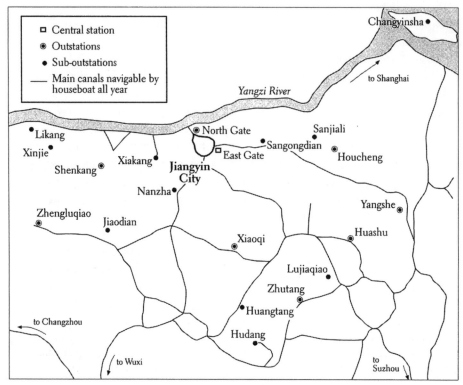

Map 3-1. The Jiangyin Field
Source: Based on undated map in Lacy I. Moffett Papers, copies in possession of author.

of their urban counterparts. The itinerating trips, as the missionary visits were called, served as the main link between these country congregations and the central station.

The Jiangyin mission field was organized in a hierarchical fashion, with the central station just outside the East Gate of the county seat controlling a network of outstations and sub-outstations in the market towns to the east, south, and west of the city. Towns with an organized group of Christians who worshipped at a chapel and had a resident preacher were outstations; sub-outstations had no resident preacher. Small pockets of unorganized Christians in other towns and villages attended church services in nearby outstations or sub-outstations until they were ready to organize more formally. These Christian congregations, including congregations with resident preachers, were all part of the mission movement and were guided by the central station. Only when a local group supported itself financially was it organized as an independent church in full control of its affairs.

After the Jiangyin Station reopened and its staff was augmented by the transfers from Wuxi in 1897, the three evangelists (Haden, Little, and

James Sprunt Male Academy high school boys preaching in local jail, with
director Andrew Allison (at left) in background, wearing hat, 1924. (Kiangyin Station
Photographs, Presbyterian Church in the United States Missions, China, Department
of History and Records, Presbyterian Church [U.S.A.], Montreat, N.C.)

McGinnis) began to preach and to distribute literature throughout the
Jiangyin field. In the city, they frequented tea shops, temples, markets,
crowded street corners, and public gathering places. One special place they
visited was the city jail. Little gained permission in 1898 from the local magistrate to conduct services behind prison walls for the inmates. About ten
inmates assembled in a small room to hear the foreign preacher. Some
of the prisoners were literate, prompting Little to leave behind Christian tracts.[8] He and his colleagues continued to visit the jail regularly
for many years to come. Women evangelists ministered separately to the
female population of the jail. The prison authorities were always cordial
to the missionaries because, as Charles Worth later noted, "we preach law
and order" and, in a material vein, because they often provided bedding
and food.[9]

    As for the "outfield work" in the Jiangyin field, Little took responsibility for
the western section, McGinnis for the southern section, and Haden for the
eastern section. After McGinnis left Jiangyin during the Boxer troubles,
Little added the southern section to his itinerating duties. Anna Sykes accompanied Little to work among the women and children, whom, according
to custom, male evangelists could not approach.[10]

Sprunt Academy brass band traveling by boat to help celebrate the dedication of a new chapel at Xiaoqi, an outstation in the Jiangyin field, 1914. (Kiangyin Station Photographs, Presbyterian Church in the United States Missions, China, Department of History and Records, Presbyterian Church [U.S.A.], Montreat, N.C.)

Outstations in the countryside were created as demand warranted. Pioneer Christians and enquirers (those with a professed interest in the Gospel and in studying to become a Christian) in an outlying town or village would travel to the main station or an established outstation for weekly services and special religious meetings. As their numbers grew and they appeared financially able to open their own chapel, they would rent quarters or acquire the use of a house in their native locale. These initial facilities often were donated by one of the more prosperous Christian converts. As church membership continued to grow, funds would be raised through a subscription drive to purchase land and build a larger, more permanent structure.

The oldest sub-outstation in the Jiangyin field was established at Sanjiali, a small hamlet about twelve miles east of the city. In the fall of 1897, a young man from that village began to come to Jiangyin regularly on foot for Sunday services. After several months, the Sanjiali enquirers numbered about ten, and the Jiangyin missionaries decided to send a Chinese assistant to the village to conduct worship services and attend to their spiritual needs. The enquirers at first rented a three-room house for five years as a chapel, one of them assuming immediate financial responsibility on the condition that three-fourths of the cost be reimbursed later by the other enquirers. When the lease was up in 1902, they erected a new building with their own labor and partly with their own funds. No records are available to determine how much of the total cost of $800 was raised by foreigners, other than a $50 con-

Crowds attending the opening of the new chapel at Xiaoqi, 1914. (Kiangyin Station Photographs, Presbyterian Church in the United States Missions, China, Department of History and Records, Presbyterian Church [U.S.A.], Montreat, N.C.)

tribution from Captain John Jürgens, a German military instructor at the Jiangyin forts.[11]

A comparable pattern of institutional development occurred at Xiaoqi, a market town ten miles south of Jiangyin. Initially, the local Christians and enquirers rented a large room in a house to serve as a chapel, and another room nearby was later rented to accommodate separate meetings for women enquirers. By 1914, the congregation launched a drive to fund the building of a two-story structure, with a 300-seat chapel and schoolroom downstairs and residences for a pastor and a schoolteacher on the upper floor. Two-thirds of the $500 construction costs came from the Chinese congregation of eighty-five professed Christians and twenty enquirers, and the remainder was donated by the missionaries. In November, the new church was dedicated in splendid fashion. The brass band from the newly established boys school at the main station came down to drum up, quite literally, crowds of curious onlookers for the three-day ceremonies. Missionaries and native preachers conducted evangelistic services, church officers were selected, and ten babies were baptized as Christians.[12]

The countryside presented a great opportunity as well as a great challenge. The urban populace was not very receptive to the Christian message in the beginning. Only after the missionaries proved themselves useful in secular ways (by offering such services as medical care, education, and peacekeeping) were they successful in the city. But in the countryside, wrote Lacy

Little in 1899, the "simple country people . . . not so hardened in sin as the upper classes . . . give more willing ears and more responsive hearts to the claims of the Gospel." At the same time, however, working with the down-trodden peasants was a daunting prospect. Climbing Flower Mountain with his friend George Worth, Little looked out over the Jiangyin countryside and brooded over the immense challenge it presented: "A feeling of oppression, accompanied by an intense longing, came over me as I contemplated the condition of these perishing multitudes. . . . It may truly be called the region of the dead, however — of the spiritually dead, whom only the Spirit of God can awake to a new life and righteousness."[13]

It would be a few years, however, before Little and the other Jiangyin missionaries could act on their grand vision of awakening the "region of the dead" to the Christian message. In 1899 and 1900, the Boxer rebels launched attacks on foreigners in China, particularly in the northern provinces. Although Jiangyin was not threatened seriously, largely due to the determination of provincial leaders in the Yangzi valley not to tolerate attacks on foreigners,[14] missionaries in the interior nevertheless evacuated their stations as a precaution. Lacy Little and Anna Sykes and her young daughter had left Jiangyin in May 1900 for home leave, and the remaining personnel (the Hadens, the Worths, and Mary McGinnis and her son James) withdrew from the field shortly thereafter. The missionaries had asked a trusted Chinese friend to frequent tea shops and gather news, and he warned them in June that for their own safety it was time to leave. As they left to board a steamer on the Yangzi River for Shanghai, a thunderstorm forced them to seek temporary shelter in a farmhouse. Its occupants were startled by the presence of the "big-nose" foreigners until the Worths' two young sons, both born in China, began chatting with them in Chinese.[15]

Station work continued under the guidance of a Chinese evangelist. Lacy Little, returning to China in October 1900 and remarrying, made two visits to Jiangyin that fall with the permission of the American consul-general in Shanghai. He discovered that no acts of violence had occurred in the area, despite rumors and posted threats, and that Chinese Christians, for the most part, had remained faithful. They had not returned to idolatry, he reported, but some had been lax in observing the Sabbath.[16] In January 1901, the Littles returned to the station, Ella Little (the former Ella Davidson of Hangzhou) being the first woman permitted to return to the interior after the Boxer uprising, and the Hadens followed in September.[17] With the abatement of antiforeign sentiment after the demise of the Boxers, the missionaries expanded their work in all directions — evangelistic, medical, and educational. A few years later, a visitor to the station concluded his report by noting, "The Kiangyin Station is aggressive all along the line of mission work."[18]

Evangelical work in the Jiangyin field expanded rapidly in the first few years of the new century. This was particularly true at the outstations, which from the start outpaced the work at the central station in Jiangyin. The eastern section, under Haden's care, grew the most. Another single woman, Rida Jourolman, joined the force in 1904 to help with the country work. Two Chinese evangelists also began to itinerate with Haden. Lacy Little increasingly devoted his time to preaching in the city and looking after the central station and itinerated only to a couple of nearby towns he had worked with from the beginning. In 1903, church membership in the Jiangyin field totaled 92, and there were 138 enquirers. By 1905, the figures had risen to 156 and 823. The great bulk of the communicants that year came from the seven outstations in the Jiangyin field, with only 14 members (less than 10 percent) recorded at the newly organized church at the East Gate station. The trend continued for the next two years. In 1907, the reported figures were 298 members (with 67, or 22 percent, at the central station) and 839 enquirers.[19]

The rapid growth at the outstations vis-à-vis the main station in these years caused some friction between the two senior members of the station, Haden and Little. The latter apparently felt that too many unsuitable enquirers in the countryside were being admitted to church membership by Haden, who was largely responsible for the outstations. Haden had a reputation for being "unusually successful in winning and teaching groups of enquirers,"[20] but his success appears to have been due to a less vigilant attitude than his colleagues in accepting members. He published a catechism in 1907, called *Outlines of Gospel Truth*, that a reviewer noted was written in very simple Mandarin and would be useful only to the very ignorant.[21] It is likely that the primer was based on his own evangelistic practices, which would explain his colleagues' complaint that too many of the converts had little understanding of the Gospel. In 1908, the Mid-China Mission discussed the matter at length and decided to transfer Haden to Suzhou and replace him at Jiangyin with Lacy Moffett. The mission also sent an official delegation to Jiangyin to help settle and reorganize the station's evangelical work.[22] Moffett's initial years at Jiangyin were spent undoing the work of his predecessor. He was quoted later as saying, "For the first ten years, we turned more people out of the Church than we took in."[23]

Lacy Moffett was the oldest of eight children. His father was a minister in Virginia who had wanted to become a foreign missionary but for a variety of reasons had never been able to accept an overseas assignment. Instead, he and his wife prepared their children for missionary work, and six of them eventually went to China as missionaries. Lacy Moffett graduated from Union Theological Seminary in Richmond in 1902 and began working among Southern Presbyterian churches with John Leighton Stuart, his roommate at the seminary who was later to become the U.S. ambassador to China, to secure recruits and support for foreign missions. Becoming close friends, in 1904 they married the Rodd sisters of New Orleans in a double wedding and then traveled to China together. Stuart was assigned to Hangzhou, and Moffett worked at the Suzhou Station for four years until he was transferred to Jiangyin, where he spent the rest of his missionary life.[24]

One of the changes Moffett introduced immediately was a monthly gathering of all Chinese and foreign evangelistic workers. These meetings, undoubtedly intended to tighten up the procedures for admitting members, usually lasted three days and took place at the main station once each quarter and at different outstations on the other occasions. When held at the central station, the entire time was devoted to Bible study and prayer, but in the country, the study and prayer sessions took place in the mornings and evangelistic work occupied the rest of the day. In the afternoons, the evangelists broke up into teams of three or four to visit Christian homes in the surrounding villages, and in the evening, they gathered to preach in the local chapel or tea shop.[25]

Very few of the initial Christian converts at Jiangyin were women (only about 9 percent in 1905).[26] Rida Jourolman and Anna Sykes worked with women in the country, but with limited success. For a time in 1906, the missionaries announced that no men would be admitted to the church who were not making an effort to instruct the women in their families in the Gospel and encouraging them to attend church services.[27] It is unknown whether the ploy worked. Ella Little at this time decided that she would open her home at the station to women and young girls who sought religious instruction. About fifty women and girls from the city and nearby villages began to attend afternoon classes, some on a daily basis but others only two or three times a week or irregularly. The average attendance on any given day was twenty-five to thirty. In the morning, Little trained three women and a few advanced girls from Christian homes who then helped her with the afternoon classes.[28]

Increased interest among Jiangyin women in receiving religious instruction prompted Ella Little to search for a separate building. In 1907, she rented a building and opened the first women's Bible boarding school in the Mid-China Mission, the Willie Moore Training School for Women. Boarders undertook a four-year systematic course of study intended to prepare them for advanced theological work at an interdenominational Bible school in Nanjing. A 1910 report listed 16 to 18 women boarders and another 75 or so who irregularly attended afternoon classes on the Bible and received some additional instruction in mathematics, geography, and writing. Little was helped at the school by Rida Jourolman and two Chinese women.[29]

In the medical realm, the transfer of Dr. George Worth to Jiangyin meant that dispensary work there, previously attended to by Reverend Haden on an ad hoc basis, could now develop systematically and professionally in the hands of a trained physician. Similar changes were occurring throughout the China missions. Typically, when a mission station first opened, it offered only limited medical care, as an adjunct to an evangelist's duties, in a small clinic or dispensary in rented quarters. As the station grew and acquired more land, larger facilities would be built within the mission compound and professionals would assume responsibility for the work.[30] The new approach also stressed the order and cleanliness that could be maintained in these new hospitals. This was important not only to provide the proper environment for medical practice but also, as Peter Buck has observed, to create "an institution in which patients could learn to become healthy citizens and good Christian ones at that."[31]

In time, the medical services offered at the Jiangyin Station became the most visible, most enduring, and most appreciated of the endeavors of the missionaries there. Through such work, Worth became one of the two senior missionaries at the Jiangyin Station and its most honored member in the eyes of the local population.[32] His association with Jiangyin lasted for four decades, and our story will highlight his career and contributions more than any other missionary at the station.

George Worth was born in Wilmington, North Carolina, in 1867. He came from a politically prominent Southern Presbyterian family (his grandfather, Jonathan Worth, was governor of the state at the time of his birth), and he had bright prospects for an illustrious and comfortable career at home. By the end of the century, however, Worth had committed himself to a life of hardship as a missionary in China, a country beset by war, pestilence, and poverty. What had caused this young Wilmingtonian to shift his field of endeavor from the Cape Fear River environs of eastern North Carolina to the lower Yangzi River region of eastern China?

Missionaries responded to a "call," a divine inspiration leading them to a life of religious service. Like David Treadup, the protagonist of John Hersey's epic novel of the missionary experience in China, *The Call*,[33] many decided on mission work after attending a series of religious rallies conducted by the Student Volunteer Movement for Foreign Missions, a group founded in 1888 under the auspices of the intercollegiate Young Men's Christian Association (YMCA). Thousands were thrilled by the group's challenge to "evangelize the world in this generation."

For Worth, the source of inspiration was basically the same. He had attended an evangelistic meeting sponsored by the YMCA in 1884 in the old chapel at the University of North Carolina (UNC) in Chapel Hill, at which his decision to become a soldier in Christ's foreign legion was made without any "mental fumbling," as he recalled later. Only seventeen at the time, Worth was enrolled at Bingham Military Academy, a noted preparatory school located in the small town of Mebane just thirty miles from the university. Dressed in his military uniform and seated at attention, he heard the preacher challenge the audience of several hundred young men: "Ask yourselves the solemn question, with God alone to witness, is there any reason why any of you should not become a medical missionary?" For nearly two minutes, Worth tightly gripped the wooden arms of his seat and was lost in thought. After the meeting was over, he turned to his good friend and classmate at Bingham, Lacy Little, and confided, "I have found my life work."[34]

For the next decade, Worth prepared for the profession he had so rapturously chosen. He enrolled at the University of North Carolina, where he was active in the Student Volunteer Movement and served as president of the YMCA in 1889–90. The YMCA first established college branches in 1877, and by the turn of the century, these branches had become the most prestigious political and social organizations on campus, taking on governing and service functions that later would be provided by student governments and student unions. Worth and Lacy Little, who also attended UNC, were singled out in an early history of UNC's YMCA as young men "who were making the YMCA begin to be a real part of college and a vital, necessary force in its life."[35] Worth helped organize a branch of the YMCA in his hometown, and at its 1889 convention, he publicly announced his resolution, formed several years earlier at the university chapel, of becoming a medical missionary. After graduating from UNC, he studied medicine at the University of Virginia and the University of New York.[36]

By 1895, Worth was ready for an assignment abroad and therefore turned his attention to choosing a marriage partner. Foreign mission boards in those days expected a male missionary to enter the field with a wife, who not only would be a personal companion but also help in bringing the Christian message to the women and children of the host country. In April, Worth announced his engagement to Emma Chadbourn, a childhood friend who also had made a public commitment to foreign missionary work. They were married in the First Presbyterian Church in Wilmington at the end of July 1895, and two days later, they left for China with the farewells of the congregation ringing in their ears.[37]

Initially, Worth had set his sights on Africa, the home of a people whose descendants in America often found their lives entwined in complex ways with white southerners. Worth had been suckled at birth by a black nursemaid of whom he became very fond.[38] His course, however, was diverted to China, which had become the centerpiece of the American missionary effort. As one Student Volunteer Movement founder put it, "China was the goal, the lodestar, the great magnet that drew us all in those days."[39] Curiously, the great rush to do mission work in China supported the age-old

Confucian notion of China as the "central kingdom," the hub of the moral universe.

Thus, the Worths found themselves in China, sent by the Southern Presbyterian mission board to Wuxi to open up a medical facility. His task was made easier when he inherited the practice of a Chinese Christian doctor who had left the profession to go into the more profitable steamboat business and had rented his clinic and equipment to the newly arrived foreigner. Worth carried on his practice in Chinese-style dress and even pinned a false queue (or braid), made from Chinese hair, to a skullcap he wore. "Going native" seemed to help him relate to his patients, although at times the people of Wuxi hurled such epithets at him as "dog" and "foreign devil."[40]

The merger of the Jiangyin and Wuxi stations reunited George Worth with his friend from preparatory school and university days, Lacy Little. After leaving UNC, Little had studied for the ministry at Princeton Theological Seminary and then had traveled to China in 1895 as an evangelist. The two men had committed themselves to doing missionary work in China together, but their plans initially had been thwarted since Worth was assigned to Wuxi and Little to Jiangyin.[41] In 1897, they happily joined forces at Jiangyin and were still together when Worth died almost forty years later.

Worth's medical work at Jiangyin began inauspiciously. He operated a rough-and-ready clinic in a rented building in the city large enough to accommodate only about fifteen patients. Its construction was so flimsy that an opium addict once kicked down the wall of his room and escaped. At first, to attract customers and potential converts, patients were given free treatment and medicine. If they were willing to listen to a sermon, they received a free meal as well.[42] Later, fees from patients who could afford to pay covered about three-fourths of the clinic's expenses. Patients brought their own bedding, clothing, and (normally) food, and relatives or friends accompanied them to nurse and feed them. The latter practice comforted the patient in unfamiliar surroundings and fit in well with the traditional Chinese orientation toward the family. It also afforded the missionaries the opportunity to deliver the Christian message to a family network rather than a lone individual.

Certain dangers were inherent in practicing Western-style medicine in turn-of-the-century China. Many Chinese, as we have seen, were quick to believe the rumors that foreign doctors were engaging in nefarious medical practices. After the Jiangyin riot of 1896, the situation had calmed down somewhat. Nevertheless, Worth encountered some trying times, particularly in connection with surgery, which was neither highly developed nor respected in the Chinese medical tradition. A patient requiring surgery often had a tenuous grip on life; if the patient should die after the doctor's operation, the

Missionaries George and Emma Worth dressed in Chinese-style clothing, with their first child, William, ca. 1896. (First Presbyterian Church, Wilmington, N.C.)

incensed relatives of the deceased might seek retribution. Worth tried to overcome this problem by requiring the patient's family to sign a contract that freed him of any responsibility for the ultimate outcome. He also at first performed all operations in public to show that no mutilation of the body had occurred. Once, during a public surgery, the patient's heart momentarily stopped beating due to a reaction to the application of chloroform. Shortly afterward, neighbors who had witnessed the successful operation and had misunderstood what had happened brought the doctor a dead woman and asked him to restore her to life too.[43]

When the Worths evacuated Jiangyin in 1900 because of the Boxer threat, they left behind the nearly completed home they were constructing with funds provided by George's father. It was finished during their absence and remained vacant until they returned in November 1903. Work at the clinic, which had been attracting a growing number of patients each year since 1897 — over 7,000 had been treated in 1899 — also stopped during this period.[44] Forced from the field, the Worths returned to America on their first furlough.

George Worth took the opportunity of being back in North Carolina to launch a plan to upgrade the Jiangyin medical facilities and put the operation on a firm financial base. He convinced the Woman's Auxiliary of the Wilmington Presbytery to assume full financial responsibility for the development of medical work at Jiangyin. The auxiliary's association with Jiangyin, and particularly with George Worth, had begun at its second annual convention, held at the First Presbyterian Church in 1889. Worth, who just that spring at a YMCA meeting in Wilmington had announced his decision to be a medical missionary, gave a short address at the convention. His future wife, Emma Chadbourn, made her public commitment to mission work at the same meeting. When they were married in 1895 and went to China as the first missionaries from the Wilmington Presbytery, the auxiliary naturally took a lively interest in their work.[45]

During their furlough in 1901–3, the Worths spoke to the women of the auxiliary at their annual meetings in 1902 and 1903, stressing the great need and great opportunity for a Christian hospital at Jiangyin.[46] Worth, in a 1904 letter to Dr. Wells of the First Presbyterian Church, outlined his plans and suggested that "it will further the work here much more for all contributions to be put into a general fund at first instead of being made for the support of cots. . . . My earnest hope is that our church and Presbytery may undertake this work. It is easily within their means and a work greatly needed."[47] This letter was read at the 1904 annual meeting, and the idea fell on fertile ground.

The auxiliary raised the $4,000 needed for the construction of the hospital by selling eighty shares of $50 each over the next two years. Subscribers received special certificates Worth had printed in Shanghai duplicating a

Patients waiting outside the first Jiangyin dispensary, ca. 1898. It was housed in a
rented one-story building, and Dr. George Worth (at left) was its only staff. (Kiangyin
Station Photographs, Presbyterian Church in the United States Missions, China,
Department of History and Records, Presbyterian Church [U.S.A.], Montreat, N.C.)

photograph of him with Chinese patients in front of the old, dilapidated
clinic.[48] The fund-raisers hoped to involve as many people as possible so that
the stake in the hospital's success and continued growth would be widespread. Eliza Murphy, who was appointed agent of the hospital fund by the
auxiliary, explained: "It is not desired for this fund to be raised by a few, but
as many persons from as many churches as possible should have a share in
the giving. The consummation of this idea would be reached if when the
Hospital is erected at Kiang Yin, its share holders would represent every congregation within our Presbytery." On another occasion, Murphy described
the auxiliary's relationship with the Jiangyin hospital as "yoke-fellows" — the
two sides were harnessed together in a common effort with equal responsibility and an equal claim to success.[49]

    With the promised support from the Woman's Auxiliary, the Worths re-
turned to Jiangyin and made plans for the construction of a new facility that
would include a dispensary, a waiting room, and a chapel. In 1905, the station purchased about two acres of land adjacent to its property outside the
city's East Gate, and in the following year, a contract was given out to local
carpenters to build a two-story hospital building along the canal that passed
by the station.[50] During construction, Worth continued to practice out of the

rented clinic in the city. The number of patients dropped off somewhat in 1905–6, probably because the anti-American boycott in protest of American exclusion laws made local residents hesitant to associate with the foreigners. No incidents were reported, but Worth took the precaution of turning over to the local magistrate human bones he used for teaching purposes. He did not want to give any cause for the revival of charges that had precipitated the 1896 riot.[51]

The new facility, named in Chinese Good News Hospital (Fuyin yiyuan), opened in 1907 and quickly became the heart of the missionary enterprise in Jiangyin. Some of the city's elite began to use its services. One official's granddaughter was treated successfully by Worth, and other officials sent some of their subordinates to the hospital to break their addiction to opium. The hospital chapel, the only one serving the Christian community at the East Gate station at the time, was used in 1907 to host the first annual meeting of the Presbytery of the Southern Presbyterian Church in China.[52] The reading room at the entrance to the hospital was stocked with Christian tracts, magazines, and Bibles. The Chinese staff included a (male) chaplain and a Chinese "Bible woman" who had been trained to present the Christian message to patients. Besides this direct proselytizing, the practice of medicine itself represented, as one mission administrator noted, "an exhibition of the beneficence of the gospel and of the mercy of God to men."[53]

As medical work expanded at Jiangyin, George Worth made additional plans and additional requests for funds from supporters back home. On his second furlough, just after the hospital opened in 1907, Worth explained its future needs. For the immediate future, he requested $25 a year to sustain each of the 25 hospital cots available for patients, or a total of $625 annually (the figure included the cost of drugs, supplies, and the wages of helpers). Also, a small capital outlay of $500 was needed to purchase some furnishings and to build two detached rooms for patients with contagious diseases. Finally, Worth appealed to the auxiliary to fund the construction of a separate women's ward, with maternity equipment, at the hospital. The estimated cost was $2,500, which apparently was raised in timely fashion, but $2,000 of the amount was spent in Jiangyin on other hospital projects because the station was prohibited by government regulations from buying additional land on which to construct the women's ward. In the end, the station decided to make do with its present property holdings and set aside space behind the hospital for the future construction of a women's ward.[54]

Support for the cots came from another source, the young people's societies in the presbytery that were under the authority of the Woman's Auxiliary. In 1902 the auxiliary appointed an agent to coordinate the efforts of these societies and to organize additional "bands," as they were often called. At the 1903 annual meeting of the auxiliary, the twelve young people's bands then in existence each adopted the support of a cot at the hospital Worth planned to build at Jiangyin. In this way, the young people became committed to the Jiangyin hospital a year before their parent organization took up the same cause. Some of the societies began to call themselves "Worth bands" in recognition of their partnership with the doctor and his work. By 1913 there were thirty-two young people's bands in the presbytery, and they had raised about $4,000 for cots in the preceding eleven years.[55]

Not long after the new hospital building opened, it was almost destroyed by a fire. At the beginning of 1909, in the early morning hours of 4 January, smoke was seen billowing out of the windows and eaves of the building. Soon flames engulfed the whole lower story. The fire gongs were struck, and the mission staff members were gratified by the quick response of neighbors and city officials to the crisis. Eight to ten fire engines arrived from the city, each hauling a 40-gallon tub of water with a two-handled pump and nozzle attached (but no hose to extend its reach). Supplementing these efforts, for two hours the station staff, friends, and neighbors slogged water from the adjacent canal in buckets, tin cans, tightly woven baskets, and the like to douse the flames. Many others came to watch the spectacle, and the district magistrate and the sheriff arrived with armed men just in case the situation got out of hand. In the end, the losses were kept to a minimum, and the hospital was reopened in March.[56]

Worth returned to America a third time at the end of 1910 to report on the work of the Jiangyin hospital and to make plans for further expansion. It should be noted that at the time, and for some years to come, no other hospital existed in the entire Jiangyin district, and even people from the surrounding districts came to the station for medical treatment. In 1910, the hospital treated over 7,100 outpatients and 166 inpatients, who paid six cents a day (if they could afford it) for the duration of their stay.[57] Also that year, the hospital welcomed its first Chinese physician, a native of Zhejiang named Wang Wanbo (whom the missionaries referred to as "Dr. King," from the translation of his surname). He had become a Christian at the beginning of the century and had studied medicine at a missionary hospital in Suzhou. He was invited to Jiangyin to fill in temporarily for Worth during his furlough.[58]

Wang's arrival underscored one of the pressing needs Worth presented to his potential backers — a second permanent physician on the staff, "an up-to-date man," he explained, "who wishes to give his life in a service that will satisfy his highest desires and tax his best talents." Worth also hoped for an operating room and additional surgical equipment.[59] Furthermore, there was still the unfinished business of a separate women's ward. Excluding the additional doctor's salary, $6,000 was needed to meet Worth's requests. After several years, the Woman's Auxiliary and one of its wealthy members were able to raise the necessary funds. The auxiliary also assumed the burden of the salary ($1,200 annually) of the doctor who was assigned in 1913 to help Worth at Jiangyin.[60]

Educational work at Jiangyin developed more slowly. The cause of mission education received a boost in 1905, however, when the Chinese government abolished the traditional education/examination system based on Confucian teachings. This created a need for a new educational system and new schools that focused on modern (and in many cases, Western) subjects.[61] In February 1906, the station rented and repaired a small building to be used as a boarding school for fifteen high school boys from Christian families. As the enrollment grew, some non-Christian students were accepted, but the overwhelming majority remained Christian. Lacy Little was in charge of the school and handled doctrinal instruction as well as physical education. He instituted a military discipline based on the manual of arms he and George Worth had learned years before at the Bingham School in North Carolina. A Chinese theological student taught Western sciences, and a Chinese scholar taught "native books" (the genre is not known) and helped the boys with their writing of Chinese characters. Students were introduced to the industrial arts and taught respect for manual labor. Religious instruction formed part of the curriculum, and all pupils were required to participate in morning and evening prayers.[62]

At first, Chinese was the language of instruction, although Ella Little helped the students with English romanization of Chinese words. The use of English in schools was debated at length in mission circles. Proponents argued that Chinese students wanted to learn English and that those who learned the language would have greater access to Christian literature (since so little of it had been translated into Chinese). Opponents reasoned that the time devoted to learning English would detract from other subjects and would result in the denationalization of Chinese youth, who would have little familiarity with Chinese literature and history.[63] Others feared that students who became too proficient in the language would abandon their interest in Christianity and "soar away" to big cities in search of lucrative jobs.[64]

Eventually, Chinese demands for English instruction became so great that most mission schools taught English, at least in the advanced classes. At Jiangyin, the teaching of English did not begin until after the 1911 revolution. One student who attended the boys school at that time complained, however, that English was taught only in a perfunctory manner and that little effort was made to explain grammatical structure. He claimed that when he and his classmates graduated from the middle school, their English proficiency was about two years behind graduates of schools where the language was taught more seriously.[65]

About the same time that the boys school was started, Ella Little began concentrating on the education of women and girls at the station. As we have seen, she first offered instruction in her home and then opened a residential Bible school for women. Starting in 1909, young girls were accepted as boarders at the school as well. The girls received the same instruction as boys at their school, except that housework (such as knitting) was substituted for industrial work.[66]

From the start, the Jiangyin schools were seen as evangelistic agencies. Earlier concerns in the mission movement that schools would drain neces- sary energy and resources from the fundamental evangelistic work had by the twentieth century given way to a need to reach youth, who could then influence the adult members of their families heretofore resistant or indiffer- ent to the Christian message.[67] Schools also fit in with the "social gospel" ap- proach to promoting Christianity that was then taking hold in the church. Instead of concentrating on saving individual souls, the "modernists" (as ad- herents of the social gospel were called) sought a total transformation of so- ciety through "good works" such as schools, hospitals, and various relief agencies. Such a transformation would create an environment supportive of missionary work as well as of individuals who converted to Christianity.

As with the medical work, this new philosophy of missions led to the ex- pansion of facilities, specialization, and the replacement of clergymen and their wives who taught part-time in the schools with full-time professionals. At Jiangyin, the Littles decided in 1909 that the buildings they were renting for the boys and girls schools, as well as the equipment, were inadequate and could not compete with the newer Chinese schools in the city. When Henry F. Williams, a representative of the Executive Committee of Foreign Missions of the PCUS, made a tour of the Mid-China Mission in April, the Jiangyin staff pressed on him the need for a larger building for the boys and an additional building for a girls school separate from the women's Bible school.[68]

At precisely that moment, and unknown to the Jiangyin missionaries, forces were at work back home in North Carolina that would solve their problems. James Sprunt, Wilmington's most illustrious and prosperous citi- zen and an elder of the First Presbyterian Church, began a sustained philan- thropic association with the mission movement in February 1909. In that month, Sprunt and his brother Alexander, who was pastor of the First Pres- byterian Church of Charleston, attended the inaugural convention of the Southern Presbyterian Layman's Missionary Movement, held in Birming- ham, Alabama. At the meetings, James was inspired, by Robert Speer among others, to pledge $10,000 to foreign missions. J. Campbell White, the found- ing general secretary of the interdenominational Layman's Missionary Move- ment, urged Sprunt to direct his entire contribution in support of a new sta- tion in Korea and to make any further donations to the same station. For the next month, Sprunt exchanged letters with White and with the chairman of the Birmingham convention to discuss the merits of this proposal. White was especially concerned that future contributions to mission work be used for the thorough cultivation of particular fields, whether in Korea or elsewhere.[69]

In the end, Sprunt accepted White's approach, but he decided to concentrate his efforts in China, not Korea, at the Jiangyin Station the First Presbyterian Church had been supporting for several years and where his friend George Worth had established a hospital. On 31 March 1909, Sprunt wrote a check for $10,000, payable to the pastor of the First Presbyterian Church, as a "special contribution to Foreign Missions, Kiang-Yin." In notifying White of his decision, Sprunt assured him that the funds would not be placed in a general fund but would be used exclusively to build a boys school and a girls school at Jiangyin to train native helpers. Furthermore, he intended to direct all future contributions to the same work, "which will of course be more interesting to me on account of my personal connection with it."[70]

Sprunt's interest in educational work was born of his conviction that Christian values must be transmitted through schools to prevent the breakdown of Christian civilization. Late in his life, in discussing the schools he funded, he suggested that an institution was "utterly worthless if its curriculum does not include instruction in the doctrines of Christ and a steady practical application of His principles straight through the whole teaching."[71] Lacy Little, the boys school director, was in total agreement with Sprunt. In a pamphlet describing the Jiangyin schools, he stated that "evangelization is the forerunner of education, and must be the keynote of every distinctively Christian enterprise of an educational nature."[72]

When the Littles learned of James Sprunt's $10,000 gift, they noted with surprise and delight that it matched exactly the estimated cost of the two new buildings they were requesting. To them, Sprunt's independently reached decision seemed to confirm the efficacy of their prayers and the workings of a providential God. After the funds became available, the station erected two substantial school buildings. The two-story dark gray brick boys school with white and red trim was completed by April 1910, but work on the girls school was postponed until 1911 because of problems with buying additional land near the boys school for its construction.

From the start, Lacy Little kept Sprunt informed of the schools' progress, and early on he sent Sprunt a copy of the architect's plans.[73] In October 1909, when asked about suitable names for the two schools, Sprunt requested that they be named after himself and his wife. The English names James Sprunt Male Academy and Luola Murchison Sprunt Academy were carved in stone above the entrances, as were their Chinese names, "Urge to Truth Academy" (Lishi xuetang) and the "Help to Truth Girls School" (Fushi nu xuexiao). The donors' portraits were displayed at the schools, and students were read some of the letters Sprunt sent to George Worth and Lacy Little.[74] After the

Sprunt Academy students in cadet uniforms and the Chinese teaching
staff (front row). (Kiangyin Station Photographs, Presbyterian Church in the
United States Missions, China, Department of History and Records,
Presbyterian Church [U.S.A.], Montreat, N.C.)

deaths of Luola Sprunt and Ella Little in 1916, brass memorial plaques were
hung in the girls school auditorium.[75] Here, clearly, was a classic example of
the personal relationship in mission funding that the Layman's Missionary
Movement had been promoting as the most effective way to expand world
evangelization.[76]

With the new facilities in place, a call went out for additional teachers to
help the Littles. Andrew Allison, with a master's degree from Tulane University in education and six years of experience in teaching and museum work
(he was a distinguished ornithologist) in the United States, arrived in September 1910 to take charge of the James Sprunt Academy. Early in 1911,
Carrie Lena Moffett, the sister of Lacy Moffett, came from Suzhou to help
Ella Little run both the Bible school for women and the girls school.[77] Forty-
seven boys and twenty-six girls enrolled in the two academies that fall.

The Jiangyin Station's expansion "all along the line" was blocked momentarily by Chinese land regulations. An article in the 1903 Sino-American
Treaty had given missionaries the right to rent and lease land and buildings

Part of missionary compound, including Bible school (at left), James Sprunt
Male Academy (in distance), and Luola Murchison Sprunt Academy for
girls (at right). (Lacy L. Little Papers, Department of History and Records,
Presbyterian Church [U.S.A.], Montreat, N.C.)

in all parts of the Chinese empire,[78] but in 1909 the station learned of an
official proclamation that prohibited the purchase of land by foreigners
within four miles of the Jiangyin forts. The present holdings of the station,
which were only two miles from the forts, would not be affected, but no new
properties could be added. The government's justification for this regulation
was that it planned to build a second string of forts on the low hills about four
miles south of the Yangzi River and thus wanted to keep this military zone
free of foreign-owned property. The station protested to the magistrate, but
he was powerless to act on this matter and unwilling to forward the complaint to the viceroy at Nanjing, Zhang Renjun. The U.S. legation in Beijing, when asked to investigate, took the position that the government proclamation did not violate any treaty.

The station sought help from the Mid-China Mission, requesting that it
ask the Chinese government to assure the station possession of its property
and to make an exception to the regulation by allowing the station to purchase five additional acres adjacent to the present property. If this request
was denied, the station asked that the mission seek government permission
and help in securing suitable land in Changzhou for a new station. The mission, in turn, referred these requests to the Shanghai consul-general, Dr. Wilder, who was sympathetic to Jiangyin's difficulties. He visited the station in
June 1910 to inspect the situation and to discuss the issue with the top civilian
and military officials in the city. Wilder also met with the leader of the city's
gentry and the missionaries' most influential supporter, Mr. Dzen. Dzen was

a former imperial censor and related by marriage to Viceroy Zhang. His advice to Wilder was to ask the viceroy to send a deputy to Jiangyin to examine the matter; if the deputy came, Dzen would use his influence to ensure that the station's requests were granted.[79]

The viceroy promised to send a deputy and claimed in a letter to the consul-general that the restriction on foreign purchase of land was the work of his predecessor, the Manchu Duanfang, who had been transferred to the province of Zhili in June 1909.[80] In late December, a deputy who was in Jiangyin on other business heard the missionaries' case at a banquet arranged by Dzen. They now asked to purchase land "in the name of the native church," hoping to avoid the issue of foreign purchase, but no official action was taken prior to the overthrow of the empire. After the revolution, the restriction was lifted, and within a few years, the Jiangyin Station experienced a building boom.[81]

4

AS BROTHERS

TO US IN

TROUBLE

The Chinese imperial state, a remarkably resilient and resourceful institution of two millennia's duration, finally collapsed in 1911 under the combined weight of Western imperialism, the rising tide of revolutionary ideas and movements, and its own anachronistic behavior. For Christian missionaries in China, it was a time of great promise. China seemed ready to accept a helping hand, and missionaries were ready to extend it. They applauded the overthrow of the old dynasty, one missionary exulting: "That regime is now, happily, shorn of its power to cripple the development of a virile people. It can never again chill China's hot yearnings after freedom, nor stand in the way of its peoples' intelligent hearing and unfettered choice of the truth as presented in the message of our gospel." Another felt "the thrill of the new hope."[1] Even after the great anti-imperialist May Fourth Incident of 1919, missionaries were being exhorted to appreciate the "grand opportunities before them in influencing and moulding [Chinese] leadership."[2]

During the first two decades of the century, the Protestant missionary enterprise in China boomed. The number of missionaries increased fifteenfold, from about 200 in 1890 to nearly 2,900 in 1915. In a comparable period, from 1900 to 1920, the number of mission stations nearly doubled (from about 340 to 675), and the number of converts almost quadrupled (from 96,000 to 366,000).[3] China was fast becoming the centerpiece of the American missionary effort, as mission boards annually invested millions of dollars for new personnel and the expansion of educational, medical, and social relief institutions. The total value of American mission property in China in 1915 was $25 million.[4] This massive assault on China by a foreign religion, however, would eventually lead to a backlash in the 1920s, when revolutionary nationalism increasingly questioned the propriety of foreign involvement in the social and cultural reconstruction of the country.

The Jiangyin Station shared in both the initial promise and the later disappointment of these times. The staff grew in number and became increasingly specialized. Opportunities to provide educational, medical, and other humanitarian services became greater, and the station's stature among the local populace was enhanced through such good works. A series of political crises from the fall of the empire to the demise of the warlords in the mid-1920s also afforded the Jiangyin missionaries an opportunity to establish a good working relationship with the city's elite and secure for themselves an honored position in the local community.

The old empire expired with barely a whimper at Jiangyin. Residents experienced some momentary anxiety as they waited to learn of the intentions of the imperial troops stationed at the forts. Schools and businesses closed, and many fled to the country. George Worth went to the forts to beg that the city be spared in the event that fighting broke out. Nothing materialized, however, as the civilian and military officials and the local gentry met and decided to join the side of the revolution.[5] The guns of the forts did boom but only to announce the end of Manchu rule. Many were ready with scissors in hand to cut off their queues, a hair style the Manchu conquerors had imposed on the Chinese, at the first sound of the guns. All of the boys at the James Sprunt Academy shed theirs, although at least one of the Chinese teachers was reluctant to do so. The only Manchu known to inhabit the city was quietly given a small amount of money "sufficient to persuade him that other regions would be more healthful for him at that particular time."[6]

Seemingly, the only difficulty caused by the transition to a republican regime was the reluctance of the people to accept the new calendar. The New Year to them meant settling their accounts, and no one wanted to move up the day of reckoning, which the switch from the traditional lunar calendar to the Western solar calendar would do. One farmer was heard to comment on another difficulty of the new calendar: "How shall we ever know when to plant wheat?"[7] The Jiangyin missionaries, of course, welcomed the new order, and they immediately perceived a friendlier attitude among the people. Andrew Allison, however, sounded a cautionary note, expressing the concern that China would follow Japan's example by accepting the West's civilization but not its Christianity.[8]

The soldiers at the Jiangyin forts were apparently an unruly lot. Six months after the revolution, in April 1912, they revolted and killed the officer who had been sent by the republican government to command them. It seems that he had arrived in the midst of a factional struggle among the officers and fell victim to their intrigues.[9] According to a missionary account, however, the soldiers justified their action on the grounds that the officer knew nothing about artillery and thus was incapable of effectively leading them.[10] The people in the city were naturally worried about how the republican government in Nanjing would respond to this incident. Many again fled the city by boat, sedan chair, or wheelbarrow — fees for all of which rose sharply — for the safety of the countryside. For others, the mission station provided a form of refuge. Children attending the missionary schools for boys and girls remained as boarders to continue their studies undisturbed. The missionaries were particularly gratified that the two granddaughters of one of Jiangyin's leading citizens and a representative to the provincial assembly were enrolled as boarders. Eventually the trouble at the fort was settled peaceably, and those who had fled returned to the city.[11]

Again in November 1913, about 400 soldiers from the forts began looting the district around the North Gate of the city. A number of homes were burned, and several citizens were wounded by stray shots. The North Gate chapel and school, a second evangelistic center recently opened by the missionaries, were entered by troops at night, but they did not disturb the property when they discovered its Christian (and Western) character. Another company of soldiers located some distance to the southwest of the city also began looting, with more devastating results. In one of the outlying towns, six people were burned to death. The main station at the East Gate was not raided, although some of the boys at the boarding school were so afraid that the director, Andrew Allison, had to sleep at the school to calm them down. Within days, the new government sent a large force to restore order, and eventually twenty officers of the marauding troops were executed. The number of cannon at the Jiangyin forts was also reduced. Property damage from the looting was estimated at $500,000, of which the government repaid $30,000.[12]

It is important to note that in these incidents involving Jiangyin's transition to a new order, the Christian missionaries for the first time took on the role of protector, however limited, of the city and some of its leading citizens. A reversal of roles was occurring. In the first fifteen years of the station's life, the missionaries had sought protection for their work from city and provincial authorities under treaty obligations; now, they were affording protection to important segments of both the Christian and non-Christian population. The opportunities for further service expanded as Jiangyin became involved in the political and military factionalism of the time. As a consequence, station personnel and city officials and gentry began to interact more frequently on political and social levels. Already in 1912, the district magistrate and Lacy Little, in turn, hosted feasts for each other. In the same year, Andrew Allison had the honor of joining city notables at a banquet for Sun Yat-sen when the ex-president of the republic visited Jiangyin.[13] Lacy Moffett also met Sun in Nanjing and was one of the first foreigners, along with his friend John Leighton Stuart, to attend a session of the new National Assembly.[14]

The mission hospital expanded its services during this period. George Worth returned to Jiangyin from his furlough in 1913, and the following spring, the foreign medical staff doubled after the arrival of Frank Crawford. Crawford's presence permitted the hospital to extend services to the country-side. Accompanied by an evangelist, Crawford began providing a series of rural clinics, one a week at three different locations every month (leaving one week free for work at the station). He treated illnesses and, when nec-essary, referred patients to the main hospital.[15] Among the Chinese staff, Dr. Wang, who was in charge of the hospital while Worth was in the United States, left in the fall of 1913 to take a special course in bacteriology in Japan. Another Chinese physician died in 1915. They were eventually replaced by two recent graduates of the Nanjing Medical School.[16]

Most significantly, the long-awaited women's ward was completed in No-vember 1915. Five hundred printed invitations to the formal opening cere-monies were sent out to the local elite, teachers and students in the city schools, and other dignitaries. Worth served as the master of ceremonies, the James Sprunt Academy brass band provided music, and many congratulatory speeches were given, including one by a local educator in the old-fashioned and little-heard classical style (*wenli*) that brought a few snickers from his compatriots in the crowd. The next day, about 300 curious townspeople came to inspect the facilities, which could accommodate about thirty pa-tients.[17] A hospital just for women was, of course, a startling sight in a land where women traditionally had very few rights or privileges. The presence of this facility gave the missionaries a greater opportunity to reach women with the Christian message. A Bible woman lived in the ward and spoke to the pa-tients regularly, and this proselytizing was followed up every Sunday after-noon with visits by one or more missionaries.[18]

Associated with the women's ward was a nurses training school, organized by Ida Albaugh, the head nurse on the hospital staff. In 1915 the first class en-rolled just three young girls, who were dressed in blue and white striped dresses and caps. But the next year, eleven trainees enrolled and thereafter the program became so popular that a second story was added to the hospital gatehouse to house the students. The training school was registered with the Nurses Association of China, which had been established in 1909 to promote high standards in this new profession and which enrolled as members all who received full nurses training. This meant that graduates of the Jiangyin program were eligible for diplomas from the association. By 1920, 52 training schools were registered with the association and it had a total of 231 members (of which 183 were foreigners and only 48 Chinese).[19]

Sprunt Academy high school students with Virginia Lee, their
English teacher. (Kiangyin Station Photographs, Presbyterian Church in the
United States Missions, China, Department of History and Records,
Presbyterian Church [U.S.A.], Montreat, N.C.)

In the early years of the republic, the schools at the station enrolled ever-
larger numbers of students and expanded their staffs. Total enrollment in 1911
was over 300, and by 1925 it surpassed 400. When the Littles, who had
founded the schools, went home on furlough in 1913, Andrew Allison took
charge of the boys school and Carrie Lena Moffett headed both the girls
school and the Bible school for women. Virginia Lee, Lula Conover, Ella
Allison, and William Cumming taught at the boys school, and Katheryne
Thompson and Jeanie Woodbridge joined the girls school staff. Moffett was
replaced as principal of the girls school in 1914 by Jane Lee (Virginia's sister).
Also in 1914, administration of the Bible school was separated from that of the
girls school, and a succession of missionary women served as its principal
over the next dozen or so years. In 1927, in response to the Nationalist movement, Chinese teachers assumed leadership of all three of these institutions
and Andrew Allison, Jane Lee, and Nell Sprunt Little (Ella Little had died in
1916 and Lacy had married Nell in 1919), then in charge of the Bible school,
all became honorary principals.[20]

As the number of station personnel grew, connections with Wilmington,
or North Carolina, or even the South, became increasingly attenuated. Of
the new educational workers, only William Cumming had any ties to Wilmington, where he was born and raised. As a teenager, he had received the

"call" to mission work during a talk by George Worth on one of his furloughs in North Carolina. The Lee sisters were from Pennsylvania. Virginia Lee taught English at the boys high school. Although Jane Lee had earned an M.D. degree from the University of Nashville, most of her missionary career was devoted to educational work.[21] Katheryne Thompson had earned a B.A. degree from Earlham College in Indiana and a teaching certificate in home economics from Drexel Institute; she also had pursued some graduate studies and received Bible training.[22] Nothing is known about Lula Conover or Jeanie Woodbridge.

Even though most of the missionaries except for the Worths, the Littles, and William Cumming had no direct links to Wilmington, all of the Jiangyin staff were "adopted" by the First Presbyterian Church in Wilmington and were referred to as "our" missionaries. For their part, the Jiangyin missionaries felt a close bond with the Wilmington church, which after all provided the bulk of the funds for the work in China, and they felt obligated when in the United States to present programs at the church.

As educational work at Jiangyin expanded, the schools took on a greater role in mission work. Every Saturday, and sometimes on Sundays, boys from the James Sprunt Academy went into the city to preach the Gospel on the streets and in temples, tea shops, and schools. They took along their songbooks and musical instruments to attract a crowd for their services. During the lunar New Year period, everyone at the station, including students from the two mission schools, helped conduct week-long evangelistic meetings in the city that often attracted up to a thousand curious onlookers. The boys and girls choirs sang hymns accompanied by a Victrola and distributed Christian tracts.[23]

The students also engaged in a variety of charitable work, mostly involving famine relief or aid to the poor in the Jiangyin area. The missionaries had been in the custom of sponsoring a feast for the students at the Qingming festival (honoring ancestors), but in 1911, the students returned the money earmarked for the feast with a request that it be donated instead to famine sufferers. In 1914, the students and staff of both schools used the money for their traditional Christmas dinner to buy rice coupons for the poor, whom they also entertained on Christmas Eve in the hospital chapel. Again at Christmastime in 1918, the students gave away over a ton of rice to 145 poor families in and around Jiangyin.[24] The Christmas gift of rice to needy families became an annual affair at the station.

One of these charitable activities surprisingly led to a school crisis in the spring of 1912. Because of a devastating flood in the Anhui province, all of the students agreed to forego the usual meal of several dishes (some vegetarian and some with meat) and a soup for just a bowl of porridge and to contribute the money saved to a relief fund. The problem arose over accountability.

Some of the students felt they were kept in the dark about how much was saved and how much was being sent to the agencies helping the flood victims. When their demands to see the account books were refused by the school director, Andrew Allison, they staged a strike of classes. Two of the "ringleaders," as the missionaries called them, were expelled, which prompted the majority of the remaining students to leave school. In the end, most of them returned, but they were forced to admit publicly at a noontime church service that they had been "taken in by the devil" and vow that they would never act in such a manner again.[25] Lacy Little's report of this disturbance, which was silent concerning its causes, stated that "it has been clearly established that the management of the school is in the hands of the *teachers* and not in the hands of the student body."[26]

A more successful event occurred in May 1911. The Sprunt Academy boys, under the direction of Dr. Wang of the hospital, staged an entertainment extravaganza to raise money for famine relief. When city leaders heard of the plans, they extended an invitation to use the largest public facility in town instead of the station's little chapel. About 1,500 people crowded into the hall attached to the Yellow Temple, which Andrew Allison ruefully noted was "full to overflowing of Buddhist idols." Ticket prices varied according to income so that the poor as well as the wealthy could attend. Although the missionaries deliberately remained in the background, they did help in various ways. The Littles provided a gramophone, Kate Moffett, Lacy's wife, and Ida Albaugh gave the students choral lessons, and Allison supplied some clothes for a skit they performed. The program was varied and included members of the Jiangyin community. In addition to all sorts of vocal and instrumental music, a young man from a prominent local family showed magic lantern slides, the science class from a city school performed chemical experiments, and the academy boys operated a tiny electric car line.

After several speeches about the plight of the famine sufferers in the county aroused the audience, a group of students performed a skit to cap their appeal for funds. A band of tattered wretches imitating the moans of famine victims appeared on the stage, eating the miserable food that was the only nourishment available in the famine-stricken areas. Another student, dressed in the Western clothes borrowed from Allison, rushed on stage in the character of a relief worker and was welcomed by the victims with exaggerated cries of joy. At that point, several Christians came forward to call for contributions. In response, "the air grew thick with dollars and smaller coins and the platform rang with them for several minutes." Pledges were also taken, and a total of $663 was sent off that night in two small handbags to be distributed to the famine victims.[27]

A few years later, warfare thrust the missionaries onto a different stage, as prominent actors in local affairs. The secession crisis of 1916, when many of

The station's motor launch, the *Wilmington*, on one of the many canals in
the Jiangyin field, 1919. (Kiangyin Station Photographs, Presbyterian Church
in the United States Missions, China, Department of History and Records,
Presbyterian Church [U.S.A.], Montreat, N.C.)

the southern provinces revolted against Yuan Shikai's monarchist movement
and declared their independence from the central government, resulted
once again in serious fighting around Jiangyin. The station this time not only
acted as a refuge from the fighting but also played a key role in negotiations
between the warring factions and provided valuable medical services to
both sides.[28]

The trouble began on 16 April when about 1,300 soldiers at the Jiangyin
forts raised the white flag of republicanism, elected a new commander — the
previous one had left the forts the day before with about 500 other men who
were unwilling to join the secession movement — and declared their independence. They also levied a tax of $25,000 on Jiangyin and, to enforce their
demand, fired one of the big guns over the city. Many residents fled the city,
but even the villages around Jiangyin were being plundered by the soldiers.
The secessionist troops seized the telegraph line and steam launches to cut
off the city from the outside. The mission station had its own motor launch
and thus possessed the only available "rapid transfer," as it were, in an area
honeycombed with canals. The launch, named the *Wilmington*, quickly became a critical resource in the ensuing fighting and negotiations.

The central government made no immediate response to the Jiangyin secession, and all was quiet in the area for a few days. Not all of the Jiangsu
province had seceded. The military governor, Feng Guozhang, was one of

Yuan's leading generals and remained loyal, as did government forces at Wuxi to the south and Changzhou to the west of Jiangyin. Hearing that these forces planned to unite to recover the forts, the new commander of the secessionists, Xiao Guangli, decided to send troops in those two directions to engage the enemy. Xiao himself led a force of over 1,000 men toward Wuxi on 23 April.

When Jiangyin civilian officials learned of this campaign, they sent a delegation to the mission station to ask the missionaries to take them in the motor launch to the camp of General Xiao so that they could attempt to prevent hostilities. Seven men set out on this mission: two representatives of the Jiangyin Chamber of Commerce, two members of the government school faculty, a representative of one of the town's prominent families, George Worth, and Lacy Moffett. Heading south along an elaborate network of canals, the delegation was unable to overtake General Xiao, who had traveled overland. They continued on to Wuxi to consult with its Chamber of Commerce and with General Su Kunshan, commander of the government troops there. General Su agreed not to attack as long as the secessionists stayed within Jiangyin County, and he allowed the Wuxi and Jiangyin delegations to negotiate with General Xiao in order to seek a peaceful solution.

This initial peace mission, however, was not successful. Before the Jiangyin delegation could reach General Xiao, fighting between the two sides began. The battle raged back and forth, but eventually reinforcements from Nanjing led to a sound defeat for the secessionists, who retreated to Jiangyin and the forts. The next day, rumors circulated that the Wuxi forces under General Su were planning to counterattack, an event that surely would bring suffering to the city, which lay between Wuxi and the forts. Panic-stricken, no one in Jiangyin seemed to know what to do next. Worth and Moffett this time set out alone in the *Wilmington* to attempt to arrange another truce, sailing under a Red Cross flag taken from the mission hospital and pretending to be searching for wounded soldiers. They discovered that the troops moving on Jiangyin were in fact not General Su's from the south but those of General Fang Gengsheng, the former commander of the forts, from the west. Fang had been given the responsibility of recovering the forts by Military Governor Feng. Locating Fang, the two missionaries secured his approval for a truce until noon of the next day, 25 April, when he agreed to meet with representatives of the beleaguered independents.

General Xiao was ready to surrender and met in the city on the morning of 25 April with the missionaries, the magistrate, and town notables to discuss the situation. Worth, Moffett, and a Mr. Tsoh representing the city went to the appointed site four miles west of the forts to discuss the terms of surrender with General Fang. The terms were generous: every man who surrendered his gun would be reimbursed, full amnesty would be granted to everyone involved, and any soldier or officer who wished to re-enlist would be permitted do so. Xiao and his chief lieutenant accepted these terms, then returned to the forts in the company of the missionaries and the town leaders to explain the situation to the soldiers. Worth at the outset stated that the missionaries were there purely as advocates of peace, not as a party to the negotiations. Tsoh then revealed the terms of surrender, which after much discussion were accepted by the secessionists.

The danger seemed averted. Overnight, however, diehard elements inside the forts, under the leadership of You Min, convinced some of the soldiers to repudiate the agreement and drive out or imprison those officers who had agreed to surrender. General Xiao had returned to the magistrate's *yamen*, and he quickly left the city on a small boat when he heard of the turnaround. At dawn on 26 April, the white flag of the independents reappeared over the forts. The mutineers, about 500–600 strong, again demanded a huge sum of money from the city under threat of bombardment. By this time, Jiangyin's commerce had been cut off and its food was scarce, its leadership scattered, its people and resources exhausted. Still, You Min pressed his demands for ransom. As the local history put it, "The city's fate rested in the bore of the cannon."[29]

General Fang, learning of the repudiation of the surrender agreement, attacked the forts with about 1,000 men at noon on 26 April and captured them by nightfall. Many of the soldiers in the forts had slipped away and surrendered, as planned, before the fighting began. Some of the mutineers held out to the end and tried to escape on junks across the Yangzi River; one boatload was sunk by a cruiser shot, and the other capsized. A handful escaped overland to the east of Jiangyin and melted into the countryside, no doubt becoming bandits or perhaps eking out a living in any number of occupations or trades on the fringes of society. The leader of the revolt, You Min, was caught and executed. General Fang was replaced as commander of the forts by one of his subordinates. The provincial military governor also assented to Jiangyin's request to reduce the number of troops stationed there and remove some of the cannon in order to reduce the possibility of future calamities.

The outcome of the battle may have been determined, and certainly the city was spared extensive damage, by the actions of one man, the artillery commander, Meng Yufa. He had decided to surrender but was forced to remain at the forts by the mutineers. When General Fang's troops attacked, the rebels, who had no training in artillery, commanded Meng and his men to fire the cannons not only at Fang but also at the magistrate's *yamen*, at one of the leading cotton mills, and at a number of other areas in the city and even the mission compound. Meng refused to carry out these orders, and the infuriated rebels threatened to kill him. Eventually, under duress, Meng's cannoneers fired twelve shots, but they caused no serious damage because they deliberately fired to miss their targets. In some cases, the shells did not even explode because Meng had tampered with the firing mechanisms. Stray cannon fire hit the bank of a pond and the courtyard of a pagoda in the city, a bridge south of the city, and the base of the city wall in the East Gate area. This last shot exploded near the mission's girls school dormitory, but this was the only danger the station experienced during the battle.

Throughout this period of fighting and uncertainty, the mission station became a haven for all classes of city residents. The wealthy at first sent their wives and children — about eighty in all — to the hospital with a variety of feigned illnesses, but when the fighting for control of the fort began in earnest, even that pretense was dropped and people of all sorts flocked to the mission compound as the safest place, "gentlemen in their silk gowns . . . not scorning to take refuge beside the poorest coolies." Refugees crowded the chapel, the hospital, and both of the middle school buildings.[30] As Lacy Moffett wrote, "We had become the protectors instead of the protected." Many soldiers from both sides and some civilians who were wounded in the fighting were brought to the hospital for treatment. A historian of missionary medicine has noted that Western medicine was more effective in the treatment of gunshot wounds than traditional Chinese medicine, which was weak in surgical work. So warfare, which was in no short supply during this period, provided mission medical institutions with the opportunity to be of great service and to command an increasing respect from their host communities.[31]

The Jiangyin elite were quick to recognize the crucial role the missionaries played during the crisis. The local gazetteer compiled shortly after the event makes ample reference to their contributions.[32] A representative from the city leaders came to the station to present formal thanks and told the foreigners: "We people of Kiangyin have awakened from a dream. We knew you missionaries were here to do good, but now we see your Christianity makes you as brothers to us in trouble."[33] The Jiangyin elite also admitted that without the missionaries as escorts and without the use of their boat, they would not have dared to travel back and forth between enemy lines.[34]

More honors were bestowed on the missionaries the following spring. On 9 March 1917, a celebration was held in the finest home in town, the residence of the Dzens, to honor George Worth for his peace efforts of the previous spring, his general contributions to the welfare of Jiangyin, and his upcoming fiftieth birthday (actually not until October, but the city elite did not want to wait that long). Huge Chinese and American flags adorned the Dzen residence, where about forty Chinese residents of the city assembled to act as hosts for the entire missionary group. With men and women dining separately in solariums overlooking grotto gardens and ponds, the missionaries were treated to a forty-course banquet, complete with toasts but, mercifully, no speeches. Those came the next day, when the second half of the celebration was conducted on the grounds of the station. Over 500 guests packed the chapel to hear speeches and applaud as Worth received a series of prized gifts: two large Chinese landscape paintings from local Christians, various silver articles from the local gentry, and four scrolls extolling his services to the community written by the district magistrate himself. Four similar scrolls were presented at the same time to the station by the gentry in appreciation for the missionaries' good work.[35]

The missionaries took heart from their increasingly warm relations with the better classes of the city and the fact that the townspeople apparently felt that "the work outside of the East Gate was really a part of their own city and not a distinctly foreign thing grafted on."[36] In the city, the missionaries felt welcome in every home and were allowed to use a large public hall for evangelistic meetings and benefit concerts for the poor. They often were asked to speak at assemblies in the government schools.[37] One of the women missionary educators was invited in 1919 to teach English five hours a week at one of the large primary schools in Jiangyin. When that school, which had been founded by some of the city elite and had a Western-style curriculum, held a gala celebration on National Day (10 October) in 1919, ten of the missionaries attended and a first for Jiangyin was recorded: at the banquet, foreign women sat at the same table with Chinese men.[38] Some girls from elite families enrolled in the girls school at the East Gate, and many scholars and gentry attended special Bible classes conducted by Lacy Little on Sunday afternoons at his home.[39]

Despite the increasing interaction and increasingly cordial relations between the missionaries and the local elite, few of the elite converted to Christianity. The missionaries hoped that community leaders would realize that their socially useful services were not distinct from their religious message, that in fact their humanitarian activities were agencies of and witness to their Christian faith. Although the Chinese elite often perceived and appreciated the connection, in the end they felt no compunction about accepting one and rejecting the other. Still, the political and financial support of this group was crucial to the work of the station and provided missionaries with the opportunity to reach out to the larger populace, if not the elite themselves, with their Christian message. Chinese commoners, long accustomed to taking their cue from the local elite, could not help but notice that the attitude and actions of the Jiangyin city leaders had changed from open hostility and opposition to Christian missionaries in the 1890s to equally open cordiality and support in the 1920s.

The gentry were especially supportive of Worth and the medical work of the station. The local elite's use and support of missionary medicine in the early republican era were in marked contrast to the early days of the station, when most of its patients were the poor and the elite held their distance. Wealthy patrons of the hospital were in the habit of commissioning handsome tablets, some five feet long, to commemorate their successful treatment, and by 1921, the hospital was running out of space to display them all.[40] Other benefactors contributed cash.[41] When Worth and his family left for home on furlough in 1921, the district magistrate, local businessmen, and gentry gave him a farewell present of an engraved silver shield mounted on a thick hardwood base about a foot in height. The inscription on the shield read, "Zealous in Holy Labor" (Shengshi xinye).[42] When Worth returned to China in 1922 with the city's first X-ray machine (a rarity at the time in missionary hospitals),[43] the city leaders had raised the necessary funds for its purchase and installation (which took Worth all winter and the next spring). The gift was presented at a gala reception in May 1923 hosted by the magistrate and the local gentry.[44] They also provided about $2,000 for the construction of another ward at the hospital for poor patients and opium addicts, designating the ward "a memorial of the days of fear and trial through which Kiangyin passed in 1916, when our hospital was the refuge to which rich and poor alike resorted to safety."[45]

Opium addiction was rampant in Jiangyin, and during the city's anti-opium campaign of the late 1910s, the foreign missionaries again had the opportunity to be of service to the local community. City leaders began rounding up all addicts they could identify and gave them a choice of either going to jail or being sent to the mission hospital for treatment at the special ward they had built for this purpose. By 1919, forty addicts from the poorer classes were being treated at the hospital at the gentry's expense.[46] The campaign was so successful that it apparently provoked a violent response from the local military commander, who was an opium smoker himself and was reputedly involved in the illegal smuggling of the drug. He threatened to kill the leaders of Jiangyin's Anti-opium Society if they continued their efforts to suppress the sale and smuggling of opium. The threat had its intended effect: city officials and gentry temporarily abandoned the anti-opium drive and were too intimidated even to register a protest with higher authorities.

Consequently, George Worth, who had been named honorary president of the society, decided to act on behalf of his Chinese colleagues. He traveled to Shanghai at the end of January 1919 to contact a special commissioner from Beijing who was spearheading the government's renewed anti-opium efforts. Worth arrived just in time to witness the spectacular burning of 1,206 chests of opium worth $25 million that the government had purchased from foreign dealers. (The Opium War had been fought eighty years earlier over the Chinese seizure and destruction of about $10 million worth of British opium.) The next day, 28 January, he met the special delegate, who advised him that the Beijing government would investigate the situation in Jiangyin.

Miss Sen and her "family" of poor and orphaned girls, 1920s. (Lacy L. Little Papers, Department of History and Records, Presbyterian Church [U.S.A.], Montreat, N.C.)

Later, instructions were sent to the local commander not to interfere with the anti-opium work.[47]

Another social concern of the Jiangyin missionaries were the poor and orphaned children in the area. Jiangyin, like all cities of some size, maintained a home for abandoned babies. It accepted several hundred babies a year, but about half of them died while in the care of the home. In 1917 the trustees of the home asked the missionaries to manage the operation. They declined to accept this responsibility, but one of the graduates of the hospital's nurses training school agreed to take charge and Worth acted as adviser and visiting physician to the home.[48] At the station, two evangelists, Anna Sykes and a Miss Sen, provided a comfortable home for a number of poor and orphaned young girls whom they encountered during their itinerating trips into the countryside. After Sykes left Jiangyin, Marion Wilcox, who arrived in 1924, continued the work with Miss Sen until the home was closed during the unsettled political conditions of 1927.[49]

Throughout the 1920s, Worth and the hospital staff battled a series of epidemics in cooperation with the local public health society. In 1919–20, the ninety beds in the hospital were in constant use by flu victims and by patients with spinal meningitis, an outbreak of which killed hundreds. In 1923, the scare was smallpox. Two years later, Jiangyin was in the midst of a cholera epidemic that totally occupied the hospital doctors and nurses. A campaign was launched to warn people of the dangers of uncleanliness. Large, bright-colored posters depicting how flies acted as carriers of the disease were displayed throughout the town. Then in 1926, scarlet fever killed a number of people, and the hospital helped vaccinate about 500 people.[50] The hospital received recognition for its medical contributions in 1923 when George Worth was elected honorary president of the public health society, which was actually headed by one of the Chinese doctors on the staff.

When Ida Albaugh left Jiangyin in 1919, no one with the necessary training was available in the entire Mid-China Mission to replace her, and consequently the nurses training school at the hospital was in danger of losing its registration. The Worths delayed their scheduled furlough for over a year to help out at the school in hopes of averting disaster. It was to no avail: in 1921, the Nurses Association of China disaccredited the school. As a result, the hospital suffered a blow to its prestige in the eyes of the local Chinese. In addition, most of the Chinese graduate nurses transferred to other hospitals where they earned higher salaries. It was only in 1924 after Margaret Dixon, a graduate of the Hahnemem Hospital Training School for Nurses in Philadelphia, joined the staff that the school was restored to its former standing.[51]

The hospital experienced other personnel problems. After Frank Crawford transferred to Jiaxing in 1919, George Worth was once again the only foreign doctor at the station. He was overworked and exhausted from his many duties. In 1921, on the eve of his much-awaited furlough, he relinquished the superintendency of the hospital to the head Chinese doctor, L. Y. Nyi. In 1925, Charles Voss, a graduate of Tulane Medical College, arrived and took over surgical duties from Worth, but Voss became seriously ill in 1926 and returned home. Emma Worth died that same year, and Margaret Dixon left China in 1927, never to return.[52] Thus, once again, only Worth and two Chinese doctors continued to provide medical services, and the nurses training program was placed in jeopardy.

The mission hospital and its auxiliary operations were part of an elaborate and costly enterprise, which required a constant struggle to raise the funds needed to keep it going. Only about a quarter of the missionary hospitals in China in the 1920s were self-supporting (excluding the salaries of the foreign staff, which were usually paid by the foreign mission board of their denomination).[53] The others, including the hospital at Jiangyin, had to supplement locally raised funds with support from church organizations back home. By the 1920s, fees from Chinese patients at the Jiangyin hospital covered about 70–80 percent of annual expenses, with the remainder provided by local supporters and the Woman's Auxiliary of the Wilmington Presbytery of North Carolina. The 1923–24 (April–March) fiscal year can serve as an example. Total hospital expenditures came to $17,138 that year. About 6,650 patients paid fees totaling $11,898, the Wilmington Presbyterial Auxiliary provided $3,000, local donations and miscellaneous income amounted to $323, and the shortfall of $1,917 was covered by monies carried forward from the previous year.[54] It was not until the 1930s that the hospital could become self-sufficient.[55]

The auxiliary's association with the Jiangyin hospital went back to 1904, as we have seen. Its investment in the medical work continued throughout the life of the station and came close to totaling $100,000. In the early republic and warlord eras discussed here, the major expenses the auxiliary supported were the construction of the women's ward in 1915, the salary of Dr. Crawford from 1913 to 1919, part of the salary of trained nurse Ida Albaugh from 1909 to 1919, and the construction of a residence in 1923 for the two Chinese doctors who up to that point had occupied private rooms in the men's ward. Finally, from 1922 on, the auxiliary pledged an annual amount of about $1,600 to cover general maintenance expenses.[56] In addition to these cash contributions, women of the auxiliary from 1924 on prepared White Cross supplies (such as bandages, gowns, and baby layettes) for the hospital.[57]

The missionaries' last opportunity for Christian service to the Jiangyin community prior to becoming targets of the Nationalist revolution came in January 1925 on the eve of the station's thirtieth anniversary. As in 1916, the city was fought over for control of its strategic forts, this time by competing warlord factions, and again the missionaries were indispensable intermediaries in negotiations and provided refuge and medical care to victims of the fighting.[58] The battle over Jiangyin was part of the larger second Zhili-Fengtian war of 1924–25, which resulted in the capture of the Jiangsu province by the Fengtian, or northern, forces.[59] Even before the conflict reached Jiangyin, missionaries there became involved. At the request of the civilian governor of the Jiangsu province, a group of missionaries and Christian Chinese engaged in relief work in late 1924 among the civilian population in the war zone, about ten miles wide and fifty miles long, stretching along the Yangzi River between the city and Shanghai.[60]

Jiangyin was one of the last cities in the province to be taken by the attacking northern troops, commanded by General Pih. From 24 to 30 January 1925, the battle raged between General Pih and General Wang of the southern (Zhili) forces. The northern forces attacked from the west and took control of the forts on the second day of battle, then surrounded the city, where General Wang held out, hoping for reinforcements from Wuxi. Cannon shot and prolonged rifle and machine gun fire inflicted much damage on the city and even the missionary compounds. One shell blew off the top of the pagoda in the middle of the city, and another destroyed the roof of the city temple. Sections outside the North and West Gates were burned, and the city and compound walls were pockmarked by bullets. One of the women missionaries was narrowly missed by a three-inch shell; she later found the brass head of the shell and displayed it on a redwood stand in her home.[61]

Roof of city temple destroyed by shells during the warlord conflict of 1925. It was a
good target because it was tall, its walls were red, and it had a gilded roof. (Kiangyin
Station Photographs, Presbyterian Church in the United States Missions, China,
Department of History and Records, Presbyterian Church [U.S.A.], Montreat, N.C.)

Girls at the Luola Murchison Sprunt Academy were reported to be "deftly
preparing hospital supplies, singing 'Nearer my God to Thee,' while rifles
cracked, machine guns puttered, and bullets sang past or pierced the wall behind which they sat."[62] While the station was under fire — George Worth
later counted 114 bullet marks within just one of the station's compounds —
none of the missionaries were injured and no thought was given to evacuat-
ing. A representative of the city's gentry urged the missionaries to call upon
the American consul in Shanghai to dispatch a gunboat to protect both the
station and the Chinese. The appeal was rejected by the missionaries for fear
that the consul would order them to withdraw to safer ground. Mail and telegraph service had been disrupted by the battle, and the station had not yet installed a radio, so the consul was unaware of the station's difficulty. The missionaries preferred it that way, determined to stay on and be of help.[63]

The station was not in the direct line of fire between the two competing
forces, and military commanders had by then become accustomed to avoid-
ing the East Gate section of the city in battle so as not to endanger the foreigners. The mission compounds thus became a ready refuge for city residents, over 1,600 of whom crowded inside the station walls during the last
week of January. The station had obtained a large supply of rice, vegetables,

Red Cross workers trained at the Jiangyin hospital collecting corpses after the
warlord conflict of 1925. (Kiangyin Station Photographs, Presbyterian Church
in the United States Missions, China, Department of History and Records,
Presbyterian Church [U.S.A.], Montreat, N.C.)

and fuel because of the Chinese New Year (which began on 24 January), so
the missionaries were able to serve three simple meals a day to their guests,
some days cooking about 500 pounds of rice. An additional 300 people
sought refuge two miles away at the North Gate chapel under the care of its
Chinese pastor and a missionary assistant.[64] Hundreds of soldiers and civilians received medical treatment at the station hospital, where additional
makeshift beds were assembled by laying boards between chapel pews. Although a couple of relief societies existed in the city, their founders apparently viewed them more as a way to afford themselves protection as noncom-
batants than as service organizations to help those wounded and dislocated
by war. These societies were vying for official recognition from Red Cross authorities but without success because of their irregular operations. Consequently, the hospital staff took charge of Red Cross work, training a squad of
volunteers in first-aid techniques for treating the numerous wounded in the
city. The staff provided another service by delivering two babies among the
refugee population in the compound.[65]

One of the oddities of the battle for Jiangyin was the presence among the
northern forces of over 600 White Russians who had joined Zhang Zuolin's
Fengtian army in Manchuria. They were tough fighters and acted as a vanguard for the northerners, who numbered about 900 men, in capturing the

forts. The Chinese greatly feared the Russian soldiers. Their wounded were cared for separately, first at the North Gate chapel and later at one of the missionaries' homes rather than the hospital, to avoid trouble. The commander of the Russians was grateful for the special treatment and promised to commend the Jiangyin missionaries to the American consul in Shanghai.[66]

After the northern invaders captured the forts on the second day of fighting, 25 January, the three senior missionaries at Jiangyin, Lacy Little, George Worth, and Lacy Moffett, at the request of city leaders, began to seek a way to facilitate peace. First they contacted the beleaguered general of the southern forces inside the city, but he was noncommittal about a negotiated settlement. A second effort on 26 January was also unsuccessful. The missionaries then undertook the more difficult task of trying to contact the commander of the northern forces in control of the Jiangyin forts. On 27 January, in the company of a delegation from the city, they carefully made their way under a Red Cross flag along paths outside the north wall of the city in search of General Pih. The peacemakers made one narrow escape when they found themselves in the line of fire between an attacking Russian soldier and the defenders manning guns on the city wall. They ducked for cover, along with the Russian, who then led the delegation to his commander. Taken by the Russian general to General Pih, the missionaries and city leaders pleaded with him to spare the city any further attack and state terms of peace they could take to the southern commander, General Wang. Pih drafted a letter outlining his terms, and after a day of indecision, Wang agreed to an armistice and to meet with his adversary.[67]

Negotiations took place on 28–30 January at Lacy Little's home within the station. Pih and Wang sat at opposite ends of a long table, with their lieutenants along either side. Armed guards stood watch outside the house. Six missionaries and a representative of the city elite sat off to the side, along one wall, observing the negotiations but not participating in them. After several lengthy sessions and one private encounter between Pih and Wang in a separate room, terms of surrender were agreed upon. On 30 January, General Pih thanked his hosts, picked up Lacy Moffett's young daughter Martha and kissed her on the cheek, and then left the missionary compound to enter the city through the East Gate and formally accept General Wang's surrender. The latter withdrew with his disarmed men and a payment of 15,000 taels of silver.[68] A resumption of fighting was narrowly averted three months later. Some of the gunners left by the northern general to guard the forts turned out to be of questionable loyalty and apparently were plotting to restore control to the Zhili faction. A contingent of northern forces surrounded the potential rebels in a surprise move, and the forts were resecured.[69]

Throughout this brief conflict, the missionaries had become indispensable actors in the drama. They were the only people trusted by all sides, their facilities provided the perfect neutral setting, and their presence guaranteed safe conduct for emissaries. Cordial relationships also developed between the missionaries and the two generals using their facilities to work out a settlement. At one point, the northern commander told George Worth, "I know what you missionaries are here for and what you are doing for my people, and it shames me to think that we are killing one another while you are trying to save as many of us as you can."[70] The defeated southern general intimated to his hosts that he might be inclined to retire to the station with his money and other loot, but they firmly rejected the overture.[71]

In the aftermath of war, the missionaries assumed leadership of the administration of relief work. Looting had been ferocious, and the shelling and shooting had caused much damage. Both the departing and the conquering forces had quartered in city homes, pilfering valuables and destroying property. Many shops were closed, with signs proclaiming, "Stock all looted; cannot do business." The post office, on the other hand, was swamped with business as soldiers brought in parcels of loot to mail home to their families.[72] Many Jiangyin residents were homeless and deprived of a livelihood. Red Cross units under Chinese control joined missionaries in dispensing relief, caring for the wounded, and cleaning up debris. Distribution of relief funds from the national and provincial governments was entrusted to the missionaries, probably to ensure that the money reached the intended parties. It should be noted, though, that the missionaries seemed to dispense larger amounts of relief to Christian families.[73]

The local gentry showed their appreciation of the missionaries' protection and help during this crisis in several significant ways. Station personnel were feted and showered with gifts, such as shields, pictures, and silk scrolls. Commemorative stone benches were placed on the grounds of the girls school, and a deep well was dug at the boys school and named "Source of Knowledge" (Siyuan).[74] Perhaps most important and symbolic of all was the gentry's participation in the station's thirtieth anniversary celebration in April 1925. The Jiangyin Educational Association granted the use of the public recreation grounds in the middle of the city, on which the northern troops had been conducting military drills but which they relinquished for the event, for a week-long series of evangelistic and celebratory meetings. A large tent, borrowed from the Southern Methodist mission in Suzhou and shipped to Jiangyin on a canal boat, was erected that could seat over a thousand guests. Above the gateway to the grounds, a mass of paper flowers formed the background for large white Chinese characters that read, "The Thirtieth Anniversary of the Christian Church in Jiangyin." Just inside the gateway, a book room was erected, where a large number of congratulatory scrolls from Jiangyin organizations and individuals were hung.

江陰基督教惠老會卅週年紀念暨公眾團代表攝影

Delegation from the gentry who attended the thirtieth anniversary celebration on
7 April 1925 of the founding of the Jiangyin Station. The Jiangyin magistrate is
seated in the center of the first row, holding a derby. The three missionaries standing
in the second row on the left are (left to right) William Cumming, Lacy Moffett,
and Lacy Little; in the back row is Charles Worth. (Kiangyin Station Photographs,
Presbyterian Church in the United States Missions, China, Department of
History and Records, Presbyterian Church [U.S.A.], Montreat, N.C.)

The first day of the meetings, 7 April, was given over entirely to the anniversary celebration itself. A large group of city notables, including the district magistrate, paraded into the tent with a body of police escorting their
gifts. They were greeted by the contrasting sounds of the brass band from the
James Sprunt Academy "puffing and clanging out a vigorous welcome" and a
Chinese orchestra "playing a high wailing melody." The gentry presented
the missionaries with a silver tablet over a foot high and four feet long bearing the following inscription (as translated from the Chinese by Lacy Little):

> Confucius said, "Attain unto love [ren]."
> Mencius said, "Obtain righteousness [yi]."
> Succeed without seeking praise.
> God is supreme.
> Thirty years of strenuous toil.
> Behold this Cross!
> The American Presbyterians have come to Kiangyin to preach the truth
> and proclaim the purpose of the Lord to save the world, to establish

schools for the enlightenment of the people, upbuild hospitals for the healing of the sick, to nourish the infirm, care for the young, minister to the afflicted and provide for the poor. There is not one of these agencies that does not reveal a heart of love.

When the community was in peril the leaders in the Church, with no fear of danger, exerted themselves to bring about peace, causing the hearts of the people to overflow with gratitude.

On this Thirtieth Anniversary, we respectfully present this tablet to your flourishing Church in token of our everlasting remembrance.

Presented by the Mayor of Kiangyin and all the public organizations of the city.[75]

After the presentation, station personnel gave brief histories of the evangelistic, medical, and educational work of the mission, interspersed with music. Dinner was served to a large number of Christians from the countryside and many of the city guests, and then a procession including the academy band and several hundred pupils took the gifts to the station compound. The rest of the week was devoted to religious meetings, with services in the mornings for Christians and evangelistic talks in the afternoons for reaching nonbelievers.[76]

One final token of Jiangyin's gratitude and esteem was the paving in 1926 of the dirt road leading from the East Gate of the city to the station and beyond, thus symbolically incorporating the station more directly into the life of the city. The project cost $2,000, which was paid for entirely by one of Jiangyin's wealthiest citizens. As a permanent reminder of the station's recent contribution to the city's well-being, the paved road was named "Peace Road."[77] The engraved tablet (installed in a room at the hospital) and the paved road stood as two tangible reminders of the station's place in the community.[78] To Lacy Little, in particular, and to the spirit of R. A. Haden, who had died in 1917, a casualty of World War I, the honors bestowed on the station must have vindicated their efforts of thirty years before when the gentry's opposition and a devious plot had caused them to flee for their lives.[79]

Although perhaps not on a par with its contributions to peacemaking, the station in late 1925 installed a radio in Worth's office in the hospital that proved invaluable to both the missionaries and the city. It apparently was the only radio in Jiangyin, and a reporter from the daily newspaper in town came to the station every morning to listen to the Chinese version of the news broadcast from Shanghai (an English version was aired in the evening). Items of interest were then published in the newspaper under the heading of "Radio News." Station personnel meanwhile distributed their own summaries of the news each day in the boys and girls schools. Besides receiving transmissions from Shanghai, the radio could also pick up broadcasts from

Jiangyin Station missionaries and guests, assembled in the Worths' front yard,
April 1925. In the back row, from left, are Charles Worth (second),
Katheryne Thompson (fourth), Lacy Little (eighth), Nell Little (ninth),
George Worth (tenth), Marion Wilcox (eleventh), Andrew Allison (twelfth), and
Lacy Moffett (sixteenth); in the middle row are Virginia Lee (far left), Emma Worth
(third), Jane Lee (fourth), and Ella Allison (far right). (Kiangyin Station
Photographs, Presbyterian Church in the United States Missions, China, Department
of History and Records, Presbyterian Church [U.S.A.], Montreat, N.C.)

Japan and Manila and thus provided the station with more current news
of the outside world than was available in local newspapers. The missionaries also appreciated the accurate information concerning the time and enjoyed listening to the church services and concerts that were broadcast on
the radio.[80]

At the time of the anniversary celebrations in 1925, the Jiangyin Station
had reached the pinnacle of its success in China. In numbers alone, more
missionaries were assigned to the station than ever before or after. The entire
PCUS world missionary effort reached its prewar peak in 1925,[81] and the
church was able to support twenty-three missionaries at Jiangyin. Four were
engaged in strictly evangelistic work, nine were in education, five were at the
hospital, one was an accountant, two were wives temporarily devoted to raising small children, and two were on home leave. The foreign staff was aided
by about twenty-five Chinese workers: pastors, evangelists, Bible women, and
colporteurs (traveling salesmen distributing Christian tracts). About 1,000
professed Christians and almost that number of enquirers attended the four

organized churches and sixteen chapels throughout the Jiangyin field. The hospital at the East Gate treated thousands of patients, the two high schools at the central station enrolled over 400 boys and girls, lower schools run by country chapels taught about 300 students, and the Bible school trained about forty women. The Christian mission's prestige and influence had also never been higher.

In taking stock of the Jiangyin Station's activities and accomplishments during the early republic, it should be noted that the missionaries' ability to be of service to their Chinese host communities depended in part on their special position as foreigners. Although no American or other foreign troops were stationed in the immediate vicinity of Jiangyin, the presence of such forces not far away in Shanghai and other major cities, and the availability of foreign gunboats that could patrol the Yangzi, enhanced the prestige and authority of the missionaries. In time, during the nationalistic storms of the 1920s, the treaty privileges foreigners had acquired and assumed in the century after China's defeat in the Opium War of 1839–42 hung like an albatross around the necks of the missionaries. Many of the American missionaries in China and their denominational boards back home, in fact, renounced such privileges and supported Chinese demands for treaty revision. But without the protection of their home government, they in turn could not have played a protector's role in their local Chinese communities.

The northward march of revolutionary forces in 1927 temporarily drove the Jiangyin missionaries, like so many of their colleagues elsewhere in China, out of their station to the safety of Shanghai and other coastal cities. Many returned, but relations with the Chinese, Christian and non-Christian alike, changed drastically, and their work never again approached the same centrality in local community life it had gained in the years from 1912 to 1925. In the early republic, the particular combination of circumstances — political disorder, the persistence of treaty privileges, an openness to Western ideas — encouraged Christian missionaries to extend humanitarian aid and the Chinese to accept it. The Jiangyin group had the opportunity to aid the Chinese on a number of occasions, and their secular endeavors in peace-keeping and providing refuge, medical care, and social welfare established them and the station as respected institutions in the local community.

5

THIS
PRECOCIOUS
CHILD

RESPONSE

TO CHINESE

NATIONALISM

The fratricidal warfare of militarists may have led to an enhanced role for missionaries, but the Nationalist revolutionary struggle with the militarists and the subsequent establishment of the Nationalist government at Nanjing confronted the missionary movement with some urgent problems. Foremost among them was the evacuation of stations and the protection of lives and property during the revolutionaries' Northward Expedition. Antiforeign and anti-Christian sentiments were common components of the revolutionary movement in the 1920s and became especially strong after the May Thirtieth Incident of 1925. The foreign missionaries scattered throughout the country were in a particularly vulnerable position. Once the immediate personal danger was past, missionaries faced challenges to their work from the new regime, even though its leader, Chiang Kai-shek, became a professed Christian. Christian propagation was allowed, but increasing pressure was applied to turn over administrative control of Christian institutions to the Chinese.

In the changed political climate after the May Fourth Incident of 1919, when students in Beijing protested their government's inability to protect the national interest against depredation by Japan and other foreign powers, the mission movement increasingly came under attack from nationalistic elements in society. Mission schools, in particular, aroused the opposition of nationalists who came to view them as insidious underminers of Chinese values, in effect another arm of Western imperialism in China. One of the first complaints accused mission school authorities of prohibiting their students from joining in patriotic demonstrations that arose in the wake of the May Fourth protest.

Students at the Sprunt Academy organized a student union that held demonstrations to arouse the masses in support of the anti-Japanese boycott. On one occasion, the students engaged in a fistfight with a traitorous merchant and his accomplices who were trying to bring in three boatloads of Japanese yarn. Several student leaders were injured in the fray. When they appealed to the courts, the merchant was ordered to pay a fine, which the students placed in their union's fund. The school authorities, however, were not happy with this turn of events. Using such slogans as "In saving the nation, you must not forget your studies" (Jiukuo buwang dushu) and "Scholars are pure and upright and do not get involved with politics" (Wenren qinggao buwen zhengzhi), they forced students back into the classroom.[1]

Missionary educators professed that they did not relish the idea of their students parading the streets to stir up anti-Japanese and anti-imperialist hatred, a decidedly un-Christian activity in their eyes. They urged instead that students "demonstrate true patriotism by good deeds," such as engaging in first-aid work, eating thin rice gruel for one meal a day and giving the money saved to the cause, or visiting homes in the company of Bible women to warn women of the dangers to the nation. Some disruption of classes did occur, but Jiangyin escaped the worst of the nationalistic storms for the time being.[2]

Despite these criticisms, the Jiangyin mission schools were generally respected in the community. When a new, privately subscribed school was established in the city in 1920, it operated on principles that reflected Western and Christian influences. Among other things, English was taught, women served as teachers and on the management committee of the school, experimental science was part of the curriculum, students were involved in governance, and physical drills were instituted.[3] The last feature had been an integral part of the mission schools from the start, and whenever the Sprunt Academy boys held a drill, it would attract large crowds from the city schools.[4] As for student governance, the boys school practiced self-government in the form of a "school city" that trained the students in managing school affairs.

In the 1920s, a broad-based anti-Christian movement arose in China's metropolitan centers. The first institutional expression of opposition to Christianity came from the Young China Association, organized in 1919 to help build a strong, modern society through scientific inquiry. For a brief time in 1920 and 1921, the association limited membership to those without any religious faith. Controversy over this provision sparked a great debate on religion that attracted many of the leading intellectuals of the New Culture and May Fourth periods. Chen Dexiu, Hu Shi, Cai Yuanpei, Zhu Zhixin, Zhou Zuoren, Wu Zhihui, and many other radicals, anarchists, liberals, and Marxists opposed Christianity (and other religions) as superstitious, unscientific, and a hindrance to social progress. Prominent Western philosophers, such as Bertrand Russell and John Dewey, were often cited to bolster their position.[5]

Anti-Christianism moved beyond intellectual discourse to become a protest movement in the spring of 1922 in response to three events.[6] One was the publication that year of a book reviewing the progress of Christian mission work in China. It carried the inflammatory title of *The Christian Occupation of China* and displayed a map showing the geographic distribution of mission forces.[7] The belligerent imagery of the title and the map provoked anger and alarm. A second publication that year focused on Christian education in China and recommended further expansion[8] at a time when Chinese educators and patriots were striving to create a national school system. The third event provided the anti-Christians a target for their resentment. When the World's Student Christian Federation announced its plans to convene a conference at Qinghua College in Beijing, radical students in Shanghai founded the Anti-Christian Student Federation to protest and try to prevent the gathering. The federation in early March circulated a proclamation that launched the anti-Christian movement and set the tone of its rhetoric. Part of the document linked Christianity to capitalism and Western imperialism:

> The capitalists from various countries have established churches in China, for the sole purpose of cajoling the Chinese people to welcome capitalism; they have also established the YMCA in China, for the sole purpose of bringing up docile and faithful walking dogs for themselves. In short, their aim is to suck dry the blood of the Chinese people. Therefore, we are opposed to capitalism; and at the same time we must be opposed to the current Christian religion and its churches which support capitalism while cheating the ordinary people.[9]

The language of this document suggests a Marxist-Leninist influence, and some evidence supports the charge of Communist responsibility through the active involvement of the Socialist Youth Corps.[10]

Nationwide, students responded to the Shanghai broadside by organizing antireligious and anti-Christian associations. The Grand Anti-Religion Federation formed in Beijing to counter what it called "the spreading infection of religious poison" (a caption it gave to a reprint of the map found in *The Christian Occupation of China*). The Christian students proceeded with their meetings at Qinghua on 4–9 April, but the Grand Anti-Religion Federation held a counterconvention at Beijing University to hear, among others, Cai Yuanpei, the prominent revolutionary and educator, attack religion and religious education.[11] The spring protest movement, however, being primarily a student affair, fizzled out as summer and school vacations arrived.

This initial anti-Christian movement did not have any noticeable effect on educational work at Jiangyin, which was prospering and branching out in new directions. To accommodate increasing numbers of students at the boys school (230 students were enrolled in 1923), a new three-story dormitory was added on to the Sprunt Academy. The girls school enrolled about 150 students that same year. On Sundays, Andrew Allison led some of the boys in street preaching or visiting the jails to hand out religious tracts. The girls participated in Gospel teams of six students and two teachers each that preached in nearby villages. Lacy Little began operating a "mass education" night school in the city for men and boys, ranging in age from twelve to forty, based on the thousand-character course developed by James Yen and the YMCA.[12] The student association at the boys school used some of its funds to erect a memorial tower to Sun Yat-sen in a city park, which was renamed Zhongshan Park in his honor.[13] An organizational change was effected in the schools in keeping with the recommendations of the Chinese government. Both the boys and girls academies were divided into three-year junior and senior middle schools.[14]

The graduates of these schools were beginning to make their way in the world. Many of them had become teachers at mission schools in Jiangyin and elsewhere, while others became doctors, nurses, and hospital directors. Some graduates were in graduate school or were studying for the ministry. Even though their total numbers were not great, the schools' alumni included people who became prominent in the fields of medicine, education, science, industry, and religion. Some became active participants in the revolutionary movement, several even losing their lives in that cause.[15]

When the anti-Christian movement revived in 1924, it focused less on the superstitious and unscientific nature of religion and more on Christianity as an agent of Western imperialism.[16] This new perspective on Christianity was spurred on by an increasingly organized and politicized sense of nationalism. China's attempts to end extraterritoriality and other treaty rights had been rebuffed at the Washington Peace Conference, and agents of the new Bolshevik regime in Russia took advantage of Chinese discontent by helping organize the forces of revolution in China.

Unquestionably, the greatest impetus to the growth of Chinese nationalism and the renewal of the anti-Christian movement was the May Thirtieth Incident of 1925, in which British police in the Shanghai International Settlement killed and wounded over a score of Chinese demonstrators. Anti-imperialist protests exploded instantly throughout China. In Changsha, for example, marchers in a protest demonstration on 1 June carried placards with exhortations such as "Kill the white man," "Down with imperialism," and "Down with Christianity." The Yale-in-China and Standard Oil complexes in Changsha were threatened by mobs, but the presence of Japanese, British, and American gunboats on the Yangzi River and the protection afforded by local Chinese authorities prevented any injury to foreigners.[17]

Jiangyin remained relatively quiet in the immediate post–May Thirtieth period. The local populace continued to be friendly to the missionaries, no doubt remembering the latter's contributions to the community's well-being during the warlord conflict earlier in the year. Students in the mission schools, whose opening that spring had been delayed by the fighting, paraded and made speeches, but classes were not disrupted as they were at many other places, and commencement exercises were held as usual.[18] In the fall, however, the students were not so docile. Toward the end of October 1925, some unspecified antiforeign disturbance at the senior high school of the boys academy led to the expulsion or withdrawal of about two dozen students, including the captain of the soccer team.[19] Several of the missionaries, not fully aware of the depth of nationalistic feeling sweeping the country, blamed the trouble on "hot-air patriots" who were "hyper-sensitive about . . . national dignity" and on "that school of hate, the May Thirtieth School at Nanking, where special inducements are offered to students from Christian schools." They also suspected the work of Russian Bolshevik agitators behind the disturbances.[20]

Despite such reservations about Chinese nationalism, most American missionaries in China and their denominational mission boards back home had come to believe that extraterritoriality and other treaty privileges defended by foreign governments were detrimental to their work, and they supported Chinese demands for treaty revisions.[21] But this attitude did not spare mission compounds at Jiangyin and other areas of central China from receiving the full force of antiforeign and anti-Christian sentiment that accompanied the Northward Expedition of 1926–27.

Because of Jiangyin's strategic location, the city and the station expected trouble as the combined revolutionary forces of the Nationalists and the Communists moved northward from Canton to challenge the warlords for control of south and central China. Already in late 1925, an advance political worker for the Nationalist movement, assumed to be a "Bolshevik," had come to Jiangyin and had begun urging people not to pay their taxes.[22] A year later, Andrew Allison reported that "the country is quiet enough in actuality, but the people are uneasy, and rumors of approaching trouble — nobody can say just what — are rife."[23] By the end of 1926, the station braced for the worst. Reports of disturbances and antiforeign outbreaks in neighboring provinces left the missionaries in no doubt as to the fate of Christian institutions after the arrival of the revolutionaries, which they expected within a month or so.[24]

By January, the American consulate general in Shanghai was advising the missionaries to prepare to withdraw if the situation worsened. At the time, the missionary and Chinese staffs of the station had considered the possibility of the missionaries' evacuation and had discussed placing control of station affairs in the hands of the Chinese. By the time a second urgent message arrived from the consulate just before the Chinese New Year (on 2 February in 1927), the station had created a provisional Committee of Control composed of fifteen of the strongest Chinese leaders representing all aspects of the station's work. It was given complete authority over the station until the missionaries could return. The Americans wanted to stay on and help out as in 1925, but the Chinese Christians advised them to leave for their own safety and in order to remove a possible source of trouble for the community. A visitor from Shanghai also urged immediate departure before the steam launches stopped for a few days during the New Year's festival. Before leaving, the missionaries also visited the Jiangyin magistrate and requested that he look after station property while they were gone. He, in turn, urged them to return as soon as possible after the New Year holidays, and the city gentry gave George Worth over $400 to buy hospital supplies in Shanghai.[25]

Most of the Jiangyin missionaries (twenty in all, including families) sojourned in Shanghai alongside refugees from throughout the interior, but Charles Worth, the second son of George and Emma Worth, and his family continued on to Japan to visit relatives.[26] In mid-February, some of the men made short visits to the station to consult with their Chinese colleagues, presumably about trouble that had arisen to challenge the provisional Committee of Control. A number of the James Sprunt Academy students influenced by the revolutionary ideology had imprisoned their principal and two of the preachers at the station for three days. After the situation was resolved, additional missionaries, including two women — a nurse and an evangelist — returned to staff a skeletal operation.[27] As of March, seven missionaries manned the station: George and Charles Worth, William Cumming, Andrew Allison, Lacy Little, Margaret Dixon, and Marion Wilcox.

The missionaries thought the revolutionary armies would bypass Jiangyin. They knew that twenty-five miles to the southeast, at Wuxi, the northern forces had gathered to resist the advance of the southerners. They also had heard that the entire area was heavily mined. Thus checked, the southerners would, the missionaries expected, move to another front for the critical battle.[28] But on 22 March 1927, Nationalist soldiers marched into Jiangyin.

The revolutionary armies demanded occupancy of all the station buildings and residences, but Chinese members of the hospital and school staffs who had joined the Nationalist Party in hopes of protecting the Christian work at Jiangyin persuaded them to occupy only the boys school and two foreign residences and to quarter only a handful of the medical corps in the hospital instead of a full regiment.[29] The missionaries vacated the two foreign residences, locked their belongings in the attics, and handed over the keys to the officer in charge. Despite the latter's assurance of protection of their personal property, within hours the attics were broken into and the contents carried off by soldiers. Most of it was sold as loot the next day in city stalls. The soldiers also inflicted extensive damage on some of the station buildings. The desks, furniture, windows, and doors of the James Sprunt Academy were all destroyed and burned as fuel.[30] Andrew Allison, a dedicated ornithologist who sent specimens to the Smithsonian and the Philadelphia Academy of Sciences, had just completed a natural history museum at the academy—his "heart's pride and joy." He was preparing for its formal opening when disaster struck: the soldiers completely gutted the facility.[31]

Communist agents among the occupying forces tried to recruit boys and girls from the mission schools and the Chinese staff of the schools and hospital into their ranks, but they met with limited success. The girls listened mutely to members of the political delegation that came to their school but refused to shout their anti-imperialist and anti-Christian slogans. A teacher from the closed boys school took the platform and, to the consternation of the delegation, proclaimed that the Nationalist constitution promised religious freedom and that these girls could not be hindered in the practice of Christianity. The head male nurse at the hospital was quoted as telling them, "You may take my life, if you wish, but nothing, nothing, shall ever induce me to have a part in anything which opposes the Lord Jesus Christ."[32]

The missionaries clearly blamed the excesses of the National Revolutionary Army and the revolutionary movement on the Communists in their midst. In a letter to his home congregation in early February, George Worth bitterly condemned them as "a most efficient, but thoroughly unprincipled, secret propaganda organization [that] has strewn the land with millions of lying slanders, false charges of every sort against all foreigners, especially the British, and against the Christian church, both protestant and Roman Catholic, [and] has revived long-dead prejudices." And, he noted, "it is all directed by very shrewd, experienced Russian propagandist experts." He did not, however, denounce the revolutionary upheaval going on around him and effecting changes in the missionaries' relations with Chinese Christians. The latter, he stated, "like all patriotic Chinese, . . . are imbued with nationalist sympathy, but it is of the kind we thoroughly approve of, just the same sort of national pride, and desire for national advancement that every right minded person must have."[33]

A native of Jiangyin later recalled that the Communist-inspired peasant movement in the Jiangsu province began in his city and that he heard as a boy that members of this movement were responsible for the burning and looting of missionary property in March. One of the leaders, Miao Xueqin, was later arrested for land seizures and murder. He was executed and his corpse was dragged through the city streets behind a rickshaw. Another Communist leader of the peasant movement, Qian Zhengbiao, had been a student at the James Sprunt Academy many years earlier but had been expelled for his role in the 1912 controversy over flood relief funds. Qian also was cap-tured later and executed.[34] The destruction of a country town east of Jiangyin and the abuse of a Chinese Christian pastor there were reputedly the work of a "Communist uprising" but were more likely perpetrated by Nationalist rev-olutionary forces. Later, local Nationalist Party officials apologized and re-instated the pastor at his church, offering to decorate the church in red and to explode firecrackers for the occasion.[35]

On the morning of 25 March, three days after the arrival of the revolution-ary forces, the Jiangyin missionaries met with the Committee of Control to discuss whether their presence at this time put the Christian community in jeopardy and hindered the work at Jiangyin. The committee insisted that this was not the case and urged the foreigners to stay, which they gladly agreed to do. Immediately after this decision, however, word arrived over George Worth's radio about the Nanjing Incident of the previous day (24 March), in which an American educator and five other foreigners had been killed and much of their property destroyed by soldiers (usually reported to be Com-munist)[36] of the Revolutionary Army. That evening, the radio broadcast the cryptic message from the American consulate general in Shanghai, "William is ill; operation necessary." By prearrangement, this message meant that Americans should evacuate from China's interior.[37] Charles Worth, who heard the message, quickly rounded up Dixon and Wilcox at the hospital and brought them to the Worth residence, where the five men were staying. After further hurried consultations with their Chinese colleagues, the Amer-icans decided to leave early the next morning for Shanghai.

American authorities dispatched a destroyer to pick up missionaries at Jiangyin and Taizhou,[38] but the Jiangyin group, at least, made their way to Shanghai by less imposing means. With the aid of Chinese Christians, they secured a large junk for the hundred-mile trip down the Yangzi River. The junk was to pick them up five miles from Jiangyin so as to avoid embarking in sight of the revolutionary soldiers occupying the city. The party divided into two bands for the overland walk to the point east of Jiangyin where the junk awaited them. One group, composed of Charles Worth, Lacy Little, Mar-garet Dixon, and Marion Wilcox, arrived downriver without incident, but George Worth, Andrew Allison, and William Cumming were accosted by two soldiers just outside the city. Their lives were threatened and many valu-ables were taken, including some watches, rings, and George Worth's gold-rimmed spectacles, but they were allowed to continue on. On board the junk, the party reached Shanghai safely after running aground once and be-ing fired upon several times.[39]

It has been estimated that about 8,000 Protestant missionaries were pres-ent in China at the time of the Nanjing Incident. Of that number, about 5,000 left China (many never to return), about 1,500 took refuge in Shanghai, and another 1,000 escaped to other coastal cities. Only about 500 remained at their stations in the interior.[40] One American expressed the bewilderment and bitterness of many when he wrote, "I am through with China. I have given the Chinese the best effort and the best years of my life. . . . Everything that I had in the world is gone. My wife and myself have been driven out like dogs. I am going back to God's country by the first boat I can get, and never return. I'm through."[41] On the other hand, from a safer distance, many mission leaders and organizations adopted the view that in the long run the Christian movement in China might be strengthened by this crisis. As one foreign missionary society secretary stated, "While the situation gives great cause for concern and is exceedingly serious, yet eventually it may give opportunity for desirable reconstruction of the work with larger Chinese direction."[42]

Many of the Jiangyin staff decided to take their home leave at this juncture, but others remained in Shanghai to await improved conditions and the chance to renew their work. Three of the men visited the station in August and four made a second journey in January, but it was not until February 1928 that the station was reopened with four men and three women.[43] In their absence, the Revolutionary Army had occupied all but one of the missionary homes and were using the Bible school chapel every day for their military training lectures. The boys school was closed and heavily damaged, but the girls school continued to operate without interference. Evangelistic work in the city, in the country outstations, and at the central station chapel also was continuing to be carried on by the Committee of Control.[44]

A month after the missionaries returned, they were forced out again, this time by the threat of a Communist offensive in the area. The revolutionary movement had split in the summer of 1927, and the Communists were driven out of the cities and into the mountains of south-central China, where they established new revolutionary bases away from the main population centers. Still, an occasional "Red scare" struck Jiangyin, as it did in March 1928.

The Communists began by attacking several of the country towns to the south and east of the city.[45] The most significant action took place at Xiaoqi, where a force of about 2,000 looted and set fire to the northern half of the town. Reports indicated that the attack was orderly and well planned. An advance company of younger men ran through the streets brandishing swords or meat cleavers and shouting, "Kill, kill, kill." This was enough to terrify the populace and make them run for cover. Then an incendiary unit followed and began to torch the town. Next came the main unit of more experienced soldiers armed with pistols. Finally, a medical unit arrived to attend to the dead and wounded. Any cash looted from shops and residences was turned in to the leaders, who later used it to purchase weapons and ammunition. All other loot was carried away by individual soldiers, who were allowed to dispose of it as they saw fit. Residents of the southern half of Xiaoqi, separated from the northern portion by a stone bridge, were able to repel the attackers. One of the wealthy families had organized a local militia, armed it with a machine gun, and barricaded the bridge with barbed wire, forcing the Communists to retire without capturing any further booty.

After the country campaigns, the Communists announced they would next attack Jiangyin itself. All the rich families vacated their residences and went to either Shanghai or Suzhou. The magistrate appealed to Nanjing to send troops to protect the city, and eventually the government sent a battalion of about 500 men, half of which were billeted in the boys school at the station.[46] The government troops fanned out into the countryside to attack the Communists, break up their meetings, and arrest as many of them as possible. The campaign culminated in a fierce battle at the outlying town of Houcheng, which was the center of Communist activity in the area. Government forces surrounded the Communists and dealt them a devastating blow: about 100 were killed and another 200 wounded. After this defeat, the Communist movement in Jiangyin was crippled. Local authorities began rounding up suspected radicals, and some were summarily executed. Outwardly, calm returned to Jiangyin, but there was concern over the future. As George Worth concluded in his lengthy report on the turmoil, "The seeds have been too well planted to allow a quick removal."

Although some Christian churches and homes were destroyed in the fighting in Xiaoqi and Houcheng, the Communist attacks were not part of any deliberate anti-Christian program. The Communists' main purpose seemed to be to improve their financial resources by robbing the rich. At Xiaoqi, Communist soldiers passing a Christian church were overheard to comment that the church members were "ordinary people and we ought to leave them alone" and, "Oh, this is the Christian church. They have no money. They are alright."[47]

The Communist threat at Jiangyin lasted only a few weeks; by April, most of the missionary staff returned. But their momentary absence as well as earlier evacuations only heightened the unresolved issue of devolution, that is, the transfer of authority from Christian missionaries to their Chinese colleagues. In writing about this issue, historians have emphasized the hasty and ill-prepared transition that occurred perforce in the wake of the Nanjing Incident and subsequent revolutionary activity that drove the foreign missionaries away from their posts throughout China. Although they recognize that the more liberal missions had begun the process of transferring authority earlier, they note that little had been accomplished before the upheavals of 1927.[48] An illustration of the gap that existed in many missions between the foreign staff and the Chinese prior to 1927 is found in the following recollection of a missionary educator:

I never forget the first mission meeting we had in 1925. We had the meeting at the summer resort up above Foochow [Fuzhou]. It's where all the missionaries went to escape the heat. The annual missionary meeting was held on the porches around in the settlement. They made every appointment of the Chinese church in that meeting — who would be principals of the academies, who would be heads of the hospitals. There were no Chinese there at all. That was in 1925. Then, of course, came the Nationalist government, and the requirement that the Chinese would be at the head.[49]

At Jiangyin, devolution began relatively early, from the start of the 1920s. This was partly due to the progressive attitude of the missionaries there. Ella Allison wrote in a 1915 station report, "Any voluntary step on the part of the Chinese themselves, and apart from the suggestion of the foreigner, to do independent work gladdens my heart; for it seems to point forward to the good day — (when will it come?) — of an independent, self-supporting church." Her foreign coworkers at Jiangyin often repeated these sentiments in their letters and reports throughout the 1920s and 1930s. To cite one example, George Worth noted in 1927 that the nationalistic upheavals of the time would require a change in the conduct of Christian work in China. The prospect did not alarm him: "*They* [the Chinese] must increase and *we* must decrease. It is what we have worked for and prayed for, and now we must welcome it." [50]

More decisive than the missionaries' outlook in initiating a transfer of authority to the Chinese was the personnel situation at Jiangyin. Transfers, temporary reassignments, furloughs, and illnesses had reduced the missionary forces to a bare minimum in 1920, at which time the numbers were less than half of what they had been a few years earlier. All the work of the station was suffering as a consequence.[51] In such straits, and with some trepidation, the missionaries transferred more responsibility — but not authority — to their Chinese colleagues. In 1920, the boys school at the station and the country evangelistic work were left without direct foreign supervision. One of the remaining missionaries, Virginia Lee, noted that "this is an ideal toward which we have been working carefully — but this 'is so sudden' that some of us feel decidedly apprehensive of the outcome." The following year, formal control of the hospital was transferred to the Chinese as Dr. Nyi took over the superintendency from George Worth.[52]

The experience gained in the early 1920s by the Chinese staff encouraged the Jiangyin missionaries to let them continue to shoulder greater responsibility for the administration of the station, including playing a role in the disbursement of funds. This was particularly true for evangelistic work since the growing membership rolls throughout the Jiangyin field required more

Three generations of a Christian family at Jiangyin, 1920. The grandfather (second from right) was an elder of the church, and his son (at right) was a deacon. (Kiangyin Station Photographs, Presbyterian Church in the United States Missions, China, Department of History and Records, Presbyterian Church [U.S.A.], Montreat, N.C.)

attention than the foreign evangelists could provide. Lacy Moffett in 1922 admitted to being "agreeably surprised and delighted with the way the Chinese workers have carried the work while so many of us have been absent," and he noted a growing self-reliance and leadership among Chinese Christians in evangelistic work.[53] A 1923 station report provided examples of this leadership: an association composed of Chinese preachers and church officers in the field had largely assumed the administration of evangelistic work; a joint committee of evangelistic and educational workers was directing the lay schools at outstations in the field; both of the city churches (the original one at the East Gate and a second one in the North Gate area) were under the care of ordained Chinese pastors; and several of the outstation chapels were also entirely administered by Chinese.[54] Also in 1923, a new residence was built for the two Chinese doctors who shared the management of the hospital with George Worth. Worth underscored the significance of this event: "Our two Chinese doctors with their families are now happily settled in the new houses, which are as *well built and as pleasing to look at as the dwellings occupied by the foreign missionaries.* This great advance over their former condition has given our doctors a prestige and dignity which they fully deserve and which has also added to the standing of the hospital." [55]

Thus, at Jiangyin, the personnel crisis of the early 1920s rather than the exodus of foreigners in 1927 precipitated the first steps toward devolution, but not without concern, as we have seen. The formal transfer of authority over the whole station to the Chinese, however, came only after the Nationalist revolution of 1925–27. In January 1927, as already noted, temporary control of all of the work at the station was vested in a newly organized Chinese Committee of Control. The committee conducted the affairs of the station for the remainder of 1927 because of the missionaries' withdrawal to Shanghai.

The Chinese Christians assumed their new responsibilities with a degree of hesitancy and uncertainty. In a manifesto published in a Shanghai missionary journal, they vowed to "maintain things temporarily" until the missionaries returned and to gain experience in "preparing for the future dawn of the self-supporting Church ('indigenous' Church) in China." [56] Members of the committee also occasionally traveled to Shanghai to confer with the missionaries.

Despite these seeming insecurities, the missionaries were quick to praise their Chinese colleagues. After a visit from five Chinese representatives in June who reported on their progress in the midst of the revolutionary upheavals, Andrew Allison wrote: "All the years we have spent in looking and planning toward the turning over of responsibility into Chinese hands never accomplished half so much as the few months that have passed since the end of January, with the thing actually done; and whenever we go back, and under whatever circumstances and conditions, the relations with the Chinese . . . will never be just as they were before, but higher and farther ahead, and closer and more confidential." Further on, he states, "Our Chinese friends . . . have been growing in a way beautiful to see." [57] A similar sentiment was expressed by a missionary in western China: "We . . . imagined that turning things over to the Chinese would take about five years. As a result of the evacuation of the missionaries it actually took only about three weeks." [58]

The foreign staff returned to Jiangyin in mid-February 1928. In March, they decided to petition the Mid-China Mission to sanction the organization of a permanent Joint Committee of Control at the station. Their request, the first of its kind among Southern Presbyterian missions in China, met with some skepticism and resistance among other missionaries but was finally approved. On 24 May 1928, the Joint Committee was established, with a membership of eleven Chinese Christians and six missionaries. A quorum of eleven was set so that the Chinese members could carry on without further reorganization if the foreigners had to leave again. From that point on, the Joint Committee became the ultimate authority at Jiangyin, and members of the Chinese majority were expected to take the lead in governing the station.[59] Chinese Christians were appointed as principals of the various schools and as superintendent of the hospital, and the missionaries who had formerly headed these institutions were to serve in an advisory capacity.

The organization of the Joint Committee, however, did not settle the question of who was leading the Christian movement in Jiangyin. Many hindrances still blocked the full implementation of a devolution policy. A number of historians have noted that throughout China the missionaries displayed a general reluctance to relinquish responsibility even after the creation of joint governing boards.[60] This reluctance was based on several concerns of the missionaries. Since the bulk of financing for their enterprise in China came from abroad, the missionaries felt a certain "trust" had been given them to ensure that these funds were expended according to the wishes of the home constituencies. Missionaries also had some doubts about the survival of religious values in schools and hospitals once foreign control was eliminated. Would the Chinese lose sight of the ultimate purpose of these Christian institutions, that is, the promotion of the Gospel? Furthermore, some missionaries were not convinced that Chinese Christians were ready to assume full responsibility for an independent church. Chinese Christians sadly took note of this fact. One of them wrote in 1927 that missionaries "are puzzled as to what to do with this precocious child [the Chinese church] on their hands. They want it to grow and yet cannot quite make up their minds whether or not it would be safe to take away entirely their own guiding hand."[61] This lack of faith in the Chinese was revealed strikingly even as late as 1935 in a letter George Worth sent home. In it, he declared that the Chinese church was in a "dependent stage, more or less, like our growing children."[62] It is not surprising, then, that missionaries continued to exert their authority on governing boards, even though they constituted a numerical minority, and in schools and hospitals.

Missionaries could also exert influence through membership in local churches. The Southern Presbyterians were one of the first denominations to take the position, in 1876, that it was not proper for missionaries to become voting members of church courts in mission lands and that churches growing out of missionary activity "are free born, and have the inherent right of self-government" as well as the freedom to determine their own form of church organization. The secretary of foreign missions declared at the same time that "all foreign mission work is pioneer and preliminary, having as its objective the establishment of self-governing, self-supporting and self-propagating native churches."[63]

Ultimately, however, a majority of Southern Presbyterian missionaries did become voting members of Chinese churches. At a 1901 conference in Shanghai, Southern Presbyterians went on record as favoring dual membership in a home presbytery and in a Chinese presbytery on a special basis. By the 1920s, many missionaries maintained such a dual membership, while others, especially newly arrived missionaries or children of missionaries, became full members of local churches.[64] At Jiangyin, Reverend Haden's children became members of a country church in 1907, and two of George Worth's sons, William and Charles, became members of the East Gate church in 1909.[65] When the Jiangyin Presbytery was organized in the 1920s, most of the missionaries at Jiangyin were admitted to membership while still retaining membership in their home churches.[66] Presumably, missionaries felt that membership in local churches best expressed their desire to work closely and cooperatively with Chinese Christians,[67] but membership also gave them a chance to guide the Chinese church in its infancy and retain a measure of influence.

Another problem was the slow development of a Chinese ministry that could relieve missionaries of pastoral work. It was only after 1920 that the number of ordained Chinese ministers exceeded ordained foreigners.[68] Jiangyin, however, seems to have done well in this area. In the early years of this century, Jiangyin produced more candidates for the ministry than any other station in the Mid-China Mission.[69] The station was particularly proud of Pastors Tsiang and Wu, who had been chosen to direct the East Gate and North Gate churches, respectively. Tsiang Z-dzi and Wu Me-peh were natives of a small market town four miles west of Jiangyin. They first heard the Gospel in 1897 when they were twelve years old from Lacy Little on one of his itinerating trips. After education at the Jiaxing boys school (before the Jiangyin school was opened), Hangzhou Christian College, and Nanjing Theological Seminary, they returned to their native region as coworkers at the station. Tsiang was installed as the first Chinese pastor of the East Gate church in November 1917. A few months later, after a new election at the church, all six members of the governing board of elders were Chinese. About the same time, Pastor Wu took up his duties at the North Gate church.[70] Several of the country chapels also had Chinese pastors by the mid-1920s.

The real sticking point in the creation of a Chinese-controlled church was funding. The initial costs of establishing Christianity in China were borne by foreign mission boards, which not only supplied and paid for the foreign preachers but also built the churches and subvented medical care and schooling. Chinese converts were generally not in a position to finance these operations. One American denomination reported in 1926 that less than 15 percent of its associated churches in China were self-supporting.[71] Mission boards and home supporters were understandably reluctant to relinquish control while still footing the costly bill of maintaining the enterprise. As one missionary educator put it, "He who pays the piper can — whether he really does so or not — always call the tune."[72] The growing influence of the social gospel or liberal wing of the mission movement throughout the early decades of the twentieth century only compounded the problem. The emphasis on education and medicine led to the establishment of an increasing number of expensive schools and hospitals. As early as 1907, the Mid-China Mission of the PCUS began to study the issue of self-support and drew up guidelines to facilitate future Chinese support, but in 1930 the missionaries were still bemoaning their failure to realize this objective.[73]

The missionary operation at Jiangyin was an elaborate one, with several schools, a hospital, two city churches, and a host of churches and chapels in the surrounding countryside. The expense of maintaining these institutions and funding the large staff they required was beyond the reach of Chinese congregations. The nature of the station's sources of funding paradoxically also retarded the effort to promote self-support. George Worth, who served for forty-one years in China, entirely supported himself and his family (two members of which also served for a time at Jiangyin) out of a fund endowed by his father. As already described, James Sprunt repeatedly made large donations to the educational work at Jiangyin, and the Woman's Auxiliary of the Wilmington Presbytery generously supported the medical work of George Worth. With steady support from such sources, the pressure to secure local funds abated. At Jiangyin, as at other mission stations, as long as missionary preachers, educators, and doctors continued to serve and to attract funds from home constituencies, then full self-support and self-governance were beyond the grasp of the Chinese, no matter how fervently the missionaries themselves desired it.

Whereas self-governance was mainly an issue within the Christian church in China, the question of religious instruction in the schools brought missionaries into conflict with governing authorities. Nationalists viewed education as a prerogative of the state and insisted that all private and foreign schools register with the state and abide by certain regulations; failure to do so would jeopardize their accreditation and the career aspirations of their graduates. In the early republican era, some mission schools began to register with the Beijing government and operate under a series of restrictions forbidding compulsory religious ceremonies or teaching and discrimination in the admission or treatment of non-Christian students.[74]

The growing anti-Christian and antiforeign movements of 1919–25, briefly reviewed at the outset of this chapter, led to renewed and more insistent demands for educational autonomy. Various educational and political organizations took up the issue. The National Association for the Advancement of Education at its first annual meeting in July 1922 aired a proposal by Hu Shi, one of the New Culture leaders, that no religious education be allowed in kindergartens or elementary schools. At annual meetings in 1924 and 1925, the association again took up the issue and urged the government to require the registration and regulation of all foreign schools and to ban all religious teaching in the schools.[75] The Young China Association, which was instrumental in the anti-Christian movement of the early 1920s, issued a book in October 1923 denouncing Christian education in China. In the following summer, delegates at its fifth annual conference adopted the following resolution: "We strongly oppose Christian education which destroys the national spirit of our people and carries on a cultural program in order to undermine Chinese civilization."[76] In October 1924, the National Federation of Provincial Educational Associations adopted a resolution that foreign schools in China should operate under strict control of the Ministry of Education and in conformity with its rules, with no religious instruction or compulsory attendance at religious ceremonies.[77]

The National Conference of Student Unions at its annual meeting in August 1924 launched a "restoration of educational rights" movement with branches in every province. The objectives of this movement, as expressed in a Fujian provincial committee's document, were Chinese control of school administrations and curriculums; the appointment of Chinese directors of schools and Chinese heads of instructional departments; the prohibition of religious education; the restoration of student freedoms, particularly their right to participate in patriotic political movements; and student participation in school administrations.[78] The Anti-Christian Student Federation was revived, and its members published tracts, pamphlets, and newspaper articles and staged lectures, parades, and demonstrations to get their message across. "Student storms" of protest disrupted many Christian institutions in this period, pitting nationalistic-minded Chinese students against their Western administrators. In 1924 and 1925, one dramatic tactic was to declare Christmas week a time to stir up trouble and to distribute anti-Christian postcards bearing such slogans as "Christianity is a tool of imperialism," "Christianity fools the feeble-minded young students," "Christians conspire with despicable vagrants and outlaws," and "A clean sweep of all Christian influences in China."[79]

The two revolutionary parties of the 1920s, the Nationalist and Communist Parties, saw in the burgeoning anti-Christian movement an opportunity to broaden their appeal and increase their membership, particularly among the mobilized youth and student groups. The Nationalist Party's second congress in January 1926 endorsed the attacks on mission schools and labeled the schools "the tongues and claws of imperialism." Some Nationalist leaders, however, were ambivalent toward Christianity because the founder of their party, Sun Yat-sen, was a Christian and because many members had graduated from mission schools. Furthermore, they feared antagonizing foreigners at the time of the Northward Expedition against the warlords. Chiang

Kai-shek, in command of that campaign, promised protection to missions as long as they did not oppose the revolutionary movement. The Communists adopted a similar stance. At its third congress in 1923, the Communist Party passed a strong anti-imperialist resolution that opposed the establishment of foreign schools and the teaching of religion in schools. In July 1926, the party decided to depict the Christian church as "the vanguard of imperialism" in its propaganda apparatus but to do nothing to "create any opportunity of actual conflict with the Church."[80] The linkage between the revolutionary parties and the anti-Christian agitation of the students changed the tenor of the movement. It became part of the intense anti-imperialist fervor that gripped China for several years in the wake of the May Thirtieth Incident of 1925.

The arguments advanced in support of these attacks on mission schools were mainly nationalistic. Foreign-controlled schools undermined the state's prerogative to educate its own citizens as it saw fit. The students attending such schools became denationalized, losing their identity as Chinese, and were often poorly trained in the Chinese language, literature, and culture. The Chinese staff in these institutions were subordinated to their foreign superiors and given insufficient responsibility in the administration of the school. The subjects the schools taught and the values they imparted were "foreign" and unsuited to China's needs. In addition, many opposed the schools because they taught a religion they considered superstitious and irrational. Many Chinese Christian educators, such as Timothy Lew (Liu Tingfang), had to admit the cogency of some of these arguments.[81]

The growing concern of Chinese educators and the organized pressure applied by key groups in the academic and political realms prompted the Beijing government to issue new regulations in November 1925. These regulations required that all private schools (Chinese as well as foreign, although the latter were the real target) have a Chinese president or vice president and a majority of Chinese on the board of directors. Further, schools were prohibited from spreading religious propaganda and from requiring attendance in religion courses, and school curriculums were to conform to Ministry of Education guidelines. The revolutionary government in the south issued similar sets of regulations in 1925 and 1926, with the added stipulation that schools hold ceremonies honoring Sun Yat-sen and offer study programs on the Three People's Principles. Chiang Kai-shek's new Nationalist government issued a set of regulations for school registration in February 1928 that conformed to previous regulations, but in 1929 the Ministry of Education in Nanjing added two new requirements. In March, it called for compulsory military training in all senior middle schools and colleges, and in August, it prohibited any religious activities in the primary schools. Government regulations also stated that graduates of unregistered schools would not be granted the same rights and privileges (such as voting, applying for government positions, and receiving government scholarships) that students of registered schools enjoyed.[82]

Missionaries in China were of divided opinion on how to respond to this series of registration regulations. Most had little trouble implementing the requirements for Chinese control and leadership in the schools, but many found it difficult to accept the restrictions on religious instruction and preferred to close down the schools rather than operate on a secular basis. Chinese Christians, on the other hand, were generally in favor of keeping the schools open. They reasoned that students in the mission schools would at least not receive a steady dose of anti-Christian teaching and that their religious training could be fostered through the churches or in other nonschool settings. The Chinese Christian Education Association urged all schools to register and to follow as many of the regulations as possible while awaiting further discussion with the government over the objectionable restrictions.[83]

The U.S. government took a cautious position on the matter of school registration where its citizens were concerned. The American position was clarified in July 1927 in correspondence between the secretary of state and the minister in China. Each educational institution was to make its own decision whether or not to register, and given American extraterritoriality rights, the Chinese government had no right to make registration compulsory. Should the Chinese government try to force a missionary school to register, American authorities in China would represent the missionaries, if they desired, before the Chinese government. In May 1928, the secretary of state expressed his hope that missionaries, Chinese Christians, and the Chinese government could work out a set of regulations satisfactory to all parties. He warned, however, that any missionary group that did transfer control must then look primarily to the Chinese government for protection. Finally, in November 1929 the Department of State announced its belief "that American citizens and organizations would not be justified, under present conditions, in contesting the right of the appropriate Chinese authorities to prescribe the method in which such schools shall be conducted."[84]

Two fundamental principles were at stake — and working at cross-purposes — in the school registration issue: nationalism and religious freedom. The Chinese were insisting on the right to determine their own educational practices without foreign interference, while Western missionaries were determined to preserve the right, supported by treaties, to propagate their religion without state control. Chinese Christians were the critical group caught in the middle of this impasse, but they held the key to the resolution of the problem. Missionaries' opposition to registration hinged on their presumed right to practice and preach religion in the schools, but as long as foreigners controlled these schools, the issue of religious freedom was overwhelmed by Chinese concerns about national pride and autonomy. As one American-trained Chinese political scientist wrote at the time, "The [Christian] movement is treated in China not so much as a religious or a social problem, but as an international political issue."[85] Once control was transferred, Chinese Christians could and did appeal to their government for the right of religious freedom without the debate being muddied by questions of nationalism. In short, only Chinese Christians, not Western missionaries, could win religious rights in China.

By 1929, about 70 percent of the approximately 200 Christian middle schools in China had registered or were in the process of doing so. Congregational and Methodist schools most readily accepted the necessity of registering and abiding by government regulations, whereas Presbyterian schools were the most opposed.[86] The two Southern Presbyterian missions in China, the North Jiangsu Mission and the Mid-China Mission, met jointly in February 1926 in Shanghai and went on record as opposing registration. The Mid-China Mission, to which the Jiangyin Station belonged, maintained this position for the next few years, affirming that its fundamental aim was "spreading the Gospel in and through all its institutions" and that schools were "primarily agencies for bringing students to the Truth of God and strengthening them in it."

Their Chinese counterparts, however, were more willing to compromise. In 1927, the Mid-China Mission transferred control of its schools to educational boards appointed by the Chinese Presbyterian church, and in the following year, the boards came out in favor of registration. They also redefined the purpose of schools as "general education" and "the development of Christian character" rather than "Christian education," as the missionaries preferred to define it. This new formulation allowed students to take elective religious courses and attend religious ceremonies on a voluntary basis. By 1930, the mission finally adopted this position and accepted the fact that three of its schools at Jiaxing and Hangzhou had registered with the Chinese government. The mission now conceded that Bible study and religious ceremonies should take place only on an elective basis, and it urged each station to open Sunday schools.[87]

The remaining two schools in the Mid-China Mission, the senior high school for girls and the junior high school for boys at Jiangyin, were unregistered and determined to stay that way. The boys school had been heavily damaged by the revolutionary forces in March 1927 and remained closed until the fall of 1929. Andrew Allison, who was no longer its director but still exerted authority as adviser, explained his reluctance to reopen:

The regulations of the Government for the conduct of Mission schools are such that we feel it will be very hard to maintain their real Christian character, and the general temper of students — especially boys — and of the officials, is such as to make it still harder. . . . We cannot consent to having the schools founded for the training of children in the knowledge of God run as agencies for party propaganda, and to have regular required worship and Bible courses forbidden while the near worship of Sun Yat-sen is compulsory, and the teaching of the principles of the People's Revolution [Sanmin zhuyi] by a member of the [Nationalist] Party [is] a basal part of the course.[88]

When classes began in 1929, only twenty-five boys attended, and the school encountered difficulties in finding teachers, undoubtedly because it was still unregistered.[89] The girls school at Jiangyin continued to operate throughout this period and resisted takeover by the revolutionaries. The school was encouraged, in fact, to follow this course by the attitude expressed by a Chinese educator in neighboring Jiaxing who reportedly warned missionaries: "The political instructors required by the government regulation came to lecture in our schools, and tell the students that freedom is the order of the day—that they are under no obligation to obey the teachers or the school rules, etc.; and the consequence is that we have no discipline, and a wretched atmosphere. Open your school; but *don't register*, for if you put yourself under government regulations you will have endless trouble."[90]

The failure of these schools to register was attacked by the Jiangyin press and by local educational authorities. Representatives of the city's Board of Education visited the station several times after 1927 to urge the schools to make Bible study and chapel attendance voluntary. In 1929 they suggested that the Bible classes at the schools be given another, less offensive name, but the Joint Committee of Control refused to make even this conciliatory gesture.[91] Their defiant position was stated clearly by Andrew Allison: "It seems to many of us that a mistake has been made in allowing any concessions at all in any Christian schools, where there is no doubt that registration or attempted registration with the government has brought about many compromises in the religious life and work within the schools. . . . The Bible and the preaching of the Word must have their just place as the very foundation of Christian schools."[92] City inspectors also checked on schools' compliance with the requirement that they hold weekly memorial services for Sun Yat-sen, the 1911 revolutionary leader and founder of the republic. Again, the station adamantly refused to conduct the service, which required bowing to Sun's picture, on the grounds that it was a form of idolatrous worship.[93] In 1931, the Christians were told that "no school unregistered before 15 August shall be permitted to receive any new pupils, or go on [with] class this fall term," but the schools opened as usual and ignored the local educational committee's demand that they "fall in line." Later, the Nanjing government announced that this order had been postponed.[94]

In succeeding years, local authorities continued to press the issue, but they seemed powerless or disinclined to enforce the registration requirement. Perhaps the Jiangyin missionaries' earlier contributions to the community shielded them. It also has been suggested that inconsistent approaches among local and national party and government organs encouraged non-compliance.[95] The Jiangyin branch of the Nationalist Party often sent letters to the station calling on the mission schools to stop their religious teaching. The response of the girls school principal, Mr. Wang, to one of these communiques was, "Of course we will not answer it. Just put it away. Those men have to do something to keep their job."[96] In the end, no steps were ever taken to close down the Christian schools despite their obvious refusal to abide by government regulations.

At first, Chinese Christians joined the missionaries in resisting registration. Chinese members of the Joint Committee voted with their foreign colleagues in support of their defiant stand. The Chinese staff of the schools and the larger Christian community also shared the same conviction that the schools should provide a religious education for their pupils and continue to hold compulsory Bible classes and daily chapel. A factor strengthening the resolve of the schools to remain unregistered was the fact that Christian families continued to enroll their children in these schools. Attendance at the girls school, in fact, was at an all-time high (over 250) because it was one of the few schools still providing religious instruction. Young girls came to the Jiangyin school from such distant provinces as Fengtian, Yunnan, and Henan as well as from neighboring Zhejiang and Hunan.[97] The boys school, however, was affected adversely by remaining unregistered. Graduates of the school found it difficult to continue their education in government schools or even in registered Christian schools, where they risked being stigmatized as unpatriotic.[98] Since education was more important to the career aspirations of boys than of girls, fewer young men were willing to take the risk of attending an unregistered school.

The hospital was also affected by the registration issue because graduates of its nurses training school were not licensed by the state to practice. Several classes of student nurses were transferred to a registered school, but this left the hospital without enough nurses to provide care. Less well trained "medical assistants" were used as substitutes. The hospital leaders, worried about the effect of these steps on nursing standards in China, were all in favor of registering the school to resolve the issue but were prevented from doing so by the home mission board.[99] What made the situation even more discouraging was that a few years earlier, in 1934, the station had built a new dormitory (mainly with funds from the Wilmington Presbyterial Auxiliary) to accommodate the large number of girls entering the program. Previously, the girls had occupied cots in the women's ward due to the lack of dormitory

space. After construction of the new facility, the hospital had hoped to pro-
duce a surplus of nurses who could be placed at the small, private hospitals
springing up in the area.[100] Now they did not even have enough nurses to
staff their own hospital.

The issue of registration at Jiangyin came to a head in 1937. The Chinese
principals and staffs of the mission schools found themselves in an increasingly untenable position. One can imagine the intense pressure they experienced due to their continued defiance of government regulations. By the
summer, when the schools began planning for their fall opening, all of the
Chinese faculty members had decided it was time to either register or close
down. The missionaries, however, were divided on the issue, which led to
strained relations at the station. The Chinese became reticent to discuss the
matter with any missionaries other than those who were sympathetic to their
plight. The missionaries, for their part, were caught in a similar dilemma.
Many favored registration, but as agents of their home mission board, they
felt duty-bound to abide by the decision of that body. The executive secretary
of the Executive Committee of Foreign Missions had visited Jiangyin and
other stations earlier in 1937, and on 3 June the committee, meeting in
Nashville, reaffirmed its opposition to registration.[101]

When the committee's action was communicated to the Jiangyin Station,
the Chinese Christian leaders decided to move on their own. They organized a new controlling school board under the authority of the East China
Synod's Board of Education and planned to register and open in the fall as a
single senior middle school.[102] On 8 July, the station's Joint Committee recognized the new board and voted to transfer authority over the schools to it.
The committee further appointed one of its own members, Pastor Sun, to
serve on the board alongside representatives of the synod, the alumni associations of the schools, the Mid-China Mission, and the Chinese Christian
community.[103] The new school board met on 10 July to adopt a constitution
and to proceed with plans for registering the school through the synod. The
two mission representatives present, Charles Worth and Alex Moffett (the
son of Lacy Moffett), cautioned the board that they could only vote in favor
of the plan with the home mission board's approval, which was uncertain.
The school board, however, decided to go ahead with its plan.[104]

The missionaries left Jiangyin for their summer vacations at Moganshan
(a resort area in Zhejiang) uncertain about the future of the school. Even
greater doubt arose as the Japanese invasion of China reached the Yangzi
delta area, forcing most of the missionaries to extend their summer vacations
into the fall and ultimately to abandon their posts. Several of the Jiangyin
missionaries briefly returned to the station in the fall and witnessed the
opening of school on 15 October, but by mid-November the entire station, missionaries and Chinese Christians alike, withdrew from the city and

relocated in an outlying village. It is not known if the school had registered during its brief operation, but the Japanese occupation made the issue academic: all the school buildings were destroyed during the fighting.[105]

The following spring, the Nationalist government retreated on the issue of registration. For some time, Nanjing had been moving away from its earlier anti-Christian stance. Its leader, Chiang Kai-shek, became a Christian in 1931, and in 1934, he and Madame Chiang turned to Western missionaries for support of the New Life movement, their version of a moral reformation of China's countryside. Furthermore, Chiang's government from the outset had stripped student unions of their political functions, thereby depriving the anti-Christian and education rights movements of their most vocal and militant supporters.[106] Now in April 1938, undoubtedly to secure American support of China against Japan, Madame Chiang told a meeting of missionaries that the ban on religious teaching in the schools had been lifted.[107] Although some missionaries may have exulted in this decision, it was a Pyrrhic victory at best. The Japanese conquerors of China were more hostile than the Chinese to the Western presence, and the ultimate impact of the Sino-Japanese War was to disrupt irreparably the missionary enterprise.

On the eve of the Japanese invasion, many Christian missions, like the one at Jiangyin, had not yet completely resolved the issues raised by the national revolution. The professed goal of a self-governing, self-supporting, and self-propagating Chinese Christian church was still far from realization. Missionaries perhaps felt an understandable reluctance to abandon a project, the Christianization of a vast empire, that had become their life's work. Would the Chinese who took over be as devoted to the success of the mission as they were? In the mission schools, which were a special target of nationalistic protests, Western administrators were loath to give up religious education, which they saw as an integral part of the evangelizing mission. To sacrifice religious freedom on the altar of Chinese nationalism was a dubious proposition to them. But their resistance on the registration issue led to an estrangement from the Chinese Christian community, which was being forced to choose between its religious beliefs and the imperatives of national rejuvenation. Soon, the problematical relationship between the Christian mission movement and Chinese nationalism would be overtaken by more monumental events — the Japanese invasion of China and the Communist Party's victory in the civil war.

6

RAYS OF
LIGHT

ESTABLISHING

THE CHRISTIAN

CHURCH IN

JIANGYIN

At the beginning of 1927, on the eve of the
Nationalist uprising, the senior missionary at
Jiangyin paused to take stock of the station's
first thirty-one years. Writing for a Southern
Presbyterian journal under the title "Rays of
Light in China's Darkness" (cleverly accompanied by the culturally potent *yin-yang* symbol),
Lacy Little maintained that the powers of darkness were giving way to the light of Christian
doctrine. He cataloged the *yin* forces as "the
inherited idolatry and superstition of the cen-
turies, the gross materialism of the masses, the
covetousness and cruelty of the warlords, the
self-assertiveness and arrogance of the scholar
class and the devilish cunning of Bolshevist
emissaries."[1] But, he noted, arrayed against
this darkness were powerful countervailing
Christian forces at Jiangyin, which then con-
sisted of a hospital, a training school for nurses,
separate high schools for boys and girls, a Bible
school for women, a school for needy children, six organized churches, thirteen centers
of country evangelistic work, five ordained and
nine unordained male Chinese helpers, six students for the ministry, six Bible women, thirteen foreign missionaries, and a church membership in the entire Jiangyin field of about
1,000. The mission work, concluded Little, was
clearly in a *yang* phase of ascendancy.

Reverend Little and the rest of the staff
had labored for decades to build a Christian
church in the Jiangyin area. Direct evangelical
work, as distinct from the work taking place in
the schools and hospital, took precedence his-
torically. Although the other social gospel or
"humanist" work at Jiangyin occasionally diverted energies away from evangelism, the conflict that emerged at other stations between
"fundamentalists" and "modernists" did not
seem to surface here.[2] The staff of the schools
and the hospital always considered these institutions agencies of evangelism and dispensed

articles of Christian faith to recipients of their services along with the peda-gogy and medicine.

Perhaps another factor contributing to the absence of friction among the staff at Jiangyin were the regular prayer meetings held at the station attended by all of the foreign and native workers. It is not clear when these gatherings first began, but references to them became quite frequent in the early years of the new republic. Every day from 12:30 to 1:00 in the afternoon, the staff gathered to pray together and, reportedly unique among stations, to raise any personal issues that might be affecting the station's work. Every Tuesday, for two hours in the late afternoon, they attended a short devotional service at the chapel followed by formal reports on all aspects of the missionary en-deavor at Jiangyin and in the outstations.[3] Lacy Little referred to these ses-sions "as the secret of the fine spirit of unity that binds us together and the ex-planation to a large degree of any progress that has been made in the work of the Kingdom at Kiangyin."[4]

At first, the main centers of evangelistic work at Jiangyin were located out-side the city walls: the original chapel within the mission compound at the East Gate and a second chapel, opened in 1912, at the North Gate. In 1915, the North Gate chapel was moved to larger quarters in the same area.[5] The East Gate chapel, which could seat 600 people, was located in the hospital and was the most important organized church in the Jiangyin field. Besides its regular services, the chapel was also used for Sunday school, baptisms, weddings, funerals, Red Cross training classes, prayer services by the staff, food distribution during Christmas week, and hosting large gatherings of townspeople who came to the station for special entertainments and so-cial events.[6]

Evangelism at the hospital itself was an integral part of its work from the beginning, as noted earlier, and was the responsibility of a Chinese evange-list and a Bible woman assigned to the men's and women's wards, respec-tively. The Chinese workers, however, were often accused of conducting their evangelical work only in a desultory fashion, and the missionaries were disappointed with the results. In 1924, they implemented an organizational change in response to discussions of the problem raised at a Mid-China Mis-sion meeting. The station appointed Lacy Little to the newly created post of superintendent of hospital evangelism. Little turned over his pastoral work at the two organized churches in Jiangyin to ordained Chinese colleagues and launched an aggressive effort at the hospital. He devoted two hours every day to preaching in the wards and conversing with patients. Emma Worth di-rected evangelistic work among the women, and both Worth and Little had Chinese assistants.

To follow up on the in-hospital work, Little implemented a plan that George Worth had devised. He kept a record book, similar to a large checkbook, in which each sheet, consisting of three parts, was devoted to one of the patients that received religious instruction at the hospital. When the patient left, he or she was given one part of the record sheet, on which was printed an invitation to attend church upon returning home, the location of the closest church, and the name of that church's Chinese pastor. The second part was given to that pastor to identify the patient as a potential church member, and the remaining part was kept on file at the hospital. When the country preachers visited the station each quarter for their three-day Bible study and conference, they would report on the former patients whose names they had been given.[7]

Inside the city walls, the missionaries had preached on occasion in a large public hall near the old city temple. In 1918, that space was no longer available, having been converted into a public library. Another site in the city used for preaching was a tea shop, but this convivial gathering place was considered off-limits to women and it could not hold large crowds. In need of a facility for evangelical work in the city, the mission located a building in the center of town large enough to house a 400-seat chapel, a reading room, some classrooms, and quarters for the resident evangelist. Lacy Little opened the new street chapel in March 1919. The city magistrate attended the ceremonies, thus signaling the support of the local elite for this expansion of mission work into their city.[8]

Christian workers stopped at almost any public place or crowded street corner in the city to preach and distribute literature. In 1928, the station planned a systematic campaign throughout the city and its suburbs that engaged thirty-six Chinese assistants. The territory was divided into twelve sections, and a band of three workers was assigned to each section. Armed with propaganda leaflets, two workers covered the shops on either side of the street while the third targeted pedestrians in the middle.[9] Whenever the opportunity arose, the mission visited government schools in Jiangyin to hand out Gospel tracts and pocket-size Bibles to students and faculty.[10] Other special groups targeted by the missionaries were addicts at opium refuges and inmates in the jails.

New Year's, the most celebrated festival of China's lunar calendar, prompted special activity at the station. Early on, the missionaries began opening their homes during this period to any interested people from the city. Hundreds would crowd into the station, curious about the foreigners' home life and exotic possessions. The windup Victrola, in particular, always created a sensation among visitors.[11] By the mid-1910s, however, the station began directing its energies toward more systematic evangelical campaigns that lasted about a week and mobilized the entire Christian force. Preachers printed their texts in advance and distributed them throughout the city. The boys school band paraded the streets with banners inviting residents to attend the meetings, which were held twice a day in the East Gate and North Gate chapels and in whatever space was available inside the city.[12] The missionaries extended these New Year's campaigns to the countryside in 1919 and thereafter. Over 100 Chinese Christians went out in pairs or small bands to 600 villages, thus reaching in one week about one-eighth of the 5,000 villages comprising the Jiangyin field.[13]

The Jiangyin staff remained alert to special events or circumstances that would gather a crowd and provide an audience for their religious message. As we have seen, the New Year's festival, visits to the jail and the opium refuge, and playing the phonograph all provided opportunities for evangelizing. Similarly, movies proved very popular. When a new electricity-generating plant was installed in the city in 1918, the station was quick to schedule outdoor film screenings before the novelty wore off.[14]

Perhaps the most popular attraction at the station starred a porpoise. In 1918, some local Chinese caught this curiosity in the Yangzi River. Not knowing what type of fish it was or whether it was edible, they brought it to George Worth. He gave them $3 for the fish, which measured 8.5 feet and weighed 500 pounds. Before cutting the porpoise up to render its fat into oil, Worth hung it in a tree for several days. An estimated 10,000 people came from miles around to glimpse this strange fish. They went away not only with stories to tell their friends but also with religious tracts distributed by the missionaries.[15]

All of the missionaries at Jiangyin helped with evangelical work, even those who were mainly involved in educational or medical tasks, as we have seen, but several had primary responsibility for preaching at the central station or itinerating into the surrounding countryside. Lacy Little, the senior evangelist, by the 1920s was concentrating on work at the station hospital and in the city. His "outfield" work, as itinerating was often called, was assumed by George Worth's son Charles, who returned to Jiangyin in 1923 after graduating from Union Theological Seminary in Richmond, Virginia.[16] Lacy Moffett served as a second evangelist after 1908, when he replaced R. A. Haden, until World War II forced him to leave the field. Charles Worth was transferred to Hangzhou in the mid-1930s, but by then Andrew Allison, who first came to Jiangyin in 1910 as an educator, also was itinerating. After the Nanjing Incident of 1927, Anna Sykes and Rida Jourolman did not return to Jiangyin. Women's work thereafter was taken up primarily by Marion Wilcox, who came to Jiangyin in 1924 and remained until 1951. Wilcox, from Georgia, had graduated from the University of North Carolina in 1918, then had received theological training in New York. At Jiangyin, she lived on a houseboat with a Chinese companion, Miss Liu, which they used for itinerating in the Jiangyin field.[17]

The evangelistic staff held a series of regular meetings to report on past work, plan for future campaigns, and renew themselves through prayer and Bible study. The city workers met every Saturday afternoon for a half-hour devotional before going into Jiangyin to preach and hand out literature.[18] As noted earlier, Lacy Moffett initiated a monthly gathering of the country workers, who met for three days of prayers, reports, and exchanges of ideas. In every quarter, the monthly meeting was held at the central station once and at outstations, on a rotating basis, the other two times. There is some indication that outstations where Christian work was not going particularly well were targeted for these three-day evangelistic meetings.[19]

Some missionaries saw their "country work" as more promising than their efforts to convert the urban elites, who seemed more interested in the foreigners' hospitals and schools and other socially useful contributions than in their religion. As Lacy Little lamented, "The Confucian scholar is securely entrenched within his own self-sufficiency and feels no need of a Savior, while the new-school Chinese student is all too often imbued with agnosticism and atheism."[20] He and others believed that the rural population, being less "cultured" and thus less corrupted by modern ideas, would be more open to the Christian message. That impression seems to be supported by scattered statistical evidence of church membership. In the provinces of Jiangsu and Zhejiang, Christian missionaries were most successful in the more backward regions, whereas in counties around the more developed treaty port areas, they gained few converts.[21] A survey of communicants in the Southern Presbyterian mission fields in China in 1936 shows that 71 percent were from rural areas.[22]

All of the evangelistic staff left records of their activities, mostly in circular letters to the home board or in missionary journals. Lacy Moffett and Charles Worth, however, kept diaries that afford even more valuable personal insights into the frustrating yet at times fruitful work of spreading the Gospel in rural China. The following description of itinerating in the Jiangyin countryside relies heavily on their accounts.[23]

The process of building a Christian church began when several people became enquirers by expressing interest in receiving instruction in the Gospel. Potential converts were generated in a variety of ways. Some of the decisive factors included hearing the preaching of an itinerating missionary or Chinese assistant, reading a religious tract, perceiving the healing power of prayer, being treated for opium addiction or a traumatic illness at a missionary hospital, or attending a Christian school. Missionary notebooks and letters related stories of conversion as testaments to the power of their religion and as inspirational literature for their supporters back home.

Many of the converts seemed to have an underlying pragmatic attitude

The Reverend Lacy Moffett in the station houseboat he used for itinerating into the Jiangyin countryside. (Kiangyin Station Photographs, Presbyterian Church in the United States Missions, China, Department of History and Records, Presbyterian Church [U.S.A.], Montreat, N.C.)

toward religious affiliation. For example, Lacy Moffett told the story of Li Yaogang, a former Taoist priest. Li decided after his wife died that since Taoism could not prevent such a personal tragedy he would seek a new religion. After hearing a sermon at a Chinese Baptist church in Shanghai, he purchased some Christian tracts at the Presbyterian Mission Press, then went back to his native region to be a witness for Christianity. He became convinced of the power of his new religion when his village received much-needed rain after a steady week of prayer. Li later studied with R. A. Haden at Jiangyin, attended a seminary, became a preacher, and worked to open up several outstations in the Jiangyin field. It is said that over forty families in one market town became enquirers through his spiritual leadership and representation of the efficacy of Christian prayer.[24]

Another tale involved a woman who, although her daughter had become a Christian, was not willing to give up ancestor worship to accept the new faith. One day, at the same time that a special Christian service was being held in her town, she went to burn paper money on her mother's grave outside of town. The burning paper set fire to a nearby wooden coffin that was placed in the open aboveground. The next day the family that owned the coffin demanded money as recompense for the damage. After this incident, the woman decided that since her ancestors had no power to protect her while she was worshipping them, she would abandon ancestor worship and become a Christian.[25]

One account involved a fortune-teller and *fengshui* (geomancy) expert. A Christian family in his area had chosen a site for a new home and another had picked a burial site without consulting him. He apparently took this as a challenge to his authority and livelihood. Looking over the gravesite, he proclaimed that "if other members of that family don't die within two months I am perfectly willing to say that there is nothing to my fortune telling and to become a Christian." After nothing harmful happened to the Christian family, he remained true to his word, burned all of his books on the supernatural, and enrolled as an enquirer.[26] A perhaps more representative story of conversion based on practical results told of a woman who came to the Jiangyin missionary hospital with a badly infected arm from a wound inflicted by her abusive husband. The limb was saved and so, too, according to the account, was the woman.[27]

Not all of the Chinese who wished to become enquirers exhibited benign intentions. Missionaries were vigilant in detecting individuals or groups professing an interest in Christianity for improper motives (at least in the foreigners' eyes). The most common example were those who sought aid in a lawsuit, hoping the extraterritoriality privileges of Westerners would accrue to them as Christians. From the outset, reports from the newly opened Jiangyin field indicated that hundreds of applicants were turned away because of suspicions about their involvement in pending lawsuits or land title disputes.[28]

An example from Lacy Moffett's journal illustrates the fact that missionaries had to proceed with great care in their evangelizing work. In January 1936, the wife of a newly enrolled enquirer at one of the outstations brought a letter to the Joint Committee of Control accusing their pastor of cheating them out of some money. It seems the woman and her husband, Dzien Yao-hai, had a prospective daughter-in-law who went to Wuxi to work as a servant for a rich family named Sen. There, she was seduced by one of her employer's sons, which prompted Dzien to file a lawsuit. When no satisfactory settlement was made, Dzien enrolled as an enquirer and appealed to the local pastor to help him press his case. The pastor traveled to Wuxi and in the end collected a cash settlement from the Sen family, who in effect bought the young servant girl as a concubine for their son. Dzien, however, claimed that the pastor had falsified his expenses and unjustly withheld $80 of the settlement. The dispute dragged on into March, at which time Moffett traveled to the outstation to question the parties involved and other church members. In the end, the pastor was exonerated and Dzien was dropped as an enquirer.[29]

This story suggests the efficacy of missionary intervention in a lawsuit. The poor Dzien family from the Jiangyin countryside made little headway in forcing a settlement on the wealthier Sen family in Wuxi until a Christian representative intervened. Although the local pastor was Chinese, his connection with the foreigners' religion must have given the Sen family reason to settle to avoid any worse trouble.

Besides the advantages gained in lawsuits, Christianity could provide other material rewards. For example, converts refused to participate in local religious festivals, which they considered idolatrous, and thus were relieved of the obligation to offer tithes in support of the local deities. The right of Chinese Christians to be exempted from these obligations was protected by a government decree in 1881 and was even incorporated into the Sino-American Treaty of 1903.[30] Also, many Chinese Christians learned English and other Western subjects as a ticket to a well-paying job with a foreign or Chinese commercial enterprise or in government service. Furthermore, a position at one of the various missionary institutions (schools, hospitals, orphanages, and the like) could provide a decent livelihood. As one missionary educator put it, "The gospel is good news to the poor."[31]

Missionaries, of course, prayed for and welcomed sincere interest in their faith. But they were "vigilant gate-keepers," applying rigid membership tests to enquirers in order to prevent an influx of "rice Christians."[32] To guarantee that an applicant had a minimal understanding of Christian doctrine and displayed evidence of good intentions, a probationary period of several months, perhaps several years, as an enquirer was required. During that period, the enquirer received religious instruction and was expected to exhibit signs of having developed a Christian character.[33] At least by the 1920s, each enquirer had to sign a pledge vowing to continue to receive religious instruction and to furnish a Christian sponsor who would cosign the pledge and thus act as a guarantor of the enquirer's reliability. The station also printed up Christian calendars for distribution each New Year to all enquirers and Christians and expected them to be posted in their living rooms or reception halls.[34] An examination of an enquirer's understanding and commitment (what the missionaries called *jiu xinde*, "examination of faith and virtue")[35] was held twice yearly by the itinerating missionary in cooperation with local church officers. The missionary sought to determine the enquirer's level of understanding, relying on the local Chinese for an evaluation of how well the applicant was living up to Christian ideals in his or her everyday affairs.[36]

One of the Jiangyin evangelists recorded a delightful, somewhat irreverent, account of an examination session in a country town. One weekend in 1928, Charles Worth rode his bicycle to Houcheng, thirteen miles east of the city, where the largest church membership in the Jiangyin field had been nurtured over the preceding decade. On this occasion, Worth and several church officers examined about 100 enquirers. The questioning of one illiterate farmer, whom Worth called Everlasting Happiness, went as follows:

cw: How long have you been a believer?

eh: About four years, I suppose.

cw: And you have been examined several times before, haven't you?

eh: Yes, quite several times.

cw: And what ever induced you to believe in Jesus, what good did you suppose it would do you?

eh: Well, my wife had a devil in her, and after I had spent all the money I could get having the Buddhist and Taoist priests trying to expel the spirit, without any good coming of it all, I heard that if I tried this Jesus Doctrine it might turn the trick. And so I got Pastor Brown to come around, and after he had explained the power of Jesus, he said that if I would believe he could send the demon out of my wife. He then prayed and sang a hymn and it wasn't long till my wife was all right.

cw: That is very good, and you have believed in Jesus ever since that time; but is this all that you expect to get out of believing in Jesus?

eh: Oh, no. He will also save my soul.

cw: Yes, and after all, that is the most important, for your body can only live a few years and then you have your soul to think about for eternity. . . . Suppose your wife should get sick and die in spite of prayer for her recovery, what effect would this have on your faith in Jesus?

eh: I trust in Jesus now so that nothing can ever move me from it.

cw: Now, I understand you are a farmer, and I would like to know where you think you receive your returns from. You work, and plant, and fertilize, and cultivate, but wherein does your success or failure really lie?

eh: I rely on God for the crops I reap.

cw: Very well then, how about your church attendance? Since you cannot read, you depend entirely on what you hear for your knowledge of Christian truth. During the busy harvest season, you miss a few services I suppose, do you not?

eh: I do, because I have no time to go to church when the rice is ready to set out or the wheat ready to harvest.

cw: Ah, and you are sometimes too busy with your own affairs to attend to the worship and knowledge of the God whom you admit gives you your crops. Suppose He should say that He is too busy with watering the rice in the Wusih [Wuxi] section that He must temporarily forget the Kiangyin east country, what would be your fix?

After hearty laughter all around, the examination of Everlasting Happiness continued with questions about prayer, Christian living, the meaning of baptism and the Lord's Supper, and other matters.

This process was repeated with each candidate for church membership. Worth's conclusion provides a good summary of the examination experience:

> By the time one has, with the able assistance of the Chinese elders, gone through this process with about a hundred persons, some of whom want to do a good deal of talking, others of whom are naturally as silent as the tomb and almost have to be thumb-screwed, and with others who are so embarrassed that they forget all they ever knew, and with one or two "thrill" or "kick" hunters, and also with maybe a slightly "cracked" individual thrown in for interest and variety, you may imagine that the Session has done about two days of mighty hard work.[37]

At times, when the number of applicants was large, the literate were given written examinations in order to reduce the time required for the examination sessions.[38]

Enquirers were rarely accepted for baptism, communion, and church membership after the initial examination; normally they were received as communicants after the second or third try. In one portion of his journal, Lacy Moffett provided very precise data on this point. At one outstation about twenty-five miles east of Jiangyin, he examined a total of 80 enquirers on two separate occasions, in April and again in November of 1939. Only 16 were received into the church, 9 on their second examination, 5 on the third, 1 on the fourth, and 1 on the fifth. Of the remaining 64, most had been examined only once or twice, but 12 were still unsuccessful after three or more attempts. One of these, an old woman of sixty-four presenting herself for the sixth time, was labeled by Moffett as "crazy." Charles Worth recalled the case of one man who was finally accepted on his seventeenth examination.[39] These enquirers' examination experiences are strongly reminiscent of the fate of Fan Jin, the celebrated character of Wu Jingzi's 1740s satire, who succeeded in passing the imperial examination only after twenty attempts, but the ironic similarity was undoubtedly not intended.

Presumably, then, if an enquirer did not show sufficient understanding and Christian character by the second or third examination, his or her chances of ever becoming a communicant in the church were slim. The rate of acceptance in the instance above — 16 of 80, or 20 percent — was higher than usual. From all of the figures given in Moffett's notes in the 1930s, a more common rate was less than 14 percent (116 of 851 examined). Similarly, from available data on thirteen examinations at both the Jiangyin central church and the country chapels in the period from 1910 to 1926, the acceptance rate was 14.5 percent (238 of 1,639). Finally, Charles Worth in 1930 reported a 16 percent rate (39 of 244) in the semiannual examinations in five outstations under his care.[40]

What social groupings did enquirers and converts come from? For the most part, in the Jiangyin field, they were not from the upper classes, a fact often noted ruefully by the missionaries. Many were illiterate, according to the sketchy information available. Charles Worth's 1930 account implied a 10 percent literacy rate among the enquirers at Houcheng. In another town, Lacy Moffett noted that only 14 of 37 church members and 10 of 23 enquirers could read any form of Christian literature. When he returned a year later to examine enquirers, 4 of the 8 male candidates and all 6 of the women were illiterate. On another occasion, he noted that only 2 of the 7 enquirers could read.[41] These few samples are in line with more general figures. A survey of fifty-five rural churches in 1936 revealed a 60 percent illiteracy rate among their enquirers.[42] The occupations of most converts in the Jiangyin field were, as would be expected, not exalted. Among those mentioned in missionary letters and journals were a butcher, pig weigher, carpenter, rice shop keeper, militia drillmaster, oil mill owner, opium addict, gambler, soldier, fortune-teller, blacksmith, traditional and Western-style doctors, country schoolteacher, and farmer.[43]

One of the main requirements for church membership was the renunciation of idolatrous practices and the destruction of idols associated with Chinese religions. This meant that ancestor worship, which an 1890 missionary conference had decided contained idolatry as an essential component,[44] as well as Buddhism and Taoism, was banned. Observers have noted that it was very difficult for Chinese converts to abandon such a deep-rooted tradition as honoring their ancestors, which was as much a social and cultural act as it was an expression of religious values. The Western-educated Chiang Monlin argues in his autobiography that the Chinese were quite willing to add the Christian God to the panoply of deities they already worshipped but not to replace them entirely.[45] Emma Worth echoed these sentiments: "If they could just add Christianity to the beliefs and superstitions which already bind them they would do so readily. It is the giving up all the old ones and trusting in Christ alone for salvation that holds them back."[46]

Yet the missionaries remained adamant on this point. Ancestral tablets, shrines, kitchen gods and statues of other deities, "idol money" (paper money burned as an offering in worship ceremonies), and the like all had to be destroyed as symbolic evidence of conversion to a new, Christian life. Usually, the new convert would invite a missionary or Chinese pastor or Bible woman to come into his or her home to take away all of these artifacts of idolatry. Occasionally, converts would bravely destroy the idols themselves, as a Mrs. Tsaung did on the day she was to be baptized, using the objects to make a fire to cook her breakfast.[47]

Idol destruction itself could become an elaborate ceremony that attracted crowds and thus serve as an effective propaganda tool. In early 1941, for example, Andrew Allison was invited to consecrate the homes of two enquirers in one village. A small procession, including Allison, five or six older Christians, and the earnest applicants, made its way to the countryside. At the two homes, idolatrous pictures were taken down, one of the older members of the family handed over her long-treasured Buddhist tokens of merit, and a stone "demon shield" was toppled over. Wooden ancestral tablets were gathered together and burned, but not before the names and dates of the ancestors were copied down carefully so as not to give the impression, Allison noted, that "the new faith had any lack of proper respect." Colorful Gospel posters were put up in place of the destroyed icons of the old religions. Finally, the new believers stood before the gathered crowd to profess their faith, then joined with the other Christians present in prayer and song.[48] In another case, nonflammable and nonbreakable objects, such as a brass incense pot, were thrown into a nearby canal.[49]

Occasionally, through deception and subterfuge, new converts would avoid full compliance with the requirement of idol destruction. One participant in the 1890 conference of missionaries in China reported that in some Christian families, one of the sons would remain unbaptized in order to carry on the ancestral sacrifices. Another practice was to hide one or two ancestral tablets when the others were brought out for burning.[50]

Other tests for new Christians included attending services regularly, keeping the Sabbath as a day of rest, and upholding Christian morality—meaning no gambling, opium smoking, adultery, or concubinage. Early marriages and divorces were also discouraged. Violators of these prescriptions or a return to idolatrous practices usually led to suspension or expulsion from the church.[51] For example, in 1931 Lacy Moffett suspended three communicants: one for gambling, another for idolatry, and a third for adultery. The following year, at another outstation, two church members were admonished for selling "idol money" in their shops. They claimed it brought the highest profit of any good sold, but they were advised to get rid of the merchandise.[52] One observer estimated that one-third of all converts would leave or be expelled from the church in five to ten years, while another third would be irregular in attendance at worship services.[53] Evangelists' frustration must have been great indeed.

As much as missionaries railed against the superstitious nature of Chinese religions, some of them tolerated one similarly superstitious practice common among rural Chinese Christians—the exorcism of demons. At Xiaoqi in the late 1920s, Andrew Allison witnessed the exorcism of a peasant woman who had for some months been considered by her neighbors to be demon-possessed. Her family had invited some local Christians to pray over her rigid and deathlike form. As a crowd of gawking villagers gathered around the house, the invocation of Jesus's name had its intended effect. The woman sat up, pointed her finger out the window, and cried, "There he goes." Some of the astonished neighbors, Allison noted with satisfaction, decided then and there to destroy their kitchen gods and other idols of their folk religion.[54]

About a decade later, Allison again was present at an exorcism ritual. A twenty-year-old woman in the village of Zhangjiacun, where the Jiangyin Christian community refugeed in the early years of the Japanese invasion, was writhing in her bed. When Mrs. Wu, wife of the North Gate pastor, began praying, the tortured woman (or the malevolent spirit within her) cried out, "Let me alone; five years ago I should not have minded leaving her, but now I have no other place to go." Mrs. Wu commanded the demon to go, and the reply was, "No, I'll go into her head," after which the woman exhibited pain there. Again, the command to go, the retort of "I shall go into her stomach," and then distention of the stomach. At last, the demon reportedly left under the assault of continuous praying, and the woman achieved peace. Months later, she was identified as a faithful churchgoer.[55]

Although Allison believed in demon-possession and accepted exorcism as part of Christian work, Lacy Moffett was more dubious. On one of his trips in May 1931, he attended a church service at which the preacher held a special prayer session for a "crazy woman," whom the church officers considered demon-possessed. The pastor placed his hand on her forehead while the congregation of about 100 sang "Onward Christian Soldiers." Although the result was not recorded, Moffett dismissed the ceremony as the "savoring of superstition, too much like an incantation to cast out evil spirits."[56] It seems only a fine line of suspended disbelief separated the worship of kitchen gods and other protective deities and the invocation of Jesus to drive out demonic influences.

Beyond the primary objective of building up and maintaining church membership in the countryside in collaboration with local preachers and church officers, itinerating evangelists routinely handled other matters as they journeyed into the field. The itinerating notebook of Lacy Moffett is replete with mundane details about traveling, settling disputes among congregations over church property, checking on fund-raising campaigns, supervising church construction, and the like. Missionaries also made an effort to maintain personal contact with the Christian families in their fields as they itinerated. They often attended birthday celebrations, weddings, and funerals and visited with families in which illness had struck. At one wedding in Huashu in 1914, Anna Sykes entertained the gathering with renditions of

Chinese bride (front row, middle) with her sisters-in-law to her right and Ruth
and Emma Worth to her left; in the back row, from left, are Rida Jourolman,
Jane Lee, and Miss Yuan, music teacher at the girls school, 1920s.
(First Presbyterian Church, Wilmington, N.C.)

"Dixie" and "Ticklish Reuben" played on a Victrola she brought with her.[57]
Lacy Moffett took photographs of the families he visited, presumably to be
used to illustrate articles on mission work for the folks back home as well as
to create a personal record of his work.[58]

The Jiangyin evangelists tried to visit the Christian communities in their
fields at least twice, and sometimes as many as seven or eight times, a year.
This kept them away from the main station about half the time. In one part
of his journal, Lacy Moffett listed his Sunday engagements for the years 1931
through 1936. Not counting the months of July and August, when oppressive
heat in the valley drove all of the Protestant missionaries to mountain resorts
at Guling (modern-day Lushan in Jiangxi) or Moganshan (near Hangzhou),
or the time he spent tending to church business in Hangzhou or Shanghai,
Moffett was usually attending to his evangelistic duties about forty weeks a
year. Except for 1936, when illness kept him at Jiangyin for extended periods,
Moffett spent more Sundays in the field than at the central station. For example, in 1931 he spent 20 Sundays in the countryside and 18 in Jiangyin. In

Station houseboat on a canal in the Jiangyin field, 1920. (Kiangyin Station Photographs, Presbyterian Church in the United States Missions, China, Department of History and Records, Presbyterian Church [U.S.A.], Montreat, N.C.)

the next five years, the corresponding figures were 13/3, 25/15, 24/15, 20/19, and 19/23.[59] Charles Worth reported that he spent four to five months each year away from the station.[60]

Such extensive travel to the country required ingenuity and stamina on the part of the missionary. The usual modes of transportation were wheelbarrow, sedan chair, bicycle, bus, or on foot. Most rural roads were little more than footpaths, wheelbarrow rides were bumpy, and covering great distances on foot was an inefficient use of time. Consequently, Charles Worth bought himself a bicycle and logged about 10,000 miles every year traveling into the countryside. His rides through the countryside attracted a great deal of attention from intrigued children, who called him everything from monkey, horse, train, and "foreign devil" to Jesus and, on occasion, "bicycle."[61] The possession of a houseboat afforded deluxe travel conditions and greatly increased the missionary's ability to extend itineration into the countryside. This was particularly true in the Jiangyin area, which was honeycombed with canals linked to the Yangzi River just north of the city. Some of these waterways were tidal canals that were navigable only during periods of high water, but the main canals were usable year-round. In the 1930s, Lacy Moffett used one of the Jiangyin Station's two houseboats to reach most of the country towns under his care. Occasionally, during low tide or in order to reach a village not situated on a waterway, he would complete the last leg of his journey on foot or by wheelbarrow.

When using a sedan chair, three men usually would be hired as a carrier team. Rotating periodically, two men would carry the chair while the third rested, following on foot. Such teams could cover 25–30 miles a day, although often only with the aid of a little opium to obliterate the pain. One of Charles Worth's carriers explained that opium was available, despite being illegal, at rest stops: "Sometimes I would be so tired and my feet and shoulders hurt so badly I could hardly make it, but yet there were miles still to go before the overnight stop. I would go back to the little den in the back of the rest stop and smoke 'one pipe,' and then back to the chair and the road again. I wasnt [sic] tired anymore, nor did my feet or shoulders ache any more, I scarcely realised that I was carrying anything, I just seemed to be drifting along, — it was wonderful."[62]

When itinerating, Moffett, Worth, and their colleagues would carry a supply of Christian tracts to pass out to people they met along the road and at their points of destination. Most people would accept these tracts, whether or not they intended to read them or heed their message. At one village in 1933, Charles Worth claimed to have distributed literature to about 1,000 residents, with only one man refusing to accept it. The missionaries met little open hostility, just indifference. As Worth noted, the villagers were mainly concerned with finding their next meal.[63] Although the Chinese often called missionaries "foreign devils," they nevertheless were impressed with their willingness to "eat bitterness," that is, to travel and live simply on these itinerating trips.[64]

If visiting an area with an already established Christian group, the itinerating evangelist would stay in the home of a leading Christian. When establishing a new area, the first task was to locate a family willing to host the missionaries and act as a guarantor; the search for such a family often took quite a while. Preaching usually took place after supper, either in the host's home, if it was large enough, or in the local tea or rice shop. Bells, gongs, trumpets, and other attention-getters were used to summon crowds to the gathering, and colorful Gospel posters would be tacked up on the walls.[65] The missionary or an accompanying Chinese evangelist would speak to the crowd about Jesus, Christianity's promise of a happier life, and other Christian messages. As with religious tracts, some received these messages with indifference, perhaps playing dominoes or some other game in a corner of the tea shop throughout the sermon.[66]

Each church in the outfield was expected to conduct communion services twice a year. The itinerant preacher would visit the outstation at these times to help examine enquirers and instruct them in the proper attitude toward

Man carrying two babies in baskets to present them for baptism at the Xiaoqi church, 1914. (Kiangyin Station Photographs, Presbyterian Church in the United States Missions, China, Department of History and Records, Presbyterian Church [U.S.A.], Montreat, N.C.)

the old "superstitious" religious practices and in how to lead a new Christian life. The successful candidates would then be baptized and receive communion along with other members of the church at special services conducted by the missionary or the Chinese pastor. For the occasion, the missionaries might bring makeshift communion provisions from Jiangyin — raisins to be stewed into wine and soda crackers to be broken up for bread.[67] An account of a service held in Xiaoqi in 1917 suggests an ambiance that a Western Christian might find shocking: "The beaten earth floor of the chapel was green with mold from the dampness; . . . a dog lay under the communion table during the service; . . . a chicken was running about pecking at the peanut hulls thrown freely on the floor." The wine at this service was made from rice and was so strong that the author, Virginia Lee, thought it more fitting to call it "fire-water."[68]

The missionaries would also visit country churches to help install new pastors, elders, and deacons and to discuss church business with the officers. Money matters were a constant concern. Usually they involved the pastor's salary or fund-raising campaigns to rent or construct new chapels or repair old ones. The mission often contributed a significant amount to help cover these expenses since local Christians were hard-pressed to raise all of the

Church officers at the installation of pastor (wearing cross) at Houcheng, one of the outstations in the Jiangyin field, with the Reverend Lacy Moffett in the background, 1930s. The Chinese characters mean "Welcome." (Kiangyin Station Photographs, Presbyterian Church in the United States Missions, China, Department of History and Records, Presbyterian Church [U.S.A.], Montreat, N.C.)

necessary funds. Tithing was assessed in each drive, but it usually amounted to only a few U.S. dollars per family.[69]

One significant feature of these various fund-raising campaigns was the organization of Christian families into traditional *baojia* ("mutual responsibility") units. For instance, in 1935–36, congregations in 5 outstations in the southeastern field were organized into 32 groups of approximately 10 family heads each. The leaders of these groups were responsible for both the spiritual and the financial work of the group.[70]

An example of church construction and financing can be drawn from entries in Lacy Moffett's journal.[71] In 1930, he and other members of Jiangyin's governing body held meetings at Yangshe to celebrate the opening of a new church building. The cost of purchasing the land and constructing the building amounted to about $3,950. At the time of its opening, only about half the funds had been raised, partly from the gifts of Chinese Christians ($650) and partly from contributions by foreign missionaries and the Mid-China Mission ($1,400). The mission later decided to contribute another $1,000, but $550 of that amount was borrowed from a special account and had to be repaid eventually. The remaining amount ($900) came from personal loans extended by three members of the congregation.

Of the total cost, then, only about one-sixth was borne initially by the local congregation, which at that time numbered sixty. When all of the loans were repaid, the congregation's share of the cost was a little more than half ($2,100). Two years after the completion of the chapel, at least one of the Chinese members who had loaned money had not yet been repaid.[72] In addition to cash contributions, one member of the Yangshe church who was a carpenter donated about fifty man-days of his own and his workmen's labor toward construction. The head carpenter also slept in the building at night as a caretaker without charge for the duration of its construction. Still, the Yangshe experience is a clear case of the inability of the Chinese Christian movement to be self-supporting, even into the 1930s.

It should also be noted that most of the title deeds of these church buildings in the 1920s and 1930s were put in the name of a foreign mission or missionary, no matter who provided the funds for their construction. This practice was followed to forestall confiscation by Chinese authorities in uncertain political times; foreign property would be protected by treaty whereas Chinese property would not.[73]

Among the country Christians, week-long Bible study conferences for men were held each summer at Jiangyin, at least after 1918. The conferences were organized and led entirely by Chinese evangelistic leaders in the absence of the missionaries, who were away at that time at summer resorts. Attendance at the conferences fluctuated, depending on the weather. If there had been plenty of rain, the men would not have to stay home to pump water into the fields so a large number could attend.[74]

A separate conference was held for women each fall. At the first conference in 1918, eighty women attended from the countryside and were housed in the Bible school, in the missionaries' houses, and on the station's houseboats. Besides the services, prayers, and lectures by various missionaries, feasting and entertainment (listening to the Victrola was always a big attraction) kept the women in good spirits. A special feature was a child welfare exhibit, transported from Shanghai, that instructed mothers in how to wash, clothe, and care for their children using newfangled items such as bathtubs and playpens.[75] By 1922, the station had built a new two-story building for the women, many of whom were nervous about ascending to the upper level.[76] In 1931, work with the country women expanded. In addition to the big annual fall conference (which sometimes attracted as many as 400 women and children), the missionaries and Bible women began to offer ten-day conferences at different outstations throughout the winter and spring of each year.[77]

Occasionally, special revival meetings were held at one of the outstations.

Attendees of the 1919 summer Bible study conference at Jiangyin. (Kiangyin Station Photographs, Presbyterian Church in the United States Missions, China, Department of History and Records, Presbyterian Church [U.S.A.], Montreat, N.C.)

One in November 1932 at Huashu featured evangelist George Hudson. A tent was erected in the center of town, on the site of a former pawnshop, and 36 separate meetings were conducted. Lacy Moffett estimated the total attendance at about 10,400, of which 136 signed cards to receive further instruction.[78]

What success did the evangelists have in creating a Christian church in the Jiangyin field? At the time of the fall of the empire in 1911, there were 3 organized churches, 9 other centers of work, and 459 total communicants. By 1927, before the Nationalist revolution disrupted missionary work, there were 6 churches, 16 outstations, and 1,078 church members. The last set of statistics available reveal that on the eve of the Japanese invasion, the mission claimed 7 churches, each with its own Chinese pastor, 8 other country chapels, and about 2,000 members (by this time, nearly equally divided between men and women).[79] Lacy Moffett's notes indicate that in the mid-1930s the ratio between church membership in the countryside and that in the city was about 2 to 1,[80] confirming the missionaries' expectations that the rural population was a more fruitful field to cultivate.

Itinerating among the humbler folk in the Jiangyin countryside brought the missionaries face-to-face with the human as well as the doctrinal dimensions of the Christian penetration of China. Small Christian communities were nurtured, often with great difficulty because of the demands of the new religion as well as the persistent attraction of traditional ways. The real strength of the Chinese church came from these small towns and villages.

Hampton DuBose, one of the pioneering Southern Presbyterian missionaries in China, once surveyed the work of his denomination's Mid-China Mission and described it as a three-tiered operation encompassing the "occupied" cities. At the top was the mission staff in Shanghai that ran the managing agencies of the mission and oversaw the publishing effort. At the next level were the mission stations in the large cities such as Nanjing, Suzhou, and Jinjiang, where much of the higher educational and medical work occurred. But the great work of evangelization, he noted, took place at a third level, in the lesser cities such as Sunjiang, Jiangyin, Wuxi, and Changzhou and their dependent market towns and villages. The missionaries there, whom DuBose dubbed the "outdoor staff" of the mission, accounted for only about one-twelfth of all missionaries in the mid-China field, yet they were the laborers in the vineyards who, like Lacy Moffett and his colleagues at Jiangyin, were most responsible for bringing converts into the church.[81]

7

RIDING

THE TIGER

JAPAN'S INVASION,

COMMUNIST

TRIUMPH, AND

THE DEMISE OF

THE STATION

The storm of student protest over Japan's invasion of Manchuria in the fall of 1931 gathered swiftly and broke in the major urban centers across the land. In Shanghai and the Yangzi River delta area, students in many government and mission schools went on strike for weeks and set out by rail for Nanjing, often forcing trains to transport them for free. In the nation's capital, these students joined comrades from throughout the country in mass rallies against Nationalist government inactivity.[1] The Jiangyin Christian schools were not disrupted, but a great deal of fervent oratory was heard in the schools and in worship services. The climate of bitterness and hatred stirred up against Japan dismayed some missionaries, who wanted to counsel Christian forbearance but as foreigners hesitated to do so for fear of being branded pro-Japanese.[2]

While the students were protesting, measures were taken to prepare Jiangyin against a possible naval or air assault by the Japanese on their way upriver from Shanghai to Nanjing should war spill over into central China. The government hurriedly and belatedly undertook the renovation and strengthening of the forts that had played such an important role in earlier conflicts. Two German military advisers were sent to inspect the situation, troop reinforcements were dispatched, and several anti-aircraft guns were mounted. In addition, communications were improved with the establishment of a radio station and the completion of a thirty-mile road from Wuxi to Jiangyin and two miles farther to the rear of the forts.

The missionaries, too, braced for the expected Japanese attack. They directed Red Cross training courses for girls in the local government school as well as in their own school, the Luola Murchison Sprunt Academy. All manner of emergency and medical supplies were stockpiled at the mission station, and a twenty-foot-square Red Cross flag was stretched out flat on the mission hospital roof, where it would be plainly visible to any Japanese pilots that might fly over. The rooftops also carried bold inscriptions, written in both Chinese and English, indicating "Hospital" and "U.S.A."[3]

The Japanese invaders were not the only force threatening to disrupt the work of the station in the early 1930s. Occasionally, the Communist movement would reemerge and cause alarm. Perhaps the biggest scare came in August 1930. Frequent Communist attacks in the Jiangyin countryside had killed and wounded many villagers, some of whom came to the mission hospital for treatment. The missionaries were holding a summer conference at the station for country Christians when rumors began circulating about an impending Communist attack against the church. A few months earlier, an antiforeign and anti-Christian leaflet was distributed in the city, so the rumors were taken seriously. At the request of the Jiangyin chief of police, the conference was adjourned early to avoid trouble. The tense situation was eventually relieved when a Communist leader was caught and executed.[4] By the fall of 1931, George Worth reported positively on the changed situation: "Militant communism has simmered down, . . . so that there is much better order in the country than last year. We meet only politeness, and warm cordiality everywhere. Even the Students Union of Kiangyin, usually the least friendly body of all, have considered requesting Charlie [Worth] to act as their drill master in their anti-Japanese volunteer corps!"[5] From this time until the late 1940s, the Jiangyin missionaries had no further contact or problems with the Communists, as the Japanese menace loomed larger and larger.

Uncertainty and fear gripped the Jiangyin community throughout the fall and winter of 1931–32 as it awaited "a slap of the dread dragon's tail."[6] As in earlier crises, many of Jiangyin's residents were counting on the mission station as a refuge. A leading banker told George Worth, "If war breaks out here, we are coming flying to the Mission Compound."[7]

By late January 1932, the fighting they all expected and dreaded finally broke out in Shanghai. Tensions had mounted for some time in that city because of a Chinese boycott of Japanese goods and a strong nationalistic outcry for resistance to the Japanese advance in Manchuria. On 18 January, some Chinese workers assaulted several Japanese, two of whom were fatally wounded. Japanese citizens retaliated by setting fire to a Chinese factory, and they killed several Chinese policemen who were trying to restore order. Consultations between civilian representatives of the two sides began, but Japan's commanding naval officer used the episode as an excuse to land marines at the International Settlement to defend Japanese lives and to call for reinforcements. When the Municipal Council of the International Settlement declared a state of emergency on 28 January and activated a contingency plan for the defense of the settlement should fighting break out, Japanese forces quickly took up their positions and by the end of the day they had moved beyond the settlement into the Chinese district of Chapei. Fighting between the Japanese and the Chinese ensued and spread fifteen to twenty miles inland before a cease-fire was arranged in early March. Negotiations dragged on into May, and all Japanese troops had not withdrawn from their advance positions back to the settlement until mid-July.[8]

As the Sino-Japanese conflict spread beyond Shanghai, Jiangyin residents feared the worst, not only from any Japanese bombardment but also from undisciplined Chinese troops retreating into the area. Close to half of the population fled to their country homes, in time-honored fashion, or to other safe areas, and many who stayed sought refuge at the station. The local Red Cross Society was counting on the mission hospital to handle the expected casualties and promised an allowance for each person treated. Western-trained doctors from the city also were to be sent to help (and, incidentally, take refuge).[9]

On 14 February, the American consul at Shanghai telegraphed Jiangyin urging American women and children to withdraw to Shanghai. The recipients of the message were reluctant to follow this advice despite the possible danger that might arise should Japanese (and retreating Chinese) troops advance further up the Yangzi River. They were prepared to stay and be of service to the Chinese, who they felt expected no less. Nine staff members, mostly women and children, nevertheless left for Shanghai and Hangzhou, but six stayed on, including George and Charles Worth, Marion Wilcox, and Andrew and Ella Allison and their young son.[10]

The evacuees left on 15 February, crossed the river on a junk, and slept on board until they were picked up before daylight the next morning in mid-channel by a British steamer. Reaching Shanghai about noon, they came upon Japanese warships bombarding the city, but the shelling was interrupted long enough to let their steamship pass. The children on board were delighted to be eyewitnesses to the fighting, but their elders could only wonder at "the strange psychology of the Oriental contestants" who could maintain "punctilious observance of [the] legal fiction" that there was no war. Steamers of all nations and even Chinese merchant ships passed safely through the "war zone."[11]

In the end, Jiangyin escaped the fighting, which was confined to the Shanghai area and ended in March. But the Christian community in Jiangyin mourned the loss of one of its native sons, Pastor Tsiang, who had resigned his East Gate pastorate in 1925 to take charge of the self-supporting Fitch Memorial Presbyterian Church in Shanghai. In the Japanese marine assault on Shanghai on 29 January, Tsiang, his wife and son, and four other members of his household were seized, beaten, and marched off under guard. Repeated inquiries about the captives by Pastor Tsiang's congregation and their Western friends produced no information, and they were all presumed dead.[12]

Japan's initial foray into China, and particularly its brutal ground and air assault on Shanghai, caused revulsion in Western circles. Missionaries in China were naturally among the strongest critics of Japanese policy and ambitions and the wanton destruction and disruption of life they caused. They generally avoided, however, making strident calls for Western action against the Japanese. Many were even critical of China's internal weakness, which they felt had invited Japanese aggression.[13] Some Jiangyin missionaries adopted such a stance. George Worth, for instance, in several letters to his relatives back home, expressed outrage at Japanese behavior: "No words of hate and bitterness are sufficient to express the rage against those 'savage, barbarian dwarfs.'" But he also blamed China for the country's plight, "which has been largely created by her own devious ways," and suggested that if the Japanese "had only the wisdom and restraint and *humanity* necessary to push their political venture in a decent way, it would have been bearable." Worth's son, Charles, revealed a similar ambivalence: "The Japanese have behaved with shameless pride and cruelty and thereby lost the respect of the world, as well as the otherwise good case that they have had against China. China deserves a sound spanking for its irresponsibility and chaos of the past seven years, but it is too bad to have Japan give it to her in such a high handed manner."[14]

By 1937, when Japan launched a full-scale invasion, all ambivalence among missionaries in China had disappeared.[15] In September, a group of American and British missionaries on extended vacation at Moganshan, a resort near Hangzhou, issued a statement on the Sino-Japanese conflict. Japan was charged with full responsibility for the armed conflict, a product of its continuous aggression against China. The complaints of the Japanese about Chinese boycotts, sabotage, murders, and agitation against them were dismissed as self-serving: "Much as we deplore the growth of hatred and resentment toward Japan, we believe that in view of the Japanese treatment of China, such anti-Japanese feeling is no more than we would have expected any other people to have developed under the circumstances. . . . The actions which Japanese spokesmen so condemn are the *result of* rather than the *justification for* the Japanese military activity in China."[16] Another message, signed in October by twenty-three Southern Presbyterians in Shanghai, stated, "We are witnesses of the heroic sacrifices and sufferings of the people to whom we have been sent, in their determined oneness of purpose to preserve at all cost their national existence and freedom against a powerful and inhuman military machine."[17]

Jiangyin missionaries in their private letters condemned the invaders in even harsher terms. Andrew Allison confessed, "There are no words that would make you see the horror and evil of the beastly, brutal, incredibly false and hypocritical works and words of the invading army and their political backers."[18] Ruth Worth, daughter of George Worth, wrote at length to a friend in America about Japanese duplicity and brutality:

> Don't believe any report from the Japanese — and I don't say this in any light mood of prejudice, tho I suppose I am prejudiced against them. But we have had it proven to us too many times in recent months that this Japanese military administration is on a wild tear now, with no thought for truth or justice or sincerity, but only aiming after conquest and personal aggrandizement. . . .
>
> Recently I read a long letter written by a Y.M.C.A. Secretary who has been in Nanking all during this time along with some 20 to 30 other foreigners. His descriptions of the ghastly orgy of murder and rape and pillage that the Japanese army has been indulging in there unchecked is blood-curdling. . . . One thing which this letter impressed on me especially is the contrast between orderliness of conditions in Nanking which the Chinese maintained up until the very last . . . and the chaos and reign of terror which has been present ever since the Japanese occupation. . . .
>
> We feel that you all abroad simply don't know what is going on and that it should be known all over the world especially in view of the reports the Japanese put out about how lovely everything is and how the Chinese peasants receive them with open arms. . . . It bothers me some, what a furious and vindictive feeling I get towards the Japs.[19]

Ruth's brother Charles was driven out of mission work at Hangzhou by the Japanese offensive of December 1937. He, too, reported on Japanese slaughter and rape and concluded, "It is perfectly evident that one of the aims of the Japanese in this campaign is to discredit and, if possible, drive out the white man, especially the missionary. In practically every city in this section from which we have reliable reports they have engaged in deliberate looting and destruction of mission property."[20] The Jiangyin Station serves as a good case in point.

In 1937, as in 1931–32, the national government and the local citizenry expected Jiangyin to be enveloped by the war. The Jiangyin forts had become even more important to the defense of the Yangzi River region because the Japanese had destroyed the Wusong forts above Shanghai in 1932. President Chiang Kai-shek personally inspected the fortifications early in 1936, and later that year, all of the hills surrounding Jiangyin were being fortified and declared off-limits to foreigners (who previously had hiked and hunted there).[21] After hostilities began and the Japanese threatened the Shanghai region, Chinese forces sank twenty-eight ships in the Yangzi River near a large island just below Jiangyin in order to block the passage of Japanese warships. Navigational signs were destroyed, and portions of the river were mined. Chinese divisions arrived with field guns to help hold the area and prevent enemy troops from landing on shore for an overland attack on Nanjing, the nation's capital.[22]

Life in Jiangyin was disrupted after mid-September when the daily whine of Japanese planes and the roar of Chinese anti-aircraft guns kept people off the streets and prompted many to flee to other areas. Homes were empty, cotton fields were unattended, and demoralization set in. The missionaries took pains to assure their Chinese associates that they would stand by them. Extra food and medical supplies were stored in the mission compound in preparation for the Japanese assault.[23] Chinese defense efforts were valiant but unsuccessful. Enemy aircraft wreaked havoc on Chinese naval forces and shore batteries. Japanese land forces moved relentlessly upriver toward Jiangyin. After a five-day battle, the invaders seized the Jiangyin forts and the city on 1 December 1937.[24]

Four Western missionaries were in Jiangyin that fall. All of the foreign staff had taken extended vacations at Moganshan or Guling during the summer or had gone home on furlough because of the unsettled conditions. By September, American consuls were urging all Americans to leave the interior, but some missionaries resisted. In Changsha, Ruth Greene of the Yale-in-China staff argued that unlike in 1927, when missionaries were the target of Chinese nationalism, they were now "just part of the scheme with our Chinese friends, and our beating it for safety does take the heart out of them."[25] All of the Jiangyin missionaries at first went to Shanghai after their summer vacations rather than returning to the station,[26] but Andrew and Ella Allison, Katheryne Thompson, and Marion Wilcox then decided to return to their work. Wilcox explained that her decision was prompted by the following Chinese editorial in a Shanghai newspaper:

> The missionaries in China today are no doubt being confronted with danger. It might be easy for them to ask their government to extend a paternal hand and deliver them from destructive forces, and yet to do so would be unChristian and unworthy of their Lord. . . . By deserting at the first sign of danger, they might betray the confidence reposed in them by the Chinese converts; by remaining together with the converts, they would surely earn the undying good will as well as affection and lay the foundation for a greater claim to Chinese support in the years to come.[27]

When the four missionaries returned to the station in October 1937, they found the mission schools barely functioning. By early November, the schools closed because of the danger. On 13 November, the Joint Committee of Control, consisting of the four missionaries and nine Chinese members, met to draw up an emergency plan. They decided that the members of the Joint Committee could leave the station if the situation became too dangerous but that they should leave as a group to maintain order and good spirits. The staff of the mission hospital was to take the necessary medicines and instruments in order to carry on elsewhere. Painted on the roofs of the hospital buildings were "U.S.A." and the Chinese characters for "Hospital" ("Yiyuan") in bold white strokes, and all the buildings flew the American flag for identification.[28] Two days later, after Japanese bombing sorties began coming close to the station, a boatload of older women and young children and the medical supplies left for the countryside. The station's itinerating houseboat, which had been left unassembled after repairs to prevent it from being commandeered by Chinese troops, was now put together and another boat was hired to prepare for the final evacuation, which came a week later, on 22 November.[29]

The immediate destination of the three boatloads of about eighty Chinese Christians and four missionaries was Zhangjiacun (or "Zhang Family Village"), about fifteen miles southwest of Jiangyin. It was located behind a mountain about one-half mile from the main canal between Jiangyin and Changzhou, which the Japanese frequently used. Few Christians lived in this village, whose population was less than 300, but the resident who served as their host had sent two young daughters to board with the single missionary women at Jiangyin. He arranged lodging for the Chinese Christians in rooms throughout the village, while the missionaries remained on the itinerating houseboat, whose living quarters measured only seven by fifteen feet.[30] For nineteen months, this Christian community remained in exile, unable to return to or use its main station at Jiangyin.

A few days after the evacuation, Japanese aircraft, according to Chinese eyewitnesses, bombed the station in broad daylight despite the clear markings on the buildings and the fact that the Japanese consul had been notified of the American property in that area. The major destruction, however, came after Japanese troops were in control of the city. In the early morning hours of 8 December, they entered the mission station, piled up household furnishings, hospital beds, and school equipment, doused them with kerosene, and set them afire. Seventeen of the twenty structures were destroyed in the conflagration, with only the doctor's residence, the nurses home, and the boys school dormitory still standing, although somewhat damaged. Japanese soldiers occupied these three buildings for a while but later abandoned them, leaving them easy prey for looting by thieves referred to as "lawless elements of the local Chinese." Most of the wall around the mission compound had crumbled under the bombing, and many of the wooden

Remaining station buildings after Japanese bombing, including the doctors residence
(at left) and the nurses home, 1937. (First Presbyterian Church, Wilmington, N.C.)

gates were gone. The total damage to mission property was later estimated at
about $91,000.[31]

The city was devastated as well. Factories and mills were stripped of supplies and machinery by both the Japanese and the local Chinese. Valuable
furniture from the better homes was shipped off to Japan. The few people
left in Jiangyin were mainly in the service trades (restaurants, tea shops, bar-
ber shops, and the like), and any women remained out of sight. The under-
staffed Japanese military police (reportedly only three for the whole city)
were powerless to stop the widespread pillage and raping.[32]

Several Jiangyin missionaries tried unsuccessfully to return to the mission
station in the fall and winter of 1937–38 to assess the damage and the possibility of renewing their work.[33] The first to get back was Charles Worth, who
was no longer assigned to the station but wanted to check on the Worth family property and possessions. The Japanese authorities in Shanghai would
not allow foreigners to return to Jiangyin, but Worth was able in late January
to obtain a military pass to Wuxi. There he hoped he could convince local
Japanese commanders to issue him a pass to Jiangyin. The Japanese refused,
however, and ordered him to return to Shanghai at once.[34] Although he returned to Shanghai, Worth ultimately would bypass the authorities and
make his way to Jiangyin without their approval.

In February, the missionaries at Zhangjiacun had discovered a route to
Shanghai that avoided Japanese-controlled areas. They traveled along the

small canals to Changyinsha, a large island in the Yangzi River about thirty miles east of Jiangyin. At that point, they could board boats that sailed back and forth to Shanghai under foreign flags. Ella Allison and twenty young Chinese Christians in late February followed this route to Shanghai, where the young people were to enroll in a special middle school.[35] Charles Worth decided to retrace their steps. He left Shanghai on 7 March for Zhangjiacun to take over Ella Allison's mission duties temporarily while she "came up for air" in Shanghai, as one missionary put it.[36] From the village, Worth walked the fifteen miles to Jiangyin on 15 March to gain the first glimpse of the station since it had been evacuated four months previously. Japanese guards stopped him as he entered the city, but after some discussion with the military police office, he was allowed to visit the mission station and to post signs instructing Japanese soldiers not to disturb the premises. He also arranged for some former servants to occupy the remaining buildings and act as caretakers until repairs were made and the Christian community could return. As for the Worth family possessions, little was left to save, but he managed to retrieve the hospital bell that his paternal grandmother had donated to the station and that had pealed so loudly on the hour that it could be heard throughout the city and the surrounding countryside.[37]

At Zhangjiacun, the Christian refugees carried on their work as best they could. The Allisons taught Bible class, while Thompson and Wilcox taught English and singing to the young girls. Some of the Chinese students, in turn, spread the Christian message among the village children. Sermons were given in two village temples, where many refugees from the Jiangyin area had congregated.[38] Occasionally, some of the missionaries visited Jiangyin to join small bands of Christians in services held in the unburned boys school dormitory. Little effort, however, was made to contact Christians in the numerous outstations that had been opened in the Jiangyin field. Reports indicated that Christian worship continued in these outstations, but the missionaries saw as their primary tasks keeping together and ministering to the large refugee group at Zhangjiacun.[39]

Concern for the health of the refugees led, in part, to the decision to relocate in May 1938 to the nearby small town of Jiaodian, where an outstation had been established in 1920. Living conditions in Zhangjiacun were primitive and overcrowded, and the missionaries feared the possibility of a cholera epidemic in the summer heat. Happily, the gentry of Jiaodian invited the missionaries to settle in their town with the stipulation that medical services be offered to the community, which numbered about 5,000. The eighty or so Christians who made the move were given free use of a brand new two-story school building, unused for its original purpose because of the war. The building was converted to provide living space for twelve families, a schoolroom, and clinics. Also at the missionaries' disposal was a large temple behind the school with an attached kitchen and an open courtyard where plays formerly had been presented.[40]

While at Jiaodian, no formal classes were held for fear of inviting attention to the Christian group there. The missionaries, however, did obtain permission from the Mid-China Mission to conduct an informal school for thirty or so Christian children. It was "a household affair, and nothing has been said about it."[41] In Shanghai, the two Jiangyin academies joined with ten other missionary schools to establish a cooperative middle school in the fall of 1938 to accommodate the great number of Christian children who had refugeed there because of the dangerous conditions in the countryside.[42]

As for medical work, the expected cholera outbreak occupied the medical personnel throughout the summer and led to calls for an additional missionary doctor. Alex Moffett, the son of Lacy and Kate Moffett, who had been at Jiangyin for thirty years, arrived from Shanghai to help Dr. William Chen, formerly at Jiangyin and now director of the Jiaodian hospital. Later, Alex Moffett transferred to the nearby market town of Xiaoqi, where he supervised a branch clinic of the Jiaodian hospital set up in the home of a wealthy family.[43] Nearly 400 cholera patients were treated at the two towns that summer, with a 90 percent rate of cure. The stricken were brought in, more dead than alive, on doors, wicker chairs, large bamboo silkworm trays, and men's backs. At Jiaodian, they were crowded into the building's first-floor hallways, where they received the intravenous saline solution that saved them. "As that life-replacing fluid flows down from the flask," wrote Andrew Allison, "a few minutes show the eyes fluttering and opening, consciousness returning, color coming back to that deathly face, the wrinkled fingers filling out, and a weak but manifestly alive person taking the place before your eyes of that nearly dead creature who was placed on the bed a quarter of an hour ago."[44] Patients were sent home as soon as they began to recover in order to make room for others, but some suffered fatal relapses when their relatives failed to heed instructions on home care and sanitary precautions. The pragmatic Chinese supplemented the hospital's work with communal dragon lantern processions to appease the gods, a practice that naturally dismayed as well as intrigued the missionaries.[45]

The Jiaodian hospital and its branch clinic served other purposes. After a Japanese attack on a neighboring town, thirteen seriously wounded people were brought to the hospital for treatment.[46] The staff also provided medical care to Nationalist guerrillas, who, however, resisted inoculations on superstitious grounds, and on occasion hid them from the Japanese.[47] The guerrillas were generally friendly to the missionaries and insisted that Americans not be harmed. On one occasion, however, the relationship produced some tension. The guerrillas asked to use the missionaries' building at Jiaodian for a memorial service to Sun Yat-sen. The missionaries agreed on the stipulation that the soldiers come unarmed and that the ceremony be brief. Despite their sympathies for the Chinese struggle against the Japanese, the Western-ers were officially neutral and did not want to jeopardize their position. To their dismay, 250 heavily armed guerrillas took part in the ceremony, which took two and a half hours to conclude, as the missionaries fretted over the possibility of a Japanese foraging party showing up. Fortunately, none did.[48]

Relations with the Japanese were more problematical. During the mis-sionaries' six-month stay at Zhangjiacun, Japanese soldiers once came as close as 200 yards to the village while on a duck hunt, but they never discov-ered the Christians there. The village also was spared from the Japanese bombing sorties that attacked many nearby areas, a fact that the Christians touted as a case of divine protection. What little contact the missionaries had with the Japanese occurred during the missionaries' itinerating trips in the Jiangyin field or during their brief visits to the city itself.[49] The most trouble occurred in Xiaoqi, where Alex Moffett had set up the branch clinic. On 11 December 1938, Japanese scouts entered the town and designated the Christian chapel as quarters for the main force, which was due to arrive the next day. Alex Moffett was away at the time, and Lacy Moffett was itinerating in the countryside. When word of Japanese intentions reached Lacy Moffett and Andrew Allison at Jiaodian, they rushed to Xiaoqi to take up residence in the chapel to forestall the Japanese. The latter were surprised to find the chapel occupied, and after some discussion, they agreed to find another place in town for billeting.[50]

A more serious incident occurred two weeks later. Andrew Allison had again come to Xiaoqi from Jiaodian to keep watch on the facilities while the Moffetts were in Shanghai. On 23 December, a messenger arrived at the chapel with the dread news that a Japanese sentry had been shot and killed at a shop near the hospital clinic. The townspeople were fleeing in panic, fear-ful of Japanese reprisals, and Japanese troops were rushing to the scene armed to the hilt. Allison, as a neutral foreigner, took charge of investigating the incident. He quickly determined, to the satisfaction of the Japanese com-manding officer, that the soldier had been killed by a Chinese guerrilla while buying sugar in the shop, that the killer had escaped into the surrounding countryside, and that none of the townspeople had been involved. The Japanese troops withdrew to their quarters, and their commanding officer sat down with the American missionary for a chat. Over cocoa, they talked about the war, or the "China Incident" as the Japanese officer insisted on calling it, about Chinese loyalties to Chiang Kai-shek, and about the distinc-tions between Chinese regulars, Chinese guerrillas (also referred to as the "plain clothes army"), and mere bandits. They parted on friendly and re-spectful terms.[51]

After a year in the countryside, and after Japan's initial thrust into China had run its course, the Jiangyin Christian refugees began to plan their return to the central station. They petitioned the Mid-China Mission for repair funds, which were approved at the spring 1939 meeting.[52] With these funds and other monies made available later from the mission, Alex Moffett arranged for the three remaining buildings at the station to be repaired and made suitable for residences and renewed work. The large Christian contingent at Jiaodian moved back to Jiangyin on 21 June 1939, and other groups of Christians and missionaries who had settled elsewhere also returned to help reopen the station.[53] The boys dormitory was used to house the 8 missionaries, 3 missionary children, 18 Chinese Christian workers, and 30 schoolchildren. Classes were conducted for the younger students, while older children attended the cooperative Christian middle school in Shanghai. Bible classes of a week to ten days' duration were held in the outstations, and a clinic was reopened in the two unburned hospital buildings at the station.[54] A campaign was launched in America and among the 280 alumni of the Jiangyin schools then residing in Shanghai to raise money for a restoration of the East Gate chapel.[55]

The Jiangyin Station thus came alive again in 1939–40 with the intention of renewing its evangelistic, educational, and medical missions. The missionaries' hopes for settled conditions in which to carry on their work proved, however, to be illusory. The Japanese invasion irreparably tore apart China's political and social fabric and fostered the growth of a Communist movement that ultimately could not tolerate the missionary enterprise. Furthermore, Japan's ambitions expanded and clashed in the Pacific with the interests of the United States. In the face of these developments, the missionary position at Jiangyin became precarious. Japanese military police regularly visited the station to question the staff. Guerrilla forces still roamed the countryside and exerted their power on occasion. The station's worst moment during this period came in October 1940 when so-called "bandits" (possibly Communists) attacked the hospital in an attempt to kidnap its director, William Chen, and rob its treasury. They were unsuccessful, but Chen was severely beaten and later died from his injuries, and another Chinese doctor suffered a broken arm and collarbone. At the time, Alex Moffett was on leave, so the hospital was left with only a skeletal staff, consisting of a head nurse, an intern, and a lab technician.[56]

Shortly after this attack, the Mid-China Mission voted to instruct all stations to close down or transfer responsibility for all work to the Chinese. Missionaries were asked to evacuate by 1 December unless their presence was absolutely necessary.[57] By March 1941, only the Allisons and Marion Wilcox remained at Jiangyin, and in early December, the Allisons left for Shanghai.

On the morning of 8 December, fifty Japanese soldiers rushed into the station with bayonets drawn, fingers on their triggers, yelling like wild men. The soldiers herded Wilcox and all of the Chinese into a courtyard while they ransacked the grounds, making off with the station's two houseboats, bicycles, radios, typewriters, a sewing machine, hospital supplies, bedding, and food supplies. The school, church, and clinic were closed down. The Chinese were forced to leave with only their necessities, while Wilcox was kept under house arrest in the compound. She lived there with one Chinese woman as a companion throughout the winter. A small number of Japanese soldiers also lived on the grounds, and in March, several hundred additional soldiers arrived. Wilcox later reported that she remained well throughout this period and was not mistreated by her captors. One soldier brought her cans of fruit, and another even had chocolates brought in for her from Nanjing. Wilcox was allowed contact with the Christians outside the walls, who continued to hold religious services and opened small clinics around the city. One treasured moment came on Christmas Day 1941 when a group of Christian children braved Japanese ire by singing carols outside the wall of her residence. On 11 April 1942, the Japanese ordered her to leave for Shanghai, and on the next day, the last missionary at Jiangyin departed the city.[58]

The United States and Japan were at war. China's cause was now an American cause. In the eyes of the Japanese, Christian work by either Americans or the Chinese was intimately linked with the American military and political effort. Consequently, Chinese Christian leaders were often mistreated by the Japanese, but they managed to keep the church alive throughout the war years. With much of the Jiangyin mission hospital destroyed and the remaining buildings occupied by the Japanese, several of the Christians opened small clinics around the city to carry on medical work. Religious services were held privately in the home of one of the elders of the Jiangyin church, and school work was resumed a few years into the occupation in one of the remaining school dormitories.[59] In fact, the absence of missionaries during this period gave Chinese Christians a greater opportunity than ever to attain the professed goal of an independent Chinese church.

The story of the Christian community in the town of Huashu, located about twenty miles southeast of Jiangyin, was perhaps the most inspiring example to the missionaries of Chinese leadership and perseverance. When the Japanese reached Huashu, they forcibly occupied the church building, which had been rented for the congregation by a missionary. The Christians then rented an empty cloth factory nearby, but they were subjected to constant harassment by Japanese soldiers, who accused them of being in league with the American imperialists. The pastor's wife was once beaten, soldiers often attended services and spied on the congregation's actions, and church furnishings were plundered. Finally, in February 1942, soldiers moved into the building, disrupting the life of the pastor and his family who resided there, consuming their supplies, and even using the worship room for torturing captured Chinese guerrilla soldiers.

The Christians endured such degradation for over two years before they were able to move into a new building on land they owned. They had amassed enough funds to buy an old tea shop in a nearby town, which they dismantled, planning to use the materials to construct the new building. Church members loaded the shop's bricks and tiles onto a canal barge to transport them to the building site, but the boat sunk in the middle of the canal from its heavy load. Fearing the loss of not only their building materials but also their lives at the hands of the Japanese for impeding canal traffic, they gathered as many volunteers as they could find to salvage the bricks and tiles from the murky bottom. After four days of diving, most of the materials were recovered (and were much cleaner to boot), and in early March 1944, they completed the construction of a substantial five-room church building. When the missionaries returned to Huashu in 1947, the congregation was contemplating adding a two-story building to house a primary school and an infirmary.[60]

As the Japanese empire crumbled in Asia, mission boards in the United States made plans to renew their work in formerly occupied territories. Funds held in reserve during the war years were released to reopen and restaff the evangelical centers, the schools, and the hospitals. The Southern Presbyterians appointed a Survey Committee to visit their mission stations in China and to determine initial priorities on reopening and restaffing. The committee made its rounds in the spring of 1946, then met in Shanghai at the beginning of May to draw up preliminary recommendations. The Executive Committee of Foreign Missions, meeting in Nashville on 4 June, adopted the committee's priority lists with some adjustments and allocated $400,000 of the Far Eastern Reoccupation Fund to China, releasing 10 percent of the money immediately for the repair and rehabilitation of station buildings and residences. The remaining funds were to be held until the Survey Committee completed an overall study of the situation.[61]

Neither the Survey Committee nor the Executive Committee felt that the "reoccupation" of China by its missionaries would be easy. Their correspondence spoke of "the fluid situation" in the field because of the growing difficulties between the Nationalists and the Communists, of "considerable anti-American feeling," of Chinese Christians who thought the presence of missionaries would add to their problems, and of rampant inflation and the shortage of basic necessities. Missionaries with children particularly were urged not to consider returning to China just yet.[62] Despite these fears, and in full knowledge of the potential risks, great numbers of missionaries began to return to their stations in the fall of 1946. In October, over 400 of them sailed for the Far East on a chartered ship, the *Marine Lynx*.[63]

Only four missionaries returned to Jiangyin after the war. Marion Wilcox and Andrew Allison arrived in March 1946, and Ella Allison joined them in October. Katheryne Thompson came back on a second run of the *Marine Lynx* in December and reached Jiangyin in early January 1947.[64] Some of the other Jiangyin veterans took up assignments at other stations in the Mid-China Mission field, both because of the limited facilities at Jiangyin and because their services were needed more urgently elsewhere. The Allisons and the two women missionaries lived together on the third floor of the boys school dormitory, one of the three buildings not destroyed by the Japanese.

The Survey Committee originally recommended that the Jiangyin Station reopen either the hospital or the school but not both. The staff, however, convinced the committee to permit them to attempt to manage both. In April 1946, the hospital reopened, and by September, it was treating about 500 patients a month. Andrew Allison wrote optimistically about plans to rebuild the hospital complex and rehire a staff. New school facilities were built on the site where the James Sprunt Academy had stood. The first session of school, which was finally registered with government authorities, began in September with over 350 junior and senior high students; boys and girls attended together because of limited staff and classroom space. Enrollment continued to rise, as in other mission schools in the postwar era; by the spring session, the school had over 400 students, about one-third of them girls.[65]

The station celebrated its fiftieth anniversary, a year late, just before Christmas 1946, but apparently without any of the fanfare or demonstrative community support that attended the thirtieth anniversary celebration in 1925.[66] The annual women's conference, last held in 1936, did not resume until November 1948. One of the highlights of that conference was an address by the Christian mayor of Yangshe, a woman who had succeeded in cleaning up gambling in her town.[67] With too few missionaries available, Chinese Bible women from 1945 on annually conducted short-term Bible classes in fourteen different places in the country.[68]

Itinerating in the countryside began immediately. To replace the old itinerating houseboats seized by the Japanese in 1941, Marion Wilcox rented one from a Christian couple who did the rowing and lived in part of the boat with their three children. She happily reported on one village that prior to the war had no chapel and few Christians but now had a Christian community of fifty-nine members who had raised about $2,250 to build a new chapel that would seat 400.[69] Andrew Allison also made rounds of outlying towns, including Jiaodian, where they had refugeed during the Japanese invasion, to preach in tea shops and temples. His reports, though, were less rosy, and he claimed to have had little success.[70]

The missionaries were in the midst of a rebuilding effort at the East Gate main station in the postwar years. Work on two new missionary residences began in the fall of 1947, and the homes were ready for occupation the following February. A new dormitory for girls was opened that spring, and part of the hospital was rebuilt. By the end of 1948, two new buildings were available for the Bible school. Funds for these projects came mainly from Presbyterian congregations back home.[71]

The final project was the construction of an imposing church building at the East Gate compound. In its fifty-year history, the main station had never had a separate church; it had used the hospital chapel. In 1937, a site within the compound walls was chosen for the construction of a new and larger chapel, but the Mid-China Mission cautioned the Jiangyin Station not to make unnecessary expenditures given the uncertain political situation. Although the war in China disrupted the plans for construction, a church fund totaling close to $1,000 was collected and held in reserve. Now, in 1948, an additional $3,000 was raised. Still, the missionaries decided to wait for more settled times before building the church. The Chinese Christians of Jiangyin, however, were determined to proceed and raised their own funds to build a small church in one corner of the lot set aside for the larger structure. The chapel was completed and conducted its inaugural worship service, ironically, only after the Communist "liberation" of Jiangyin in April 1949.[72]

The rebuilding efforts, as well as the work at Jiangyin, were affected by several developments. Certainly the soaring inflation made the entire enterprise very costly when funds were converted to the local currency. A few examples from the missionary correspondence reveal how worthless Chinese money had become. Andrew Allison paid 1,000 yuan for a haircut in 1946, and Katheryne Thompson bought a can opener in Shanghai in 1947 for 4,500 yuan. A country church was built in 1947 for 112 million yuan, which equaled about $2,200 in U.S. currency, and another chapel in 1948 cost 1 billion yuan (only about $1,500). Later in 1948, a contribution from home to the building fund of slightly less than $1,000 was exchanged for 4,400 billion yuan.[73] Most Chinese contributions were made in kind (rice, jewelry, cotton goods, etc.) since inflation had made Chinese money valueless. Building materials were also scarce, one report indicating that Jiangyin was almost bare of trees, which presumably had been cut for fuel and construction. In time, rice could not be found in the markets at any price.[74]

Beyond these economic factors was the more ominous threat of political upheaval and the imminent success of the Communists. Communist victories in Manchuria and north China in 1947–48 brought them to the verge of success and presented American missionaries, and indeed all foreigners, with the urgent question of whether to stay in China or evacuate. The Communists' official attitude toward the foreign mission movement was at first somewhat restrained and tolerant. In March 1948, they announced a policy of religious freedom and protection of missionary activity as long as missionaries obeyed Chinese laws and did not engage in subversive activity. The Common Program adopted by the Chinese People's Political Consultative Conference in September 1949 included an article guaranteeing freedom of religion, and the new government reasserted this principle in April 1950. But in May, Premier Zhou Enlai met with prominent Chinese Christians and stated that, although missionaries currently in China could stay, those with technical skills being particularly welcome, no new missionaries could enter China, those who left on furlough could not return, and the Chinese church must cut its administrative and financial ties with imperialist powers.[75]

Chinese church leaders recognized that the new order would necessitate changed relations with the foreign mission movement. In December 1949, nineteen Christian leaders issued "A Message from Chinese Christians to Mission Boards Abroad." In it, they expressed appreciation to those involved in the mission movement and asserted that they saw no direct link between missionary work and imperialist policies, although they suggested that the mission movement's past entanglements with the unequal treaties gave rise to misunderstanding. They called for the complete transfer, where it had not already occurred, of responsibility for policy formulation and financial administration to Chinese leadership. Missionaries, the statement concluded, were still welcome in a service role, although in somewhat restricted circumstances because of the new political-economic environment.[76]

Clearly, the day of the missionary was drawing to a close. At the least, missionary work in China would be drastically curtailed and fraught with danger. American mission boards and the U.S. consulate began to express concern for the safety of missionaries in the interior and privately doubted if the mission movement could survive in a Communist-controlled China. For a year prior to the establishment of the People's Republic in October 1949, about half of the Protestant missionary force had already made plans to evacuate. Their reasons for leaving varied, including poor health, approaching retirement age, concern for their young children, and insufficient language skills or adjustment to the field. Many who had been interned by the Japanese did not want to risk losing their freedom again. Those who remained were influenced by their commitment to continue God's and their life's work, their loyalty to Chinese Christian colleagues, their belief that Christianity could meet the needs of the Chinese, and their hope that communism and Christianity could coexist.[77]

At the Jiangyin Station, the moment of decision came in November 1948. On 16 November, the U.S. consul-general in Shanghai urged all American nationals in Jiangsu and neighboring provinces to move to places of safety and make plans to leave China before the opportunity was foreclosed. At about the same time, the Executive Committee of Foreign Missions of the PCUS sent a cablegram to the China Mission authorizing it "to take whatever measures may be necessary for safety of our missionaries." The Ad-Interim Committee of the mission met in Shanghai on 18 November and voted to summon all mission members to Shanghai; to turn over all hospitals, schools, and other institutions to Chinese Christians; to notify the Chinese that 1948–49 appropriations to these institutions would be paid but no funds would be supplied thereafter; and to instruct each mission station to file with the local magistrate and chief of police a statement on missionary property holdings, with the request that they be protected.[78] Under the circumstances, the Allisons opted to return home since they were less than a year away from retirement. They sailed from Shanghai on 4 December, bound for San Francisco on a transport ship provided by the U.S. government.[79] Marion Wilcox and Katheryne Thompson decided to stay in order to continue their evangelical and educational work.

Wilcox and Thompson were the only foreigners in the city (of any nationality, in any occupation) when the Red Army "liberated" Jiangyin on 24 April 1949. Many residents had fled in the preceding months, and the new regime had little patience with those who now wanted to return. Most of the Christian families had stayed and continued to pursue their usual religious activities, including Bible classes and the summer conference, with little interference.[80] The Bible classes were confined to Sundays and had to be held outside the station compound. The two missionaries were restricted in their movements and work. For the first month, they received constant visits from the "boys from Shantung," as they called the Communist forces, many of whom had never seen foreigners before, who inquired about their nationality and their purpose. Neither woman left the station for itinerating trips in the countryside, considering it wiser to leave this task to Chinese preachers and Bible women. Besides, they reasoned (or rationalized), there was plenty of work to do in Jiangyin. In fact, they were required to obtain passes from the police, which were often hard to get, to travel anywhere. Residing in their own homes, they had ample food supplies and suffered no physical hardships, although they alluded to severe mental and spiritual strain. Their experience was comparable to that of most other Protestant missionaries in China at the time.[81] Educational work also was disrupted. Communist agents held indoctrination sessions and propaganda musical performances at the mission school, which left little time for studying. Many students withdrew because of the turmoil and returned home. Attendance at later sessions dropped significantly.[82]

In November 1949, Wilcox and Thompson tried unsuccessfully to obtain permission from the district magistrate to go to Shanghai for a Thanksgiving celebration with other foreigners and to attend a mission meeting. They tried again the following February and were finally granted three-week passes to the "big city." Despite the restrictions and harassment they experienced at Jiangyin, neither missionary sought to leave China or "for one instant regretted the decision to stay." They took heart from Chinese friends who stated, "You just don't know what it means to us to have you folks stick by us now."[83]

The new government's coolness toward missionaries intensified after China's entry into the Korean War in October 1950. Accusations against missionaries as agents of imperialism became strident, and many missionaries were imprisoned on charges of espionage or behavior detrimental to China. In April 1951, Premier Zhou Enlai summoned Protestant Christian leaders to a conference to work out a policy ensuring the true independence of the Chinese church from America and other Western nations. Zhou released to the group a set of government regulations demanding that "Chinese Christian churches and other organizations should immediately sever all relations with American Mission Boards." Missionaries, it stated, would either be dismissed and punished if they had worked against the new government, allowed to go home, or permitted to stay if invited by Chinese churches to work in nonadministrative positions.[84] At Jiangyin, both the schools and the hospital cut their ties with the American mission movement, and by 1952, these institutions were under the control of the local government. The hospital was renamed "People's Hospital," while the combined schools were renamed "Jiangyin No. 2 Middle School."[85]

At the same conference, the churches were encouraged to launch "accusation meetings" against erstwhile colleagues they considered guilty of illegal or unpatriotic activity. At the conclusion of the conference, the church leaders issued their own declaration supporting the government's regulations, the "Oppose-America, Support-Korea" campaign of propaganda and suppression of counterrevolutionaries, and the Three-self movement (for self-government, self-support, and self-propagation) within the Chinese church.[86]

The message was clear to all missionaries, and in the spring of 1951, a wholesale exodus began. Exit permits, although promised in the April regulations, were not easily obtained; many requests were approved only after long delays and some were even denied.[87] The Jiangyin missionaries, who had intimated in November 1950 that their stay might soon be curtailed,[88] sent their last messages home on New Year's Day 1951. They wrote about the successful country women's conference in November, the joyous Christmas celebrations, and the activities of the hospital and Bible school. They gave no indication that their lives or work were any more proscribed than they previously had been.[89]

These letters, however, concealed the fact (revealed in a later communication) that in mid-November they had decided to seek permission to leave China precisely because their activities were becoming increasingly restricted. They received frequent unexplained visits from the police, they were unable to visit the mission hospital, and after Christmas 1950, they were not permitted to teach at either the high school or the Sunday school. Chinese friends urged them to leave for their own safety and in order to lessen the danger to Chinese Christians. On 20 November, the Chinese principals of the high school and the Bible school wrote the authorities that the missionaries wished to return home on their regular furloughs. Exit permits were issued on 23 April 1951, and by the next day (on the second anniversary of the Communist entrance into Jiangyin), they were gone, thus concluding the fifty-six-year missionary enterprise in Jiangyin.[90]

The postwar years at the Jiangyin Station were merely a brief interlude temporarily suspending the demise of the Western missionary movement in China. The movement had too little time to recover from the wreckage of the Japanese invasion before being faced with the challenge of a new state power committed to the elimination of religion and particularly its foreign vestiges. Any lasting impact of Western missionaries in China would surface only after the purification and domestication of Christianity by the Chinese.

8

HANDS ACROSS
THE SEA

A SPECIAL

RELATIONSHIP

WITH THE

HOME CHURCH

Besides the impact of the demise of the Jiang-yin Station after a fifty-six-year existence on the Southern Presbyterian missionaries in China and the Christian community they nurtured, it also meant the end of an intense long-term relationship, both personal and institutional, between the station and its supporters at home. The story of the Jiangyin Station is not complete without considering this relationship and the impact it had in shaping the religious life and organizational behavior of supporting institutions and constituencies back in the United States: the Southern Presbyterian Church, the First Presbyterian Church of Wilmington, and the women of the Wilmington Presbytery.

Like other American Protestant denominations, the Southern Presbyterian church made China the centerpiece of its missionary efforts in the first several decades of the twentieth century. The church's fund-raising strategy took definite shape in 1902 with the establishment of a "Forward Movement" launched by, among others, Lacy Moffett, who later worked as a missionary at Jiangyin for several decades, and John Leighton Stuart, who later became president of Yanjing University in Beijing and then U.S. ambassador to China. They had been recruited to perform mission work by the Student Volunteer Movement but were detained at home for lack of funds. Their plan was to encourage churches, societies, and individuals to accept responsibility for particular missionaries, stations, or types of work in the field. By personalizing the relationship in this way, they hoped to raise more funds.[1]

When the Southern Presbyterians accepted responsibility for specific areas of mission work in 1907, they also adopted a "missionary platform" including the creation of the first denominational Layman's Missionary Movement to raise funds and the issuance of a call for churches within the denomination to adopt a particular overseas mission field as their special object. In response to this call, the First Presbyterian Church of Wilmington requested and was assigned the Jiangyin mission field, where one of its own members, George Worth, had been stationed since 1897 and whose medical work the Woman's Auxiliary of the Wilmington Presbytery in 1904 had agreed to support. Members of the congregation, for their part, pledged about $7,000 in support of the mission, and by the time of the Chinese revolution, the subscriptions had risen to $10,000. Finally, in 1909 James Sprunt pledged the first of many large gifts to finance the educational work at Jiangyin.[2]

Thus, by 1909, all of the institutional work at Jiangyin and most of the salaries of its missionary staff were funded either by the Woman's Auxiliary or by the First Presbyterian Church and its members. Through this "special relationship," nearly $600,000 flowed from the Wilmington area to the missionaries at Jiangyin until the station was closed in 1951. The First Presbyterian congregation hailed the Jiangyin church as its "spiritual daughter"[3] and followed its growth with parental pride and concern. They saw the station and its missionaries as extensions of themselves and participated vicariously in mission work through their yearly contributions. As Anna Sykes wrote, "We know that your hearts are with us all the times [sic], for 'where your treasure is, there will your heart be.'"[4]

A large proportion of the First Presbyterian Church's annual contributions went to pay the salaries, or some portion of them, of the Jiangyin missionaries. The cover of the church's Sunday bulletin always listed the foreign and home missionaries the church or its members were supporting in the field.[5] The Hadens received support from 1903 to 1908, when they were transferred to another station. As new appointments were made at Jiangyin, the church provided funding for all or part of their salaries. After 1908, the Littles, the Moffetts, the Allisons, Anna Sykes and her daughter, the Lee sisters, Ida Albaugh, Rida Jourolman, William Cumming, and the Chinese assistants received the church's support. George Worth and his family were funded entirely by an endowment set up by his father.[6] When his children, Charles and Ruth Worth, grew up and became missionaries at Jiangyin, however, the church provided for their salaries, mostly through pledges from James Sprunt. After World War II, the church resumed the full support of the Allisons at Jiangyin as well as Charles Worth at another station in China.[7]

The records of the First Presbyterian Church provide a detailed accounting of its annual contributions to foreign missions, all of which were earmarked for the Jiangyin missionaries (see table 8-1). The figures clearly reflect the major role the church played in funding the station from 1909 on as a result of its assumption of Jiangyin as its special responsibility and James

Table 8-1. Annual Support for Jiangyin Station by First Presbyterian Church, Wilmington

1902	$ 1,342	1927	$18,696
1903	626	1928	17,499
1904	1,387	1929	15,626
1905	1,602	1930	15,513
1906	1,610	1931	14,551
1907	2,216	1932	14,440
1908	3,381	1933	13,809
1909	11,483	1934	12,517
1910	22,009	1935	15,400
1911	14,448	1936	10,278
1912	18,279	1937	13,637
1913	15,459	1938	13,544
1914	28,654	1939	3,280
1915	17,341	1940	2,935
1916	16,769	1941	2,336
1917	23,855	1942	2,209
1918	12,044	1943	2,386
1919	13,782	1944	3,170
1920	15,450	1945	3,682
1921	18,493	1946	4,145
1922	15,420	1947	3,738
1923	18,945	1948	7,295
1924	27,005	1949	4,967
1925	19,018	1950	5,224
1926	20,277	1951	4,916
Total	$566,688		

Source: Data from First Presbyterian Church, Wilmington, *Handbook, 1892–1913* (N.p., [1913]), p. 20 (for 1902–13), and Bulletin, 30 Apr. 1916 (for 1914), Scrapbook of Church History, 1886–1938, and Sessional Records (for 1915–51), First Presbyterian Church, Wilmington, N.C.

Note: All figures reflect the amount collected as of 31 March in the respective year.

Sprunt's involvement with foreign mission work. Sprunt made his contributions through the church, which included them in its total, forwarding the entire sum to the Executive Committee of Foreign Missions of the PCUS in Nashville and ultimately to Jiangyin. Support was greatest in the early years of the republic, as station work expanded, but it began to decline gradually after the Nanjing Incident of 1927 due to rising doubts about the efficacy and propriety of undertaking mission work in China. The precipitous decline in contributions after 1938 was due to the discontinuation of Sprunt funding.

James Sprunt, an elder of the First Presbyterian Church, was one of the wealthiest merchants in the southern states. He came to North Carolina from Scotland in 1852 as a young lad, and in 1865, at age nineteen, he entered the cotton trade business with his father, Alexander. When the latter died in 1884, James and his younger brother William took over the family business and by the turn of the century built it into the largest cotton-exporting house in the United States. A local paper claimed in 1924 that "for a quarter of a century, ninety per cent of the commerce of the port of Wilmington was done by the house of Alexander Sprunt & Son."[8] By 1908, the firm annually bought about half a million bales of cotton from local producers at 115 interior stations in the Carolinas and Georgia, shipped them to Wilmington for compressing and storing (in Sprunt-owned factories), and eventually exported the cotton (in company-chartered transatlantic steamers) to numerous agencies in Great Britain and Europe.[9]

These transactions not only made James Sprunt a very wealthy man and, in the estimation of a contemporary, "a business man who is easily *primus inter pares* among all the business men of the South,"[10] but also built the port of Wilmington into one of the greatest in the South and enriched its entire business community. They also brought prominent people, including President William Taft in 1909, to his home for lavish entertainment and hospitality.[11]

Members of the Sprunt family were associated prominently with the First Presbyterian Church, serving as church officers and contributing greatly to its upkeep and improvement. As a young man, one of James's close friends in the church was Tommy Wilson, the son of the pastor, who was to become the president of Princeton and later of the United States.[12] Through the church, James began to support its foreign missionaries in China, including another friend, George Worth, at Jiangyin.

In May 1908, at a time when Sprunt and his exporting company were at the peak of their fortunes, J. Campbell White, the founding general secretary of the Layman's Missionary Movement, was a guest for three days at Sprunt's magnificent waterfront home in Wilmington. White was touring the country seeking to raise a million dollars annually from prominent businessmen for foreign mission work. In the wake of that visit, he asked Sprunt if he would be willing to undertake the annual support of the general secretary's $4,000 salary. A family in Montreal had supported White for ten years in India as a missionary, and he found such an arrangement "afforded peculiar satisfaction to all concerned. One feels he has in this way the special personal interest and prayers of his supporters, as he cannot do when his support comes out

James Sprunt, primary benefactor of the Jiangyin mission station, ca. 1920. (North Carolina Collection, Wilson Library, University of North Carolina, Chapel Hill, N.C.)

of a general fund."[13] Sprunt readily accepted the commitment, after quickly checking White's standing among prominent mission leaders, and even added $1,000 yearly for White's travel expenses.[14] Sprunt's support apparently continued until 1915, when White took other employment.

Through White and his organization, Sprunt, in his own words, "got the vision" and began a "career of stewardship" based on the notion that a person was a lifelong trustee for a portion of God's wealth and was responsible for using it wisely in support of God's cause.[15] Sprunt's stewardship began in 1909 when he undertook support of the educational work at Jiangyin. He took an active interest in the work at the station and was alert to any signs that it was not being properly supported or managed. In 1919, he and other members of the Committee on Foreign Missions of the First Presbyterian Church wrote to the Executive Committee of Foreign Missions in Nashville about appropriations to Jiangyin for the 1919–20 fiscal year. They found Nashville's method of bookkeeping confusing and were uncertain whether Jiangyin's requirements were being met by the $10,000 quota assigned to their church or whether more funds were needed. If additional support was needed, they were prepared to increase their annual budget for foreign missions.[16] Whatever quota was set, the church's contribution did increase throughout the next decade (see table 8-1).

Two years later, Sprunt was very critical of the Executive Committee in Nashville for reducing the missionary forces at Jiangyin, rendering the station helpless, in his estimation, and overworking its remaining staff. Since the beginning of 1919, Sunday bulletins at the First Presbyterian Church, which he surely read, had printed a series of letters from Jiangyin in which the missionaries complained of inadequate foreign staff and hospital equipment. In one of the letters, George Worth was uncharacteristically pessimistic and bitter about the personnel situation:

Do you know that three years ago the three hospitals of our [Mid-China] mission south of the Yangtze River had a total of six doctors and three nurses, whereas they now have a total of but three doctors and one nurse. What do you think of that for three hospitals? . . . As far as we have any information from home there is not a single doctor nor nurse under appointment for our China field, and that in despite of the fact that thousands of both doctors and nurses have just returned from the war. . . . It is a constant source of wonder to us missionaries why the mission authorities at home do not appear to have made a great effort to win many of these men and women for mission work. . . . We have eleven less missionaries at work in our sphere than five years ago. The work and responsibilities have increased but the new workers that have joined our ranks do not make up for the actual losses by death, broken health or necessary transfer to other points. The other churches [denominations] seem to be making great drives for mission causes, but we hear of nothing from our own church [the PCUS].[17]

In the winter of 1921, Sprunt received a personal account of the situation from a nephew who had just spent two weeks in Jiangyin. The young man noted the lack of personnel — only six of the normal contingent of fourteen remained — and, most alarming of all to Sprunt, described his host, George Worth, as exhausted and sickly. He also stressed that Worth's work at the hospital was hampered by the lack of an X-ray machine. "The Chinese," his nephew wrote pointedly, "know that good hospitals have X-Ray equipment, and many go to Shanghai to get the benefit of it." In a letter to his pastor, Sprunt fumed that "a hospital without water works, and an operating room without an X-Ray instrument, seem to me a lamentable reflection on our church," and he threatened to discontinue "my gift to the cause of foreign missions unless the Kiang-yin Station can be more directly under our control."[18] Sprunt was apparently unaware that the overwhelming proportion of missionary hospitals in China operated under similar, if not worse, conditions.[19]

After receiving a somewhat encouraging letter from George Worth about the station's accomplishments, despite the reduced number of staff members, and the possibility of new appointments, Sprunt's fears about his mission investment were quieted. His reply to Worth reaffirmed his faith in a God who "can use a few to accomplish the work of many. . . . If the disadvantages which have beset you in the station have been opportunities to show the delivering power of our God, we must thank His great wisdom that answers the intent of our prayers, rather than our actual requests." On a more mundane level, he expressed relief that "you and Emma have never had to relinquish your hold on the Mission through all the readjustments and the swapping around of workers."[20] Divine will was fine, but the fact that familiar, dear friends were in charge was perhaps even more reassuring.

These momentary doubts about mission management did not deflect Sprunt from his commitment to missions, and he remained a generous benefactor for the rest of his life. Ella Little once wrote that "Santa Claus has no standing at all in Kiang-Yin in comparison with Mr. James Sprunt."[21] Within a decade of his momentous decision to support mission work at the 1909 Birmingham convention, Sprunt calculated that he had already contributed about $50,000 to the Jiangyin Station, which may have been a conservative estimate.[22] After his initial $10,000 gift, he made an annual subscription through the First Presbyterian Church of $3,000–5,000.[23] He also generously fulfilled special requests, providing $5,000 for hospital equipment and expansion and $3,000 for the girls school and $10,500 for the boys school when each needed additional space.[24] In 1919, he extended a personal gift of $10,000 to the new Mrs. Lacy Little, his niece Nellie Sprunt (the daughter of his brother Alexander).[25] In 1923, he undertook the support of Charles Worth, George's son, and his new wife when they joined the staff at Jiangyin. Without such support, which probably amounted to about $2,000 a year, the Board of Foreign Missions would not have appointed them as missionaries.[26] In 1924, in one of his last philanthropic acts, Sprunt provided $7,000 for the construction of an additional residence, named after his mother, for the staff at Jiangyin.[27]

James Sprunt died on 9 July 1924, but his beneficence continued. In 1921, he had established a Benevolent Trust Fund in his name. Shortly before his death, he added a codicil to the fund that made generous provision for the work at Jiangyin. He directed that $10,000 be paid yearly, in quarterly payments, from the fund to the Jiangyin Station for a period of twenty years after his death.[28] These contributions continued until 1938, when trustees of the fund informed the pastor of the First Presbyterian Church that the poor performance of the stocks in the fund precluded any further payments. The pastor protested the termination of the payments six years before the time designated by Sprunt, but the fund simply had run out of cash and, in fact, the trustees had been loaning money to the fund for several years in order to continue payments.[29]

With the loss of these funds, the amount of church support to Jiangyin decreased significantly. From 1939 to the end of World War II, the annual contribution averaged less than $3,000. After the war, with the prospect of reopening the Jiangyin Station, church support increased to about $5,000 a year, still a far cry from the five-figure contributions made in 1909–38 when Sprunt money filled the coffers.

The Jiangyin missionaries took special pains to cultivate home support, because, to a great extent, their continued work in China depended on it. Personal ties with the home church, at Jiangyin as well as at other mission stations, were developed most regularly through routine letter writing. Mission boards asked their representatives in the field to report at least quarterly. The boards then duplicated and circulated the letters to a large mailing list that included member churches, various church agencies, and individuals interested in mission work. According to one investigator, the Southern Presbyterian Missionary Correspondence Department in Nashville sent China missionaries' letters to about 120,000 individuals and institutions. Since it is probable that most of these copies were read by perhaps as many as ten other readers, Southern Presbyterian mission letters may have reached an audience of over a million people.[30]

In their letters, missionaries frequently wrote about specific individuals who had converted or enrolled as enquirers or with whom they had dealt in some other capacity. In this way, they replaced American images of hordes of faceless Chinese people with real people whose needs could be recognized and fulfilled. Mission letters thus served as perhaps the most effective vehicles for personalizing and humanizing mission work for the home audiences, giving them a sense of participation and a stake in the work of evangelization around the world. In a lengthy letter written by Virginia Lee in April 1920, describing in detail a Chinese celebration she had attended and offering shrewd insights into the Chinese character, Lee closed with the exhortation, "That is what I want YOU to feel and know." [31]

Missionaries at Jiangyin, like their colleagues at other stations, wrote letters at a prodigious rate. In addition to those sent to the Missionary Correspondence Department in Nashville, they reported station news to PCUS journals in China and the United States (the *Bi-Monthly Bulletin*, the *Monthly Messenger*, the *Missionary*, *Missionary Survey*, and the *Presbyterian Survey*) and to general missionary publications such as the *Chinese Recorder*. They also kept up personal correspondence with friends, relatives, and financial backers (such as James Sprunt) back home. Most important of all, however, in maintaining the "special relationship" with Wilmington were the semiannual reports the Worths sent to the Wilmington Presbyterial Auxiliary and the weekly station letters sent to the First Presbyterian Church.

The information conveyed through these different avenues of communication often overlapped, but the focus of the writer and the level of specificity varied. Naturally, the personal letters dwelt on family life in China, and the Worths mainly discussed hospital matters in their letters to the women of the auxiliary. As a whole, however, these letters provide a wealth of information on the station, all facets of its work (and play), the progress of Christianity in the field, the personal stories of Chinese converts and coworkers, the relationship between the station and the local community, the social and political conditions in the immediate area, and the great events and movements of the time. This correspondence, in short, provided its recipients (and offers today's researcher) a full and intimate picture of the Jiangyin Station and its place in modern Chinese history.

As a final comment on the value of this correspondence, it should be noted that missionaries were better situated to observe the activities and attitudes of the Chinese than any other group of foreigners in China. Missionaries were driven by the nature of their work to move beyond the treaty ports into the small towns and villages of China. And unlike government or business representatives, they intended to remain in China. The average Protestant missionary in the 1920s and 1930s had approximately thirteen years of experience in China and could read and speak the language well. It is remarkable and instructive in this regard that George Worth's final conversation on his deathbed in Jiangyin in 1936 with his daughter Ruth was mostly in Chinese.[32] Missionaries, it is fair to say, were the most knowledgeable and perceptive of foreign observers in China. Through them, thousands of Americans gained their first and probably most lasting impressions of this distant civilization. At a time when public schools had not yet incorporated the study of non-Western cultures into their curricula, churches thus provided a vital educational forum in which adults and youth alike received regular lessons on China from their representatives in the field.

The First Presbyterian Church received a station letter from Jiangyin every week, written by different missionaries in turn. The earliest letters were sent in 1904 by Reverend Haden and Dr. Worth, who wrote detailed accounts of their work at the station, and were printed in their entirety in the church's manual for that year.[33] By 1908, when the church adopted the Jiangyin Station as its special responsibility, entire letters or excerpted passages were printed regularly in the Sunday bulletin — so regularly, in fact, that their absence was cause for comment.[34] Between 1908 and 1930, an average of twenty bulletins each year contained a news item or reprinted letter from Jiangyin.[35] Since the bulletin was only issued about eight months of the year (October through May or sometimes June), church members could expect to read about the special object of their prayers and support two or three Sundays a month during the active seasons of the church. On occasion, letters would be read to the congregation at Sunday services instead of being printed.[36]

The Jiangyin missionaries took their commitment to keeping the home folks informed seriously, and they posted a schedule at the station indicating whose turn it was to write.[37] When a new pastor was installed at the First Presbyterian Church in 1922, Lacy Moffett wrote to reiterate that "we in Kiangyin all prize very highly the relationship with the Wilmington Church, so much so in fact, that we are sometimes accused out here of being rather proud over it. It has been a great privilege to be taken into their fellowship as we have been, and a most encouraging thing to know how their prayers have followed us and our work — no, your work." Moffett went on to assure the pastor that they would continue to send weekly letters and any additional materials (maps, pictures, special reports, etc.) the church might request.[38] Examples of the objects the missionaries had already sent home were a blue and red silk banner adorned with tassels and Chinese characters that read "Great American Missionary Societies"; a map of the entire Jiangyin field, which the Ladies Foreign Missionary Society of the Wilmington church displayed at its meetings; photographs of station buildings and groups of Chinese Christians that, according to the pastor, "make the work there more real and definite"; and curios that were displayed annually or offered for sale as a way of raising additional funds.[39] Special "Jiangyin Nights" and "Missionary Days" held regularly at the church featured presentations concerning the work in China.

The steady reception of letters and other material at the church constantly reminded its members of their obligations to the mission in China. Although they were less frequent, personal contact between missionaries on furlough and home congregations had an equal if not greater impact. On these occasions, the work in China became a palpable reality through the presence of the missionaries. Supporters at home could discuss firsthand with their representatives abroad the problems and opportunities of the missions. Often, a furlough could be as demanding on a missionary as being on the job. In 1921, the father of Nell Little reported that she and her husband Lacy, who had come home specifically to recuperate from an illness, "are on the march constantly and have been itinerating almost as much as they do in China."[40]

Missionaries brought photographs and film footage home with them to illustrate their talks. On one of his early furloughs in 1911, George Worth gave an address at the First Presbyterian Church illustrated with "lantern slides."[41] In 1935, he prepared stereopticon pictures and a movie on Jiangyin, which he showed to many audiences on a barnstorming tour throughout the South with his daughter Ruth in 1936.[42] A few years later, a four-reel film was produced at Jiangyin for educational work back home. The footage not only shows mission work at the central station and at a country outstation but also records aspects of the daily life of the Chinese, such as rice cultivation, sericulture, canal traffic, war relief activities, and street scenes.[43]

George and Ruth Worth were not the only Jiangyin missionaries home on furlough in 1936. The First Presbyterian Church hosted four others from the station that spring—Lacy and Nell Little, Carrie Lena Moffett, and Marion Wilcox—as well as Charles and Grace Worth, formerly of Jiangyin but currently stationed at Hangzhou. During "Mission Week," from 27 April to 3 May, these missionaries used a variety of platforms to generate interest in and support for their work. Every weekday, one missionary presented a ten-minute meditation at the early morning service. George Worth one afternoon addressed the Woman's Auxiliary, which for years had supported the mission hospital at Jiangyin that he directed. A reception in honor of the missionaries was held in the middle of the week for the entire congregation. The week culminated in "Foreign Mission Day" on Sunday, 3 May, when the Jiangyin missionaries spoke in Sunday school.[44] A similarly large number of furloughed missionaries had gathered at the First Presbyterian Church in 1922 and again in 1929,[45] but usually only one or two were present at a time. Whatever the number, Jiangyin missionaries on furlough made a special point to visit the "Mother Church," as they called it, to maintain the personal relationship so important to their fund-raising enterprises.[46]

Of all the Jiangyin missionaries, George Worth held a special place in the hearts and prayers of the congregation of the First Presbyterian Church. He and his wife grew up in the church and became its first foreign missionaries. The Worths were married at the First Presbyterian Church on 31 July 1895 on the eve of their departure for China. They were honored at a farewell reception at the church the next day and were seen off by a large group of friends at the railroad station on 2 August.[47] A church historian noted that "it was through Dr. Worth's influence that the First church developed a feeling of responsibility for the entire work in [Jiangyin] and surrounding district."[48] It seemed only fitting, then, that George Worth was asked to give the address on foreign mission work in April 1917 as part of the church's centennial celebrations.[49]

The support and interest of home congregations were essential in maintaining morale and enthusiasm among missionaries. On the eve of their return to China in 1922, the Moffetts wrote:

> The fresh contact with the church at home has brought us renewed inspiration for work. We are profoundly impressed with the enlarged vision of service which has come to the rank and file of church members. . . . Our people are not only giving money in an unprecedented way for Christian work, but men and women are giving hours of time and personal effort to direct soul winning, the most fruitful and joyous of all Christian service. For this we thank God and take courage as we go back to China in your stead.[50]

And just as the routine station letters kept the people at home informed about mission work, the missionaries eagerly read letters from home for news of their relatives and friends. Such correspondence helped them maintain their personal and cultural moorings. George Worth once wrote gratefully and touchingly to his niece that her letters were like "hands across the sea and love travelling all the way around the globe."[51]

Finally, the close relationship between the "Mother Church" in Wilmington and its "spiritual daughter" in Jiangyin contributed to the vitality of each. Sustaining the foreign mission and watching it grow in size and importance gave the home church a sense of purpose and, at times, offered it a challenge. The station letters always cited statistics on the number of enquirers in the Jiangyin field and the number of new church members enrolled after each examination. These figures were used to spur the congregation to a greater effort. In a 1909 bulletin, the pastor added the following pointed observations to the latest news from Jiangyin:

> 1st. The work was started there 14 years ago, among heathen, with not a single Christian. Now they have 431 members. This church began in 1817. Now we have 683 members.

2nd. They have nine candidates for the ministry. Here at home we have not a single candidate under the care of the Presbytery, though three are about ready to become candidates.[52]

Similarly, the Jiangyin missionaries, who regularly received the home church's bulletin, relayed to local Chinese Christians news of the "Mother Church" and spoke of its many achievements and its leadership role within the Southern Presbyterian Church. When the East Gate church installed its first pastor in 1918, one of the Chinese elders urged the congregation "to press on to full self-support and beyond self-support to self-propagation, having as their ideal to be a 'Second Wilmington First Church.'"[53]

The second major source of funding for the Jiangyin Station, besides James Sprunt and the First Presbyterian Church, was the Woman's Auxiliary of the Wilmington Presbytery, which adopted the Jiangyin hospital as its special project. Mission work not only provided a source of information and inspiration for the women of the church but also helped them develop organizational skills.

Women's support of foreign missions began when the first foreign mission board was formed in 1810, at which time charitable societies organized by church women began to divert their funds to that cause. A half-century later, support of mission work was promoted more systematically with the organization of women's foreign missionary societies in most of the Protestant denominations. Between 1860 and 1910, forty-four societies were formed, with local, regional, and national structures.[54] In the journal of one of these denominational societies, the author of an 1869 article entitled "Laborers Wanted" glorified the fund-raising work of women at home: "A *few* must go forth to teach, but the *many* must *work* at home . . . to organize praying bands and working circles to earn and raise money. . . . Let every lady, who feels that *she would be a missionary*, go to work at home, and she may, by every dollar raised, teach her heathen sisters."[55] The women who did go abroad as missionaries or as wives of missionaries served as a great inspiration by maintaining a steady correspondence with their supporters at home, who by 1910 raised about $4 million for mission schools, hospitals, orphanages, asylums, and the like.[56]

These societies, by giving women the opportunity to play a vital role in expanding mission work, provided women with "a primary source of identification." With a new self-awareness and self-confidence, they expanded their vision of the world and their own lives beyond the roles of wives and mothers.[57] Women became a more active force in their churches, even though as yet they had no representation in policy-making. Male leaders were quick to recognize this development and fought to keep women subordinate ("auxiliary") to the church instead of being an independent force.

The Southern Presbyterians, who were among the last of the major de-nominations to create a women's organization, were a case in point. Local congregations had formed women's missionary societies as early as 1817, but until the 1880s, they lacked uniformity, cooperation, and higher organization at the regional (presbytery), state (synod), or denominational (assembly) level. In 1884, Jennie Hanna of Kansas City was inspired by the success of the Women's Board of the Northern Presbyterian Church (established in 1870) to attempt to create a similar integrative structure in the Southern Assembly. The secretary of foreign missions encouraged her to organize, but only at the presbyterial level. Starting in 1886, she began contacting women who sup-ported foreign missions in each of the 2,000 or so congregations within the denomination and urged them to join with other local churches to form presbyterial unions. The first two unions were established in 1888 in East Hanover, Virginia, and Wilmington.

Even this minimal step aroused conservative opposition. Many ministers never replied to Hanna's initial request for a list of names of women in their churches with whom she could correspond. The General Assembly polled the presbyteries for their positions on this controversy. Of the 68 presbyteries that responded, only about one-fourth (18) favored women's unions on all levels, whereas over one-half (39) urged that they be restricted to the session (individual church) level. Many branded the women's effort to organize as "un-Scriptural, un-Presbyterian, unwomanly" and argued that it placed un-due emphasis on one phase of church work to the exclusion and detriment of others. Some pronounced that a woman's place was in the home, in support of and subordinate to men. Women's organizations, even those supporting a church cause, would ignore this "divine" arrangement.[58]

The women's unions, however, proved too effective in raising funds to be stopped. By 1900, about 1,000 local societies and 30 presbyterial unions ex-isted; by 1910, 78 of the 84 presbyteries and 5 of the 14 synods in the denomi-nation had formed unions. Finally, in 1912, the General Assembly of the PCUS appointed a woman "superintendent" to coordinate women's unions at all levels and to organize them where they did not yet exist, in effect creat-ing a churchwide Woman's Auxiliary. Within two years, every presbytery and synod was organized and constitutions and other literature had been printed, all of which the women had accomplished on a shoestring budget, operating out of the superintendent's home with equipment and supplies provided by local auxiliaries and supportive church leaders. By 1914, the General Assem-bly recognized the financial value of the auxiliary—in 1913, it had raised about $125,000 for foreign missions, six times the amount contributed by men's and young people's societies—and furnished the superintendent with an annual operating budget.[59]

Hanna's urgent call for the formation of presbyterial unions had reached

Margaret Sprunt Hall (James's sister) of the First Presbyterian Church at the end of 1887. Hanna had sent out a circular, asking the recipient to distribute it to every church in the Wilmington Presbytery, in which she envisioned a quadrupling of women's contributions to foreign missions if only a more effective organization could be established. She challenged her readers to come to the aid of their church and its workers in foreign fields: "The constantly recurring debt on our For[eign] Miss[ions] Committee is a terrible witness to inactivity and neglect of opportunity somewhere. The women of the Southern Church are not lacking in the energy, intellect, consecration & ability necessary to organize on a sound basis. Let us try it."[60]

Margaret Hall turned out to be one of the women of energy and ability Hanna was seeking; in the next five months, she helped organize women's societies in her own and other churches in the presbytery. By the end of May 1888, the Wilmington Presbyterial Union was formed, the second union in the Southern Assembly, and representatives from eleven local women's societies attended its first convention. In its constitution, the union declared that its objective was "to support and cheer our lady missionaries in the field" and to "circulate useful Foreign Missionary literature to stimulate the interest of the women of the Presbytery in this cause."[61] In 1890, due to continuing fears about higher levels of organization in women's work, the union was dissolved and replaced by the Woman's Foreign Missionary Committee of the Wilmington Presbytery, but the nature of its work did not change and women continued to refer to their group by the earlier name. When the General Assembly approved the organization of a denominational Woman's Auxiliary in 1912, the name changed again to the Woman's Presbyterial Auxiliary.[62]

The auxiliary's support of the mission hospital at Jiangyin has been noted in previous chapters. After the hospital opened in 1907, auxiliary women exhibited a proprietary feeling about the institution they had built, always referring to it as "our hospital." At every auxiliary meeting, a photograph of the facilities was displayed and a report on current medical work and anticipated needs was made. For example, the 1912 annual meeting held on 19–21 June at the First Presbyterian Church in Wilmington presented a concentrated dose of information on the hospital and China in general. The convention program itself contained on its cover a photograph of the hospital that George Worth had brought home with him. At Wednesday evening's preparatory service, the Reverend Alexander Sprunt, the brother of James and father of Nell Little, gave an address entitled "Motive for Missionary Work." At the opening session on Thursday, Emma Worth spoke on the needs of the hospital, and that evening, the Reverend W. H. Hudson held a discussion entitled "Revolution in China." The next day, Eliza Murphy, auxiliary agent for the hospital funds, read her report on the status of fund-raising for a

Margaret Sprunt Hall, founder of the Wilmington Presbyterial Union in 1888.
(First Presbyterian Church, Wilmington, N.C.)

women's ward and other new facilities at the hospital. Rida Jourolman reported on evangelical work at the station, and Reverend Hudson again spoke, delivering an address entitled "The New Woman in New China." The convention ended Friday evening with illustrated talks on Jiangyin by Lacy Moffett and George Worth. In all, ten missionaries, four from Jiangyin, were present at the meetings.[63]

The hospital's claim on the women's attention became so pervasive that each local women's society in the presbytery was urged to set up a "blessing box" and ask its members to contribute a penny a day for the Jiangyin hospital.[64] Through such offerings, thousands of women felt they were in daily communion with *their* workers at *their* hospital at *their* station in *their* China. Is it any wonder that they were devastated by the news in early 1938 that the Japanese had destroyed the hospital in bombing raids? It was as if their own property in Wilmington had been attacked.

Matching the women in interest and commitment to foreign missions, if not financial resources, were the young people's societies in the presbytery, which began to raise money for cots at the hospital in 1903. Although the young people's contributions were modest, they provided another intense, personal link between the work in China and the support base at home. When these bands met, their members prayed for the Worths and for the patient occupying the cot provided by their small change. The young people took particular interest in the plight of their counterparts in China, such as Jin Mei, or "Golden Sister." She was a girl about four years old who had contracted measles and over a year's time grew weak from a fever, eventually dying from the long struggle. Jin Mei's story was reported to the young people of Wilmington, who included her in their prayers, and one of their number sent her a nursery book, which, however, arrived a few weeks after the Chinese girl's death.[65] In recognition of their good work on behalf of the Jiangyin hospital, the Worths in 1922 presented the young people with an engraved silver tablet they had received the year before from the Jiangyin magistrate and gentry as a parting gift on the eve of their home leave.[66]

Building the hospital was just the beginning for the women and young people of the auxiliary. As medical work expanded at Jiangyin, George Worth turned to them repeatedly for funds to buy equipment, build additional facilities, and maintain the entire plant. Their support, which amounted to close to $100,000 over the life of the station, is summarized in table 8-2.

As the sole benefactor of the hospital, the auxiliary had a special bond with George Worth similar to that between the First Presbyterian Church and the station as a whole. This relationship presented problems as well as advantages, as Worth noted in a 1924 communication with the auxiliary:

Table 8-2. Summary of Support for Jiangyin Hospital by Wilmington Presbyterial Auxiliary

1904–7	$ 4,700	Original building (men's ward)
1908–11	2,000	Waterworks; two small outbuildings
1908–13	7,000	Women's ward
1909–19	3,500	Trained nurse's salary ($350/year)
1913	3,000	Enlargement of men's ward
1913–17	6,000	Second doctor's salary ($1,200/year)
1918–19	3,600	Doctor and wife's salary ($1,800/year)
1922–52	37,000	General fund for maintenance
1923	2,200	Residence for Chinese doctors
1924–28	4,400	Additions to women's ward, waterworks
1929–34	3,800	Nurses home
1948	5,000	Rebuilding, from reserve fund
1954	11,000	Transferred to projects in Korea and Africa
1954	800	Left in reserve fund, Nashville
Total	$94,000	

Source: Data from Wilmington Presbyterial Auxiliary, Minutes of Annual Meeting (Wilmington, N.C., 1901–54).

Let it always be remembered that the Kiangyin Hospital is the child of Wilmington Presbyterial, the child of your prayers, you gave it life in 1904 and you have nourished it ever since, and never let it be forgotten that this hospital has no other source from which to draw its support. Others may appeal to the Church at large or even a great conference like that at Montreat, but it has never seemed to us proper nor loyal to our Presbyterial to ask others to undertake the nourishment of your particular child. . . . We are indeed highly favored, and we rejoice continually in it but you can see how our privilege of being in your special care carries with it a certain restriction to us, and likewise entails a definite and peculiar responsibility upon the Presbyterial.[67]

George Worth nurtured this relationship in every way possible. From the start, he sent at least two letters a year to the auxiliary, one in time to be read to the women at their annual business meeting in the spring (usually April) and the other in time for their fall Day of Prayer. These letters were distinct from those he sent to the First Presbyterian Church or to the Executive Committee in Nashville for circulation, and they naturally focused primarily on medical work. Since reports of the auxiliary meetings often were published in local papers and religious journals, the letters also helped to keep the public informed about missionary work in China. In 1932, Worth's spring letter to the auxiliary was printed in its entirety on the front page of the Sunday magazine of the *Wilmington Star News*.[68] Worth usually sent photographs along with these letters to give home supporters physical evidence of the results of their beneficence. On their furloughs, the Worths not only attended auxiliary meetings but also attempted to visit each of the several dozen women's societies throughout the Wilmington Presbytery.[69]

In his letters, Worth was profuse in his appreciation of auxiliary support. In 1934, he proclaimed its membership of over 2,200 to be "a regiment of hands across the sea" doing "grand, greathearted [work] in God's service."[70] In the last letter he sent to the auxiliary before his death, Worth professed to "have never tired, and I trust others have never tired of my expression about what a blessing the Wilmington Presbyterial has been to me, and to mine, to the Church at Kiangyin, and to the whole cause in China during the 32 years since the Presbyterial first decided to put a Kiangyin Christian Hospital on the missionary map, and to make me their representative — No words at my command to do justice to the subject."[71] After his death, one of the auxiliary women said of Worth, "He never failed in every letter, at every visit, to express to us his sense of loving obligation" and his "ever-flowing appreciation and gratitude."[72]

The women of the auxiliary did not tire of George Worth's expressions of gratitude, and they returned them in kind with wholehearted love and respect as well as financial support. The 1922 annual meeting, which the Worths attended, was dedicated to them. When the nurses home was completed in 1934, the auxiliary approved the following inscription for the cornerstone: "This building was erected by the Presbyterial of Wilmington, North Carolina, U.S.A., A.D. 1934, to the glory of God and for the benefit of the people of Kiangyin, in loving appreciation of Emma Chadbourn Worth and George C. Worth, M.D." When a commemorative tablet was engraved in Jiangyin, George Worth omitted his own name in the English version, but it does appear in the Chinese text.[73] News of his death in November 1936 was greatly mourned in Jiangyin and in Wilmington. At its next meeting, the auxiliary voted to prepare a memorial booklet containing a sketch of Worth's life and a sampling of the tributes paid to him; the remaining tributes, letters, and other memorabilia not printed in the booklet were to be preserved in a scrapbook. The women also called for subscriptions for a memorial tablet, which would be placed on a wall of the hospital, and authorized naming the tuberculosis ward (Worth's final request of the auxiliary) the Worth Memorial Building.[74]

The auxiliary's commitment to Worth and medical work at Jiangyin was the lifeblood of the organization. Its significance was clearly understood by

George Worth, founder of the Jiangyin hospital, ca. 1935.
(First Presbyterian Church, Wilmington, N.C.)

Eliza Murphy, who was in charge of the hospital fund. In her 1913 retrospective report on the fund-raising efforts, she enumerated four "distinct blessings we have received as a Presbyterial":

> In the first place, it has meant the uniting of all the forces and the enlisting of new forces. Perhaps half the people of the presbytery who are interested in missions today have become interested within the last ten years through the definite interest in our definite object.
>
> It has been the inspiration to organization. When the children's bands grew in two years from 3 to 23, the thought shining before those dear young eyes was cot-support in Dr. Worth's hospital.
>
> Figures have shown from year to year the increase in giving—the growth in "this grace also."
>
> Far beyond our taking account is the cultivation of the spirit of definite intercession and faith. We have found the high privilege of working together, praying together, rejoicing together; not only working together here, but working with those across the seas. A share in the ministry to a million people—a thousand every month.[75]

Organizational growth, inspiration, increased donations, sorority, a sense of responsibility, and an expanded view of the world—these were the fruits of a lifetime partnership with the Jiangyin mission.

Despite this very personal, exclusive relationship between the Wilmington Presbyterial Auxiliary, on the one hand, and the Worths and the Jiangyin hospital, on the other, all of the funds raised by the auxiliary had to be submitted to the Executive Committee of Foreign Missions at the Nashville headquarters of the Southern Presbyterian Church, which had the final authority to approve disbursements to Jiangyin for specific projects or expenses. This arrangement was one of the prices the women's foreign missionary societies had to pay to gain approval in 1912 for a denominational auxiliary. Another was not to work for foreign missions alone, as most of the societies had done since their inception, but to embrace all other benevolent causes of the church. Many groups offered only token support for these other causes.

Although it was not entirely true, as later claimed, that "the [Wilmington Presbyterial] Missionary Union (later the Woman's Auxiliary) [was formed] for the one express purpose of building a hospital in Kiangyin,"[76] very early in its existence the group dedicated itself to that goal. In 1911, the women were reminded that other benevolent causes of the church were supported by regular monthly collections in each congregation but that their offerings should concentrate on their special object in China.[77] When the church-wide auxiliary was created in 1912 with its mandate to work for all causes of the church, adjustments had to be made at lower levels. On the advice of the denominational superintendent, the Wilmington Presbyterial Auxiliary at its annual convention in 1914 decided "to give one dollar to each of the other causes, thereby acknowledging the claim, and give all the rest to our . . . own object already established before the 'Auxiliary' days."[78]

As for the requirement that funds be channeled through Nashville, it, of course, applied to money donated by James Sprunt or raised by the First Presbyterian Church and its agencies as well as to funds raised by the auxiliary. The local donors often suspected that Nashville was not properly managing the funds. As we have already seen, James Sprunt in 1921 complained about his lack of direct control over the use of funds for the Jiangyin Station. George Worth also expressed concern in 1932 about the committee's distribution of the annual maintenance support from the auxiliary. In a letter to the auxiliary president, he detailed the financial crisis arising from the cut in funds that the Nashville Executive Committee had imposed on all mission fields. In the previous fiscal year (April 1931 through March 1932), the hospital had received only $800, and in the 1932–33 year, he expected the payment to be cut to $450, which would have dire consequences for the hospital, perhaps even forcing it to close. Worth urged the auxiliary to use whatever means necessary to ensure that "your Hospital" received at least $800. Even that amount, however, puzzled him: "Since 1922 you have been sending Nashville for our current account the sum of $1,650. How much you were able to send last year we do not exactly know, but we do know that the Hospital received but $800 on current account."[79] Prompted by this letter, the auxiliary president reminded the Executive Committee in Nashville of the agreement made in 1922, "that all money sent in for our work at Kiangyin was to be applied to this work; the same not being subject to cut."[80]

The special relationship between Jiangyin and its home base in Wilmington was a mixed blessing for the Executive Committee and created tension between the First Presbyterian Church and the larger PCUS foreign mission bureaucracy. Although the generous support from the First Presbyterian Church, James Sprunt, and the auxiliary relieved Nashville of much of the financial burden of maintaining its mission station at Jiangyin, missionaries of independent means or with strong personal connections to a home church could be somewhat independent of denominational control. This was particularly true when the support came from trust funds (such as that of James Sprunt or the one set up for George Worth by his father) that could be used only for their stated purpose. The generous contributions of Wilmington church members to the Jiangyin Station also meant that little or no funds could be expected from them for other foreign mission projects of the Executive Committee.[81]

After George Worth's death, the special relationship between the auxiliary and the hospital became somewhat attenuated. No one at Jiangyin could

relate to the First Presbyterian Church or the Wilmington Presbyterial Auxiliary in quite the same way. Emma Worth had died a decade earlier, and
their children, Charles and Ruth, had transferred to other stations. The Chinese staff of the hospital, which was formally under Chinese control after
1927, when Dr. William Chen replaced George Worth as director, tried to
follow Worth's example in cultivating auxiliary support. In a 1929 letter, they
acknowledged "the closeness of your relations with Dr. Worth" and sought to
build upon it: "Your relations with him are your relations with us. We, your
Chinese friends, are now carrying the weight of the Kiangyin Christian Hospital. . . . Although we have never seen your faces, and between us lie ten
thousand leagues of distance, and the boundaries of many nations, yet in
Christ we are united in one." [82] In 1935, George Worth brought home with
him a silver shield inscribed "to the Wilmington Presbyterial from the Kiangyin Hospital with gratitude for your loving care of us." The auxiliary responded with a resolution of appreciation to Dr. Chen and his staff for the
support they had given Worth over the years. [83] But a hint of reserve can be
detected in the auxiliary's reaction to the assumption of Chinese direction of
the hospital. In 1927, the auxiliary attributed its lack of success in fund-
raising efforts to the changeover and expressed some concern about the direction of work at Jiangyin: "According to the latest reports, Kiangyin Hospital is in the hands of native Christians. What the outcome will be, no one
knows. We can only trust in God, and make it the burden of our prayers." [84]

The auxiliary's concern about the impact of Chinese control of Christian
institutions in China on fund-raising efforts back home was shared by others
in the mission movement. In response to the Nationalist revolution in 1927,
three informal conferences attended by over forty missionaries and Chinese
Christians were held in Shanghai from 28 February to 15 March, sponsored
by the National Christian Council's Subcommittee on Church and Mission
Administration. At a session devoted to financial matters, Lacy Moffett of
Jiangyin noted that although "the administrative control of Christian work
and financial independence are usually considered by the home church to
go together," in recent years, missionaries had shifted their position. Most
now recognized "that there must be a transition period in which control
shall be largely in the hands of the Chinese Church though still subsidized
from the mission Boards." But, the writer conceded, this sort of arrangement
created problems in "keeping active the interest of the home church and of
so presenting the situation that their interest and contributions will not be seriously impaired." [85] A year earlier, another missionary writing in the *China
Christian Year Book* reported that one American missionary society spent
71 percent of its China budget on salaries for its foreign staff and only 29 percent on other mission work. If the missionaries were to withdraw from the
field and allow the Chinese to assume more and more control, the author

mused, would American donors be willing to continue financial support as the emphasis shifted to greater funding of institutional work rather than individuals?[86]

These were serious concerns that went beyond the question of who was in charge — missionaries or Chinese Christians? The entire premise of home support for foreign missions from the late nineteenth century on was based on the need to cultivate a personalized relationship between a mission station, missionary, or particular aspect of mission work and a supporting church or individual at home. For over forty years, women of the Wilmington Presbyterial Auxiliary had developed exactly this kind of relationship with the Jiangyin hospital, forging a bond that was as much personal as it was institutional. The advantage of increased support for the hospital as long as the special relationship remained intact disappeared when the object of personal concern was eliminated. George Worth's death in November 1936 and the Japanese capture of Jiangyin about a year later placed the whole enterprise in doubt.

Throughout the unsettled times of the Japanese invasion and the Communist rise to power, the women of the auxiliary continued to raise money for "their hospital" and deposit it in a reserve fund in Nashville until a resumption of work seemed feasible. In 1942, the auxiliary's foreign mission secretary sent a circular letter to each auxiliary group in the presbytery, reminding the women of George Worth's great career in China and of their special relationship with the Jiangyin hospital. Since the auxiliary was the sole supporter of the hospital, which received no funds from the foreign mission board of the denomination, the women's societies, she stressed, must pledge all of the foreign mission money they raised in their congregations to the Jiangyin hospital fund. A local church that had a member serving as a missionary at some other station abroad, however, was allowed to contribute only half of its funds to Jiangyin. At the time, the annual fund-raising goal of the auxiliary was $2,500. Under such steady cajoling, by 1948 the women had placed about $14,500 in the reserve fund, and $5,000 had been drawn on the account for rebuilding purposes.[87]

With the ascension of the Communists to power in 1949, the auxiliary's connection with Jiangyin ended. The health bureau of the local military government took charge of the hospital in 1951 and renamed it "People's Hospital."[88] In 1954, upon the advice of Ruth Worth, the auxiliary authorized Nashville to disburse the remaining reserve funds (which by then totaled about $12,000) in support of medical work at two other missions: $2,000 for a Korean tuberculosis hospital and $9,000 to the Congo Mission, where Ruth was then located, for the construction of a needed hospital building. Worth argued that these contributions were entirely appropriate not only because the future of missions in China looked bleak but also because her parents had originally planned to serve in Africa before being sent to China[89] and be-cause George Worth's last request to the auxiliary had been for money to build a tuberculosis ward at Jiangyin.[90] It seems that even in the final dispo-sition of its funds, the auxiliary sought to honor its personal commitment to George Worth (by funding the tuberculosis ward in Korea) and his family (by supporting his daughter's work in the Congo). Although no records have been found indicating what happened to the remaining $800 in the fund, the fifty-year relationship between the Wilmington Presbyterial Auxiliary and the Jiangyin hospital came to an end.

For half a century, supporters of foreign missions in the Wilmington area raised well over half a million dollars to fund an elaborate educational, med-ical, and evangelical enterprise at Jiangyin. Jiangyin missionaries took great pains to cultivate a "special relationship" with their backers: the First Pres-byterian Church in Wilmington, the prominent cotton merchant James Sprunt, and the Wilmington Presbyterial Auxiliary. A steady flow of personal and institutional correspondence, talks and "lantern slide" presentations by missionaries on home leave, articles in religious and secular publications, the naming of buildings and organizations after leading participants in the enterprise, and the like publicized and personalized the relationship. A dense network of human connections — a "regiment of hands across the sea," in George Worth's words — was forged that sustained the Jiangyin Station.

But it did more. The support of foreign missions affected constituencies in the United States as well. The missionaries at Jiangyin were the supporters' main, if not only, source of information on China, and contact with them enriched and altered the organizational and personal lives of churchgoers in the Wilmington area. Long after the Jiangyin Station and its evangelical, ed-ucational, and medical enterprises vanished from the scene in China, the legacy of mission work in Wilmington persisted. Down to the present day, the literature of the First Presbyterian Church has continued to proudly refer to the church's historic "special concern for overseas missions." The "special relationship" had a profound impact on everyone it touched on both sides of the Pacific.

9

GOOD WORKS

MISSIONS AND

MODERN CHINA

In the 1920s, a leading Chinese Christian argued that "it is the activities of Christianity rather than its teachings and spiritual experiences that have arrested the attention of our people and have won their respect." [1] Echoing this sentiment, an American missionary wrote, "To the great mass of non-Christians our terminology, our gospel, its hopes and its demands, are meaningless and not understood save as expression is given to them in the activities of the Christian community reacting upon the life of the individual and the [Chinese] community." [2]

The outlook presented in these two comments reflects the social gospel approach to promoting Christianity in foreign lands, an approach that was very much in evidence at the mission station at Jiangyin. Essentially, the social gospel was a distinctly American effort to reorient Christianity to deal with the social and economic consequences of industrialization and urbanization in the second half of the nineteenth century. Social critics within the church saw the rampant capitalism of America's Gilded Age as a formidable obstacle to the realization of a true realm of spiritual regeneration among humankind. At the same time, biblical scholars' reexamination of the life of Jesus led to an emphasis on his ethical teachings, stripped of the theological accretions added by the Christian church as it grew and became highly institutionalized. As a result of these two new emphases, a social gospel movement developed that, on the one hand, encouraged Christians to engage in all forms of social work and, on the other hand, called for a complete reconstruction of society.

Integral to the social gospel approach was the notion that the problems of the age must be solved in a social way. In this belief, they differed from more conservative Christians who focused on individual salvation. Instead of seeking the deliverance of the few from the evils of the world, the social reformers sought a total regeneration of that world. One reformer later commented that regenerate men cannot exist without a regenerate society.[3] Only a total transformation of society could create an environment conducive to individual salvation and pave the way for the Kingdom of God on earth.

The rise of the social gospel in the American Protestant church produced an impact on the mission movement, both in theory and in practice. From its inception in 1810, the American missionary movement saw as its goal the spiritual salvation of individuals in foreign lands and thus focused on evangelism. Mission theory stressed the preciousness of every soul in the world. Rufus Anderson, the influential secretary of the American Board of Commissioners for Foreign Missions from 1832 to 1866, was the leading proponent of this view. The task of the missionary, he averred, was "that of reconciling immortal souls to God." He denounced the "civilizing" work of missions and argued that the social consequences of the Gospel would emerge in later generations through the lives of indigenous Christians. Promoting Western civilizational forms in foreign countries as a prerequisite for success in saving souls would, according to Anderson, be seen as an intrusion into the affairs of those nations and inevitably link Christianity with Western imperialism.[4]

In one sense, Anderson was far ahead of his time in emphasizing the importance of an indigenous church and in warning of the dangers of "cultural imperialism." But in another sense, his view that missions should stress preaching rather than social service represented an outmoded and impractical conception of mission work. Bringing about individual salvation by purely evangelistic means could have only limited success unless the social setting in which those individuals were trapped was overhauled. In China, these new missionary concerns converged with the stirrings of reform. Chinese modernizers in the late nineteenth century were attracted to Western forms of medicine, education, and social relief as a way of dealing with the growing problems of disease, ignorance, and hunger.[5]

By 1900, almost every major denomination with missions in China, including the Southern Presbyterians, had accepted the social gospel approach and had shifted an increasing amount of personnel and funds into educational and medical work. By the 1911 revolution, one-half of all American missionaries no longer engaged in direct evangelical work.[6]

This trend alarmed some traditionalists in the missions, although it did not seem to be a major issue at Jiangyin, and prompted them to complain about the neglect of or interference with the primarily religious nature of their work. As a practical matter, however, the mission schools and hospitals often first attracted people to Christianity and, in the end, gained for missionaries far greater respect than their religious teachings. Missionaries working in these social institutions, as at Jiangyin, saw them as evangelistic agencies and took every opportunity to spread the Christian message along with learning and medicine. As one medical administrator wrote, not only were mission doctors "blazing a trail for the preacher, but . . . their ministry of healing was itself an exposition of the Christian message."[7] This point serves as a reminder that evangelical and cultural work need not be mutually exclusive.

The growing emphasis on social reform in mission work had a number of consequences. One was an increasing professionalization and secularization of mission work. Clergymen and their wives who did part-time teaching in the schools or medical work in the clinics were replaced by full-time professionals, the products of teachers colleges or medical schools in the United States. By 1910, 70 percent of the missionary force in China were laypersons, up from about 50 percent in 1868, of which 80 percent were women.[8] Not all of these laypersons were necessarily educators or physicians; some were evangelists from the independent "faith missions."[9] Still, in the major denominations, ordained ministers increasingly accounted for a smaller percentage of the mission force, particularly those engaged in teaching or medical work.

Through these schools, hospitals, and other social agencies, missionaries became purveyors of alternate, more "modern" models of development. They transmitted to the Chinese a broad spectrum of Western civilizational values that often were in conflict with native values. Thus, as the social gospel approach gained ascendancy, the mission movement was in a position to have an impact on modernization efforts in China. But when the transmission of new ideas and institutions was backed by political and military pressure from foreign powers, a classic case of "cultural imperialism" resulted, as Anderson had foreseen.[10]

In medical work at Jiangyin and at other mission stations, the concept of institutionalized care in a hospital with a resident staff and specialized equipment and laboratories was itself a modern phenomenon. Furthermore, these mission hospitals did more than provide a new level of care; they were also used to train professional medical personnel. To give their Chinese trainees as well as themselves a sense of professionalism and an exalted status in society, missionaries formed medical associations and published medical journals. In their minds, medicine and its professional trappings (hospitals, associations, journals, textbooks) would serve as the perfect model and conveyor of modern Western scientific learning for China.[11]

Another modernizing aspect of missionary medicine was the extension of health care to new social groups, such as women, rural inhabitants, and opium addicts at Jiangyin and lepers, the blind, and the mentally ill elsewhere. The mission hospitals also promoted personal hygiene and public health.

Mission schools made an important contribution to the modernization of China as well. Perhaps their most universally recognized impact was on the role of women in society. Through mission schools, many Chinese women for the first time were able to envision themselves as participants in the political and economic life of the nation. Besides helping to popularize the notion that girls as well as boys ought to be educated, the single women missionaries who taught in these schools served as powerful role models for the female students. After graduation, many of them went on to establish careers, often as single women in the field of education like their teachers. With well-paying jobs, they gained a measure of economic, and thus personal, independence.

In curriculum matters, mission school innovations included an emphasis on the physical and biological sciences, laboratory work, medical education, mathematics, and so on. Schools focused on these subjects as a way of introducing the methods of scientific inquiry, or as one mission study of education put it, "to create a reverence for the authority of facts, rather than of ancient and traditional opinions." [12]

Beyond academic subjects, mission schools served as models in the physical and moral development of their pupils. The value of physical exercise (often in the form of martial drills), recreation, and personal hygiene was stressed. Teachers also emphasized the importance of character development and the individual personality, which was particularly significant to women and children. Moral cultivation, besides inculcating general Christian values, included encouraging students to become involved with their communities in social welfare projects (such as the charity work of the Jiangyin schools).

The educational contributions of the missionary movement were offset, however, by one major drawback. Rufus Anderson was correct to warn of the dangers inherent in cultural work (or a "civilizing" mission, the more invidious term used by some missionaries). Such secular work, and particularly education in Anderson's mind, amounted to cultural intrusion and would lead to a reaction among the host communities. This result became readily apparent in China in the 1920s. In the changed political climate after the May Fourth Incident of 1919, mission schools increasingly became the target of anti-imperialist groups.

Finally, the social gospel approach led to the creation of an increasing number of expensive institutions, such as schools, hospitals, and orphanages, that Chinese Christians were unable to support by themselves. The continuing need for support from mission boards back home prevented the realization of a self-supporting church, and this helped perpetuate the perception of Christianity as a foreign religion. Thus, the social gospel impeded the growth of an indigenous Christian church in China.

To conclude, through the "good works" promoted by the social gospel, missions made major contributions to China's modernization, many of which were recognized and welcomed by the Chinese. At Jiangyin, the missionaries' medical work, as well as their peacekeeping efforts during several warlord conflicts, elevated the mission station and its foreign staff to a respected position in the local community and afforded them a greater opportunity to propagate the Christian religion. But much of the goodwill they gained by these activities was dissipated in the controversy over the issue of government regulation of mission schools. Education, which was more directly involved in the transmission of cultural values than other secular activities, provoked a nationalistic backlash that created strains both within the Christian community and between it and the larger society.

In the end, the logic of the social gospel — that a cultural makeover of a non-Christian society (which implied Westernization) was a prerequisite or at least corequisite for the evangelization of that society — positioned the mission movement in China to serve as a catalyst for modernization but also exposed it to the corrosive effects of a virulent nationalism. The American missionary movement fell into a trap from which it could never extricate itself.

NOTES

ABBREVIATIONS

The following abbreviations are used throughout the notes.

AMP   Alex Moffett Papers, copies in possession of author.

ASSP   Alexander Sprunt and Son Papers, Manuscript Collection, Perkins Library, Duke University, Durham, N.C.

CL   China Letters, 1919–51, Missionary Correspondence Department, Board of World Missions, Presbyterian Church in the United States, Department of History and Records, Presbyterian Church (U.S.A.), Montreat, N.C. (all letters were written from Jiangyin unless otherwise noted and were sent to the board for circulation to member churches).

CWP   Charles W. Worth Papers, in possession of Mrs. Charles W. Worth, Wilmington, N.C.

DHR   Department of History and Records, Presbyterian Church (U.S.A.), Montreat, N.C.

FPCW   First Presbyterian Church, Wilmington, N.C.

FRUS   U.S. Department of State, *Papers Relating to the Foreign Relations of the United States* (Washington, D.C.: Government Printing Office, 1861–1932).

LMP   Lacy I. Moffett Papers, copies in possession of author.

MSHP   Margaret T. Sprunt Hall Papers, Department of History and Records, Presbyterian Church (U.S.A.), Montreat, N.C.

RWP   Ruth Worth Papers, copies in possession of author.

SHC   Southern Historical Collection, Wilson Library, University of North Carolina, Chapel Hill, N.C.

WPF   Wilmington Presbyterial Files, Women of the Church Synodical and Presbyterial Collection, Department of History and Records, Presbyterian Church (U.S.A.), Montreat, N.C.

CHAPTER ONE

1. In the romanization of Chinese personal and place names, I have retained many spellings as transcribed in the missionary accounts, but where Chinese characters were used or the people and places are well known, I have rendered them in pinyin. I used familiar older spellings, however, for Canton, Chiang Kai-shek, Sun Yat-sen, and James Yen.

2. Ernest Thompson, *Presbyterians in the South*, 2:301; G. Thompson Brown, "Overseas Mission Program," p. 162.

3. Reed, *The Missionary Mind*, p. 19, table 2.

4. This briefly sketched background is treated in depth and with great facility by Jonathan Spence in *The Search for Modern China*.

5. Virginia Lee letter, 9 Nov. 1926, CL.

6. Emma Worth letter, 31 Mar. 1921, CL; Lacy Moffett letter, in Bulletin, 25 Mar. 1923, FPCW.

7. On the Qing conquest of Jiangyin, see Wakeman, "Localism and Loyalism."

CHAPTER TWO

1. Lacy Little, *Rivershade*, p. 5; R. A. Haden, "Kiangyin Station," p. 177; Bear, "Mission Work," 2:395, 407; Presbyterian Church in the United States, Executive Committee of Foreign Missions, *Minutes of the China Mission*, 1895, p. 56; *Chinese Recorder* 26, no. 7 (July 1895): 345.

2. See Junkin, *For the Glory of God*.

3. Dean, "Sino-American Relations," pp. 83–84.

4. R. A. Haden, "Kiangyin Station," p. 177; Presbyterian Church in the United States, Executive Committee of Foreign Missions, *Minutes of the China Mission*, 1895, p. 56.

5. Presbyterian Church in the United States, Executive Committee of Foreign Missions, *Minutes of the China Mission*, 1895, pp. 56–57; *Missionary* 29, no. 1 (Jan. 1896): 9, and no. 2 (Feb. 1896): 88.

6. R. A. Haden, "Kiangyin Station," pp. 177–78; Lacy Little, *Rivershade*, pp. 5–7.

7. Lacy Little, "Flower Mountain," p. 221.

8. Chinese sources refer only briefly to this incident. See, for example, *Jiaowu jiao'an dang*, ser. 6, vol. 2, doc. 635, p. 833, and Shen Songshou, "Jiangyin nao jiao'an." The following account thus relies on the full reporting of American missionaries and diplomats.

9. Lacy Little, *Rivershade*, pp. 8–9; A. C. Jones to Charles Denby, Jinjiang, 20 May 1896, in *FRUS*, 1896, pp. 72–73.

10. Polachek, "Moral Economy," p. 812 (n. 2); Wu, *International Aspect*, pp. 55–56.

11. Feuerwerker, *Foreign Establishment*, p. 39; Hunt, *The Making of a Special Relationship*, pp. 154–55; Wu, *International Aspect*, pp. 28–30.

12. *Jiaowu jiao'an dang*, ser. 5, vol. 1, docs. 244, 264, 272, pp. 171, 198, 204.

13. Arthur Smith, *China in Convulsion*, p. 39.

14. Hemenway, *Memoir*, p. 27.

15. Lacy Little, *Rivershade*, p. 7. See also Charles Worth, "Recollections of a Happy Life," p. 5, CWP.

16. A. C. Jones to W. W. Rockhill, Jinjiang, 24 July 1896, in *FRUS*, 1896, p. 75.

17. Reported in Arthur Smith, *China in Convulsion*, pp. 86–87.

18. Shen Songshou, "Jiangyin nao jiao'an," p. 99.

19. *Missionary* 29, no. 6 (June 1896): 248. Jürgens later contributed funds for building a chapel at one of the outstations (ibid. 36, no. 5 [May 1903]: 224).

20. "The Kiangyin Riot"; *Chinese Recorder* 27, no. 6 (June 1896): 311–12; Lacy Little, *Rivershade*, pp. 9–10; Charles Worth, "Recollections of a Happy Life," p. 5, CWP; Ruth Worth interview by author, Wilmington, N.C., 10 Dec. 1982; Charles Denby to Richard Olney, Beijing, 23 May 1896, and A. C. Jones to Charles Denby, Jinjiang, 20 May 1896, in

FRUS, 1896, pp. 71–73; S. H. Chester report, in *Missionary* 31, no. 2 (Feb. 1898): 58. The local gazetteer (*Jiangyin xianzhi*, 1920 edition) is silent on this incident, although it briefly describes the early history of the station (chap. 3, p. 20).

21. "The Kiangyin Riot," p. 349; A. C. Jones to Charles Denby, Jinjiang, 20 May 1896, in *FRUS*, 1896, p. 73.

22. A. C. Jones to Charles Denby, Jinjiang, 20 May 1896, in *FRUS*, 1896, pp. 72–73.

23. Charles Denby to Richard Olney, Beijing, 23 May 1896, in *FRUS*, 1896, pp. 71–72.

24. Hunt, *The Making of a Special Relationship*, p. 162. See ibid., pp. 158–67, for an extended discussion of U.S. policy during this period.

25. Ibid., pp. 72–73.

26. Arthur Smith, *China in Convulsion*, p. 69.

27. *Jiaowu jiao'an dang*, ser. 5, vol. 1, doc. 274, p. 205, vol. 4, Chronology, p. 38.

28. *FRUS*, 1896, pp. 58, 63–64, 1897, pp. 62–63, and 1898, p. 209; Hunt, *The Making of a Special Relationship*, p. 167; Young, *Rhetoric of Empire*, pp. 84–87. The International Protocol of 1901 (the Boxer Settlement) further confirmed the responsibility of high officials (*FRUS*, 1901 Appendix, pp. 316–17), and article 14 of the Sino-American Treaty of 1903 granted missionaries the right to rent or lease property in perpetuity (Wu, *International Aspect*, pp. 34, 255–56).

29. "The Kiangyin Riot," p. 349; Charles Denby to Richard Olney, Beijing, 23 May 1896, and A. C. Jones to W. W. Rockhill, Jinjiang, 29 Aug. 1896, in *FRUS*, 1896, pp. 71, 79. On the role of the *dibao* in missionary cases, see Sweeten, "Ti-pao's Role," esp. pp. 14, 20–21.

30. W. W. Rockhill to A. C. Jones, Washington, D.C., 22 July 1896, in *FRUS*, 1896, p. 74.

31. W. W. Rockhill to Charles Denby, Washington, D.C., 24 July 1896, in *FRUS*, 1896, p. 75.

32. Lacy Little, "Riots," pp. 263–64.

33. "The Kiangyin Riot," p. 350.

34. Details of the plot as revealed at the trial are in A. C. Jones to W. W. Rockhill, Jinjiang, 24 July 1896, in *FRUS*, 1896, pp. 75–77.

35. R. A. Haden, "Kiangyin Station," p. 178; A. C. Jones to W. W. Rockhill, Jinjiang, 24 July, 29 Aug. 1896, in *FRUS*, 1896, pp. 77–78, 79–80; Shen Songshou, "Jiangyin nao jiao'an," p. 99.

36. R. A. Haden, "Kiangyin Station," p. 178; Charles Denby to Richard Olney, Beijing, 13 Aug. 1896, in *FRUS*, 1896, pp. 78–79.

37. Charles Denby to Richard Olney, Beijing, 13 Oct. 1896, in *FRUS*, 1896, pp. 80–81.

38. Lacy Little, "A Visit to a Chinese Prison"; R. A. Haden, "Kiangyin Station," p. 178; Charles Worth, "Recollections of a Happy Life," pp. 5–6, CWP.

39. A. C. Jones to W. W. Rockhill, Jinjiang, 29 Aug. 1896, in *FRUS*, 1896, p. 79; correspondence between Charles Denby and the U.S. Department of State and the Zongli Yamen, Mar.–May 1897, in *FRUS*, 1897, pp. 99–102.

40. A. C. Jones to W. W. Rockhill, Jinjiang, 24 July 1896, in *FRUS*, 1896, p. 78.

41. R. A. Haden, "Kiangyin Station," p. 178; R. A. Haden, "Encouragements at Kiangyin," pp. 265–66; *Jiaowu jiao'an dang*, ser. 6, vol. 2, doc. 636, p. 910.

42. P. Frank Price, "China Conference," pp. 309–10. The tiger as a symbol of the antiforeign and anti-Christian movement seems to have gained some currency. For a similar allegory about the experience of a Baptist mission in South China, see Lipphard, *Out of the Storm*, pp. 70–71.

CHAPTER THREE

1. Presbyterian Church in the United States, Executive Committee of Foreign Missions, *Minutes of the China Mission*, 1898, p. 30; *Missionary* 31, no. 1 (Jan. 1898): 19, and no. 6 (June 1898): 266; R. A. Haden, "Kiangyin Station," pp. 178–79; Lacy Little, *Rivershade*, p. 13; *Bi-Monthly Bulletin*, o.s. [1898], pp. 9–10.

2. Lacy Little letter, 27 Jan. 1898, in *Missionary* 31, no. 5 (May 1898): 224; Bear, "Mission Work," 2:529; *Chinese Recorder* 28, no. 10 (Oct. 1897): 493–94.

3. Hunt, *The Making of a Special Relationship*, p. 155. See also Latourette, *Christian Missions*, pp. 417–20; Feuerwerker, *Foreign Establishment*, pp. 49–50; and Forsythe, *Missionary Community*, pp. 10–13.

4. Andrew Allison letter, 6 Feb. 1939, and Charles Worth letter, 11 May 1925, CL.

5. DuBose, *Preaching in Sinim*, p. 54.

6. *Report of the Student Volunteer Convention of 1891*, quoted in Varg, *Missionaries*, p. 60.

7. Published in Shanghai by the China Continuation Committee, a forerunner of the National Christian Council in China.

8. *Chinese Recorder* 30, no. 8 (Aug. 1899): 406–7.

9. Charles Worth letter, 21 Aug. 1930, CL.

10. *Bi-Monthly Bulletin*, o.s. [1898], pp. 10–11, and 1899, pp. 13–14; Bear, "Mission Work," 2:551, 3:264–65.

11. R. A. Haden letter, 20 Dec. 1897, in *Missionary* 31, no. 6 (June 1898): 265–66; R. A. Haden letter, 31 Oct. 1898, in *Bi-Monthly Bulletin*, o.s. [1898], p. 11; Mary McGinnis letter, 7 Mar. 1899, in *Bi-Monthly Bulletin*, o.s., 1, no. 3 (1899): 13; Eugenia Haden letter, Feb. 1903, in *Missionary* 36, no. 5 (May 1903): 224.

12. Ella Little letter, in *Missionary* 36, no. 2 (Feb. 1903): 75–76; *Missionary* 43, no. 5 (May 1910): 236; *Bi-Monthly Bulletin* 7, no. 1 (Jan.–Feb. 1915): 583; *Missionary Survey* 5, no. 10 (Oct. 1915): 736–39.

13. Lacy Little, "Flower Mountain," p. 222.

14. For example, Governors-general Zhang Zhidong and Liu Kunyi issued proclamations in June 1900 denouncing the Boxers and promising protection to all foreigners (*FRUS*, 1900, pp. 254–55).

15. Charles Worth, "Recollections of a Happy Life," pp. 7–8, CWP.

16. Lacy Little, "Notes from Kiangyin," p. 73.

17. Lacy Little, *Rivershade*, p. 20; Bear, "Mission Work," 3:70–71; Ella Little, "Resuming Work."

18. *Bi-Monthly Bulletin* 1, no. 2 (Jan.–Feb. 1906): 30.

19. *Missionary* 39, no. 12 (Dec. 1906): 549–51; Bear, "Mission Work," 3:277.

20. *Chinese Recorder* 48, no. 4 (Apr. 1917): 256.

21. *Chinese Recorder* 39, no. 1 (Jan. 1908): 45.

22. Bear, "Mission Work," 3:269, 272–73.

23. Charles Worth, "Lacy I. Moffett," p. 2, LMP.

24. Ibid., p. 1; Shaw, *An American Missionary in China*, pp. 18–20; P. Frank Price, *Our China Investment*, pp. 67–68.

25. *Missionary* 43, no. 5 (May 1910): 236; Charles Worth, "Lacy I. Moffett," p. 3, LMP; Kate Moffett letter, *Bi-Monthly Bulletin* 9, no. 3 (May–June 1917): 946; Lacy Little, *Rivershade*, p. 41.

26. *Missionary* 38, no. 9 (Sept. 1905): 443.

27. *Missionary* 39, no. 12 (Dec. 1906): 550–51.

28. *Bi-Monthly Bulletin* 2, no. 1 (Jan.–Feb. 1907): 12; Bear, "Mission Work," 3:282.

29. Lacy Little, "A Year at Kiangyin," pp. 597–98, and *Our Kiangyin Schools*, pp. 2–3.

30. Cheung and New, "Typology," p. 36.

31. Buck, *American Science*, pp. 21–33.

32. See, for instance, laudatory articles on George Worth and the hospital by contemporary Chinese in *Jiangyin wenshi ziliao* (Jiangyin historical materials): Yang and Chen, "Jiangyin xian Fuyin yiyuan jianshi," and Xie, "Huaerde ho Jiangyin Fuyin yiyuan."

33. New York: Penguin Books, 1985.

34. Wilmington Presbyterial Auxiliary, *Worth Memorial Booklet*, pp. 20, 22.

35. Woollcott, "Fifty-four Years of the Y.M.C.A.," p. 290.

36. *North Carolina Presbyterian*, 2 Apr. 1896.

37. First Presbyterian Church, Wilmington, *Record and Manual, 1895–1896*, pp. 15–16.

38. Wilmington Presbyterial Auxiliary, *Worth Memorial Booklet*, p. 22.

39. Sherwood Eddy, quoted in Varg, *Missionaries*, p. 3.

40. George Worth, "Wearing Chinese Dress"; Charles Worth, "Recollections of a Happy Life," p. 3, CWP; Ruth Worth interview by author, Wilmington, N.C., 10 Dec. 1982.

41. P. Frank Price, *Our China Investment*, pp. 49–51; Mrs. J. A. Brown, *Wilmington Presbyterial Auxiliary*, pp. 71–72; Wilmington Presbyterial Auxiliary, *Worth Memorial Booklet*.

42. Murphy, *Kiangyin Hospital*, p. 3; Wilmington Presbyterial Auxiliary, *Worth Memorial Booklet*, p. 17.

43. Chester, *Lights and Shadows*, pp. 76, 77.

44. Bear, "Mission Work," 2:552, 3:35, 277–78.

45. Mrs. J. A. Brown, *Wilmington Presbyterial Auxiliary*, pp. 21, 71–72.

46. Ibid., pp. 37, 39.

47. First Presbyterian Church, Wilmington, *Manual, 1904*, pp. 28–29.

48. Ibid.; Mrs. J. A. Brown, *Wilmington Presbyterial Auxiliary*, pp. 21, 37, 71–72; Murphy, *Kiangyin Hospital*, pp. 3–4; Wilmington Presbyterial Auxiliary, *Minutes*, 1905, pp. 17–18, 1906, p. 18, and 1907, pp. 17–20; Margaret Sprunt Hall, "Sketch of Woman's Foreign Missionary Union of Wilmington Presbytery," 1911, pp. 5–6, WPF.

49. Wilmington Presbyterial Auxiliary, *Minutes*, 1906, p. 18, and 1921, p. 18.

50. Bear, "Mission Work," 2:277.

51. *Bi-Monthly Bulletin* 1, no. 2 (Jan.–Feb. 1906): 22, and no. 4 (May–June 1906): 76; Presbyterian Church in the United States, Executive Committee of Foreign Missions, *Annual Report*, 1906, pp. 26–28.

52. George Worth to Wilmington Presbyterial Auxiliary, 7 Jan. 1909, WPF; Murphy, *Kiangyin Hospital*, p. 4.

53. Chester, *Medical Missions*, p. 7; Murphy, *Kiangyin Hospital*, p. 4; Bulletin, 13 Dec. 1908, FPCW.

54. Wilmington Presbyterial Auxiliary, *Minutes*, 1907, pp. 19–20, and 1910, pp. 21–22; Murphy, *Kiangyin Hospital*, p. 4; Bear, "Mission Work," 3:279; Mrs. J. A. Brown, *Wilmington Presbyterial Auxiliary*, p. 73.

55. Wilmington Presbyterial Auxiliary, *Minutes*, 1903, pp. 13–15, and 1913, p. 20.

56. Bulletin, 21 Feb. 1909, FPCW; *Bi-Monthly Bulletin* 3, no. 6 (Jan.–Feb. 1909): 169–71, and no. 7 (Mar.–Apr. 1909): 216.

57. *The Kiangyin Hospital*, pp. 2–4.

58. *Missionary Survey* 6, no. 11 (Nov. 1916): 856–58.

59. *The Kiangyin Hospital*, p. 3.

60. Wilmington Presbyterial Auxiliary, *Minutes*, 1910, pp. 17, 21–22, 1911, pp. 4, 6–7, 1912, pp. 12–13, and 1913, pp. 15–16; *The Kiangyin Hospital*, pp. 3–4; Murphy, *Kiangyin Hospital*, pp. 4–5.

61. On educational reform in the late Qing period, see Bastid, *Educational Reform*, and Borthwick, *Education and Social Change*.

62. *Bi-Monthly Bulletin* 2, no. 1 (Jan.–Feb. 1907): 12; Lacy Little, *Our Kiangyin Schools*, pp. 1–2; "Data Respecting the Christian Schools."

63. Latourette, *Christian Missions*, p. 443.

64. Hu, "Wo zai Jiangyin," p. 180.

65. Ibid.

66. Jane Lee, *Kiangyin Girls' School*, pp. 2–3; Lacy Little, *Our Kiangyin Schools*, p. 2.

67. China Educational Commission, *Christian Education*, p. 34; Rawski, "Elementary Education," p. 136.

68. Lacy Little to James Sprunt, 10 May 1909, and Ella Little to James Sprunt, 13 May 1909, ASSP; Lacy Little, *Our Kiangyin Schools*, p. 3.

69. See correspondence between James Sprunt and J. Campbell White and Charles Rowland, 23, 25 Feb., 2, 5, 10, 13, 22, 29 Mar. 1909, ASSP.

70. Canceled check dated 31 Mar. 1909, and James Sprunt to J. Campbell White, 2 Apr. 1909, ASSP.

71. James Sprunt to George Worth, 9 May 1921, ASSP.

72. Lacy Little, *Our Kiangyin Schools*, p. 1.

73. First Presbyterian Church, Wilmington, Bulletin, 2 Jan. 1910, ASSP; *Bi-Monthly Bulletin* 4, no. 1 (Jan.–Feb. 1910): 18, and no. 3 (May–June 1910): 77; Lacy Little, "A Year at Kiangyin," p. 597; Lacy Little report, in *Missionary Survey* 1, no. 2 (Dec. 1911): 103.

74. James Sprunt to Margaret Sprunt Hall, 1 Oct. 1909, ASSP; *James Sprunt*, pp. 73–74; Chen Xikang and Chen Liangheng, "Jiangyin Lishi zhongxue jianshi," p. 46.

75. *Bi-Monthly Bulletin* 9, no. 3 (May–June 1917): 946; Miao, *Jiangyin jinshi lu*, pp. 93–94 (chap. 2, p. 5); Sessional Records, 1 Apr. 1917, FPCW.

76. Chester, *Behind the Scenes*, p. 39; Ernest Thompson, *Presbyterians in the South*, 3:126–27; Stuart, *Fifty Years*, pp. 30–33.

77. *Missionary* 43, no. 1 (Jan. 1910): 5–6; Lacy Little, *Our Kiangyin Schools*, p. 4; P. Frank Price, *Our China Investment*, pp. 77, 87; Presbyterian Church in the United States, Board of World Missions, *In Memory of Missionaries*, pp. 10–11, 29–30.

78. Varg, *Missionaries*, p. 125; Wu, *International Aspect*, pp. 34, 255–56.

79. *Bi-Monthly Bulletin* 4, no. 4 (July–Aug. 1910): 101–3.

80. Lacy Little, "A Year at Kiangyin," pp. 596–97.

81. *Bi-Monthly Bulletin* 4, no. 7 (Jan.–Feb. 1911): 183–84, and 6, no. 4 (July–Aug. 1914): 505; *Missionary Survey* 1, no. 2 (Dec. 1911): 103; Notes, 16 Jan. 1916, Scrapbook of Church History, FPCW.

CHAPTER FOUR

1. Varg, *Missionaries*, pp. 136–37. For the almost universally positive response of one American Protestant church to the 1911 revolution, see Metallo, "Presbyterian Missionar-

ies," pp. 158–59. On the Southern Baptist reaction, see Rubinstein, "Witness to the Chinese Millennium," pp. 150–57.

2. *Chinese Recorder* 50, no. 8 (Aug. 1919): 518–19 (the author is Julean Arnold, not a missionary but a U.S. commercial attaché); Virginia Lee letter, "White and Gold," received at Nashville, Apr. 1920, and Emma Worth letter, 10 Nov. 1920, CL.

3. Hogg, "Role of American Protestantism," p. 376; Varg, *Missionaries*, p. 89.

4. Hunt, *The Making of a Special Relationship*, p. 293.

5. Jiangyin newspaper, quoted in Wilmington Presbyterial Auxiliary, *Worth Memorial Booklet*, p. 17; Bulletin, 17 Dec. 1911, FPCW.

6. Hu, "Wo zai Jiangyin," p. 178; *Missionary Survey* 1, no. 6 (Apr. 1912): 433; *Bi-Monthly Bulletin* 5, no. 1 (Jan.–Feb. 1912): 30–31.

7. *Bi-Monthly Bulletin* 5, no. 1 (Jan.–Feb. 1912): 30, and 5, no. 8 (Mar.–Apr. 1913): 211. Even into the 1920s, the rural Chinese were ignorant of the new calendar, and the Jiangyin Station announced its events using both calendars (Emma Worth letter, 5 May 1920, CL).

8. Bulletin, 7 Jan. 1912, FPCW.

9. Miao, *Jiangyin jinshi lu*, pp. 41–43 (chap. 1, pp. 21a–22a).

10. *Bi-Monthly Bulletin* 5, no. 3 (May–June 1912): 77–78.

11. Ibid.; Miao, *Jiangyin jinshi lu*, pp. 41–43 (chap. 1, pp. 21a–22a); Xie, "Huaerde ho Jiangyin Fuyin yiyuan," p. 121.

12. *Bi-Monthly Bulletin* 5, no. 12 (Nov.–Dec. 1913): 380; Jiangyin Station letters, quoted in Bulletin, 21 Dec. 1913, 4, 25 Jan. 1914, FPCW; Miao, *Jiangyin jinshi lu*, pp. 43–47 (chap. 1, pp. 22–24).

13. Lacy Little letter, quoted in Bulletin, 1 Dec. 1912, FPCW. At the time, Sun was apparently making the rounds of several mission institutions (see Metallo, "Presbyterian Missionaries," p. 162).

14. Bulletin, 5, 12 May 1912, FPCW.

15. Lacy Little, *Rivershade*, p. 15; Frank Crawford letter, in Bulletin, 19 Dec. 1915, FPCW.

16. *Bi-Monthly Bulletin* 5, no. 12 (Nov.–Dec. 1913): 381, and 7, no. 4 (July–Aug. 1915): 673.

17. Bulletin, 16 Jan. 1916, FPCW; *Missionary Survey* 6, no. 5 (May 1916): 335–39.

18. Frank Crawford report, in Wilmington Presbyterial Auxiliary, *Minutes*, 1917; Ruth Worth interview, Wilmington, N.C., 8 Jan. 1980, pp. 4–5, in North Carolina's China Connection Archive, North Carolina China Council Papers, in possession of author.

19. *Bi-Monthly Bulletin* 7, no. 4 (July–Aug. 1915): 672–73, and 10, no. 2 (Mar.–Apr. 1918): 1042; Wilmington Presbyterial Auxiliary, *Minutes*, 1917; Yang and Chen, "Jiangyin xian Fuyin yiyuan jianshi," p. 59; Balme, *China and Modern Medicine*, p. 147.

20. Lacy Little, *Rivershade*, pp. 24–31.

21. P. Frank Price, *Our China Investment*, pp. 64, 149.

22. Katheryne Thompson to Creighton Lacy, Sioux Falls, 20 Dec. 1951, in possession of Creighton Lacy.

23. *Bi-Monthly Bulletin* 5, no. 3 (May–June 1912): 78; no. 8 (Mar.–Apr. 1913): 211–12; and 6, no. 1 (Jan.–Feb. 1914): 398; *Chinese Recorder* 44, no. 4 (Apr. 1913): 255–57.

24. *Bi-Monthly Bulletin* 4, no. 9 (May–June 1911): 241; 7, no. 1 (Jan.–Feb. 1915): 583; and 11, no. 1 (Jan.–Feb. 1919): 1156.

25. Hu, "Wo zai Jiangyin," pp. 182–83.

26. Lacy Little letter, 17 June 1912, in *Bi-Monthly Bulletin* 5, no. 4 (July–Aug. 1912): 103–4.

27. *Missionary* 44, no. 7 (July 1911): 343–44; *Bi-Monthly Bulletin* 4, no. 9 (May–June 1911): 257.

28. The following description of the secession crisis is based on two very detailed accounts, one in English and one in Chinese. The missionary report is found in a Lacy Moffett letter, in *Bi-Monthly Bulletin* 8, no. 3 (May–June 1916): 804–8. The Chinese account is presented in Miao, *Jiangyin jinshi lu*, pp. 51–64 (chap. 1, pp. 26a–32b). These two sources essentially corroborate each other, with only slight discrepancies in dates; I have followed the missionary account in dating events.

29. Miao, *Jiangyin jinshi lu*, pp. 59–60 (chap. 1, pp. 30a–30b).

30. Presbyterian Church in the United States, Executive Committee of Foreign Missions, *Annual Report*, 1917, p. 62, quoted in Bear, "Mission Work," 4:181.

31. Cheung, *Missionary Medicine*, pp. 74, 79.

32. Miao, *Jiangyin jinshi lu*.

33. Lacy Moffett letter, in *Bi-Monthly Bulletin* 8, no. 3 (May–June 1916): 808.

34. Ibid.; George Worth letter, 1916, quoted in Murphy, *Kiangyin Hospital*, p. 12.

35. *Bi-Monthly Bulletin* 9, no. 2 (Mar.–Apr. 1917): 913–15; *Missionary Survey* 7, no. 7 (July 1917): 494–95.

36. *Bi-Monthly Bulletin* 9, no. 2 (Mar.–Apr. 1917): 913.

37. Lacy Little, *Rivershade*, p. 49.

38. *Bi-Monthly Bulletin* 11, no. 4 (Sept.–Oct. 1919): 1234; Virginia Lee letter, "White and Gold," received at Nashville, Apr. 1920, CL.

39. Lacy Little, *Rivershade*, pp. 50–51; *Bi-Monthly Bulletin* 9, nos. 4–5 (July–Oct. 1917): 968; *Missionary Survey* 8, no. 2 (Feb. 1918): 99–100.

40. *Bi-Monthly Bulletin* 8, no. 3 (May–June 1916): 808, and 9, no. 2 (Mar.–Apr. 1917): 913–15; *Missionary Survey* 7, no. 7 (July 1917): 494–95; Bulletin, 17 Apr. 1921, FPCW.

41. See, for example, Bear, "Mission Work," 4:184, and *Bi-Monthly Bulletin* 11, no. 4 (Sept.–Oct. 1919): 1234–35.

42. Mrs. J. A. Brown, *Wilmington Presbyterial Auxiliary*, p. 70. This shield is now held by the First Presbyterian Church in Wilmington.

43. Balme, *China and Modern Medicine*, pp. 104–5.

44. *Bi-Monthly Bulletin* 13, no. 3 (Mar.–Apr. 1923): 1462, and no. 4 (May–June 1923): 1487; Lacy Moffett letter, in Bulletin, 25 Mar. 1923, FPCW; Emma Worth letter, 10 July 1923, Mrs. George C. Worth Folder, FPCW.

45. George Worth letter, in Bulletin, 3 Nov. 1918, FPCW. See also Lacy Little, *Rivershade*, p. 49; Murphy, *Kiangyin Hospital*, p. 7; *Bi-Monthly Bulletin* 9, nos. 4–5 (July–Oct. 1917): 968; and Williams, *In China*, p. 43.

46. *Bi-Monthly Bulletin* 11, no. 1 (Jan.–Feb. 1919): 1156; station letters, in Bulletin, 26 Jan., 16 Mar. 1919, FPCW.

47. George Worth to sons, Jiangyin and Shanghai, 24–28 Jan. 1919, RWP; Presbyterian Church in the United States, Executive Committee of Foreign Missions, *Annual Report*, 1920, pp. 61–62, quoted in Bear, "Mission Work," 4:183; station letter, in Bulletin, 4 May 1919, FPCW.

48. Emma Worth letter, in Bulletin, 16 Mar. 1919, FPCW.

49. Lacy Little, *Rivershade*, pp. 44–47; Ruth Worth interview, Wilmington, N.C., 8 Jan. 1980, in North Carolina's China Connection Archive, North Carolina China Council Papers, in possession of author.

50. Emma Worth letters, 5 May 1920, 23 Mar. 1923, 25 Aug. 1925, CL; *Monthly Messenger* 17, no. 3 (Mar. 1926): 1784.

51. Mrs. J. A. Brown, *Wilmington Presbyterial Auxiliary*, pp. 75–78; Emma Worth letters, 23 Mar., 26 Nov. 1923, CL; George Worth to Wilmington Presbyterial Auxiliary, 28 Mar. 1924, WPF; P. Frank Price, *Our China Investment*, p. 132.

52. Bulletin, 3 Apr. 1921, FPCW; Emma Worth letter, 25 Aug. 1925, and Jane Lee letter, 7 Dec. 1926, CL; Murphy, *Kiangyin Hospital*, p. 9; Hudson, "Southern Presbyterian Church in China," p. 256.

53. Balme, *China and Modern Medicine*, p. 188.

54. George Worth to Wilmington Presbyterial Auxiliary, 28 Mar. 1924, WPF.

55. Yang and Chen, "Jiangyin xian Fuyin yiyuan jianshi," p. 62.

56. Susan E. Hall, "Sketch of the Woman's Auxiliary of the First Presbyterian Church, Wilmington, N.C., 1817–1934," pp. 7–8, Histories of Churches and Woman's Work in Wilmington Presbytery, FPCW; Wilmington Presbyterial Auxiliary, *Minutes*, 1908, p. 18, and 1922, p. 2; Murphy, *Kiangyin Hospital*, p. 8; George Worth to Wilmington Presbyterial Auxiliary, 28 Mar. 1924, WPF.

57. Susan E. Hall, "History of the Woman's Auxiliary of Wilmington Presbytery, Synod of North Carolina, 1922–1938," p. 3, WPF; Bulletin, 13 June 1926, 28 Apr., 19 May 1929, FPCW.

58. Breslin, *China*, pp. 47–48, argues that American Catholic missionaries' efforts at mediation and providing protection to refugees during warlord strife were only successful if an American military force was nearby. This does not seem to have been the case at Jiangyin, where the missionaries were successful despite the absence of such forces. In a general sense, of course, the presence of foreign forces in China and the treaty privileges of foreigners certainly enhanced the missionaries' ability to act.

59. Ch'i, *Warlord Politics*, pp. 223–24; Lacy Little letter, "War at Kiangyin," 4 Feb. 1925, CL.

60. Charles Worth letter, 10 Nov. 1924, CL; Bulletin, 4 Jan. 1925, FPCW.

61. William Cumming letter, 9 Feb. 1925, in *Monthly Messenger* 16, no. 2 (Feb. 1925): 1666, 1670; Jane Lee letter, 10–17 Nov. 1925, CL; Xie, "Huaerde ho Jiangyin Fuyin yiyuan," p. 121.

62. Egbert Smith, *Essential Facts*, p. 8.

63. Lacy Little letters, "War at Kiangyin," 4 Feb. 1925, and "Three Testing Times at Kiangyin," 27 Mar. 1925, CL.

64. Andrew Allison, "War Experiences," pp. 374–75; William Cumming letter, 3 Feb. 1925, and Emma Worth letter, 4 Feb. 1925, CL; Xie, "Huaerde ho Jiangyin Fuyin yiyuan," p. 121; Yang and Chen, "Jiangyin xian Fuyin yiyuan jianshi," p. 60.

65. Lacy Little letter, "War at Kiangyin," 4 Feb. 1925, CL; Emma Worth letter, in *Monthly Messenger* 16, no. 2 (Feb. 1925): 1670; Jane Lee letter, in Bulletin, 16 Nov. 1924, FPCW; Yang and Chen, "Jiangyin xian Fuyin yiyuan jianshi," p. 60.

66. Andrew Allison, "War Experiences," p. 376; William Cumming letter, 3 Feb. 1925, and Emma Worth letter, 4 Feb. 1925, CL.

67. Lacy Little letter, "War at Kiangyin," 4 Feb. 1925, CL; Xie, "Huaerde ho Jiangyin Fuyin yiyuan," p. 121; Yang and Chen, "Jiangyin xian Fuyin yiyuan jianshi," p. 60.

68. Lacy Little letter, "War at Kiangyin," 4 Feb. 1925, and Emma Worth letter, 4 Feb. 1925, CL; Charles Worth, "Recollections of a Happy Life," pp. 28–29, CWP; Andrew Allison, "War Experiences," p. 376.

69. Virginia Lee letter, 4 May 1925, CL.

70. Charles Worth, "Recollections of a Happy Life," p. 30, CWP.

71. Andrew Allison, "War Experiences," pp. 375–76; Lacy Little letter, "Three Testing Times at Kiangyin," 27 Mar. 1925, CL.

72. Andrew Allison, "War Experiences," p. 418; Emma Worth letter, 4 Feb. 1925, CL.

73. Andrew Allison, "War Experiences," pp. 417–18; Egbert Smith, *Essential Facts*, p. 4; William Cumming letter, 11 Nov. 1924, CL; Emma Worth letter, in Bulletin, 10 May 1925, FPCW.

74. Jane Lee letter, 10–17 Nov. 1925, and Lacy Little letter, 15 Oct. 1926, CL; Chen Xikang and Chen Liangheng, "Jiangyin Lishi zhongxue jianshi," p. 48.

75. Lacy Little, *Rivershade*, pp. 50, 53; Kiangyin Station Photographs, Presbyterian Church in the United States Missions, China, DHR.

76. Station letters, in Bulletin, 17 May, 7, 14 June 1925, FPCW.

77. Lacy Little letter, 15 Oct. 1926, CL; *Monthly Messenger* 16, no. 6 (June 1925): 1709–10, and 17, no. 5 (May 1926): 1798.

78. The honors bestowed on missionaries for their peace work were not unique to Jiangyin. In nearby Songjiang, residents erected a pavilion in honor of a Methodist missionary for his aid and protection during the same warlord conflict. Several years later, they successfully resisted an effort by local Nationalist officials to tear it down and replace it with a memorial to Sun Yat-sen (Burke, *My Father*, pp. 289–309, 336–41).

79. Haden died when the ship he was taking to visit relatives in Switzerland was torpedoed in the Mediterranean; it was reported that he drowned while trying to rescue other passengers (*Chinese Recorder* 48, no. 3 [Mar. 1917]: 144–45).

80. William Cumming letter, 11 Dec. 1925, in *Monthly Messenger* 16, no. 10 (Dec. 1925): 1749–50; Emma Worth letter, 26 Jan. 1926, CL; station letters, in Bulletin, 24 Jan. 1926, 17 Apr. 1927, FPCW.

81. G. Thompson Brown, "Overseas Mission Program," p. 163.

CHAPTER FIVE

1. Chen Xikang and Chen Liangheng, "Jiangyin Lishi zhongxue jianshi," p. 47.

2. Bear, "Mission Work," 4:173–74, 176; Virginia Lee letter, Aug. 1919, CL; Jane Lee, *Kiangyin Girls' School*, pp. 5–7.

3. Virginia Lee letter, "White and Gold," received at Nashville, Apr. 1920, CL.

4. See, for example, an account in *Bi-Monthly Bulletin* 4, no. 9 (May–June 1911): 240–41.

5. Yip, *Religion*, pp. 19–22; Kiang, *Student Movement*, pp. 54–60; Shaw, "Reaction," pp. 159–74; Lu, "Anti-Christian Thoughts," pp. 139–43, 175; Lutz, *Chinese Politics*, pp. 33–39; Jonathan Chao, "Indigenous Church Movement," pp. 99–101; Chang, "Anti-Religion Movement," p. 463.

6. This was noted contemporaneously by Donald Richardson, a Presbyterian missionary and dean of the Nanjing Theological Seminary at the time of the March 1927 attack on foreigners (*Church in China*, pp. 95–96).

7. The book was edited by Milton Stauffer and published in Shanghai in 1922 by the China Continuation Committee, a forerunner of the National Christian Council in China.

8. *Christian Education in China*, a report for the China Educational Commission published in New York in 1922 by the Foreign Missions Conference of North America.

9. Lu, "Anti-Christian Thoughts," p. 122. See also Yip, *Religion*, p. 23, and Yamamoto and Yamamoto, "Anti-Christian Movement," pp. 133–34.

10. Jonathan Chao, "Indigenous Church Movement," pp. 141–46.

11. Lu, "Anti-Christian Thoughts," p. 118; Kiang, *Student Movement*, pp. 62–66; Yip, *Religion*, pp. 23–24; Lutz, *Chinese Politics*, pp. 59–64; Jonathan Chao, "Indigenous Church Movement," pp. 136–39; Chang, "Anti-Religion Movement," pp. 459–60, 467.

12. *Bi-Monthly Bulletin* 13, no. 5 (Sept.–Oct. 1923): 1511–12, and 14, no. 1 (Jan.–Feb. 1924): 1556–57; Katheryne Thompson letter, 16 May 1923, and Emma Worth letter, 31 Mar. 1924, CL; *Presbyterian Survey* 14, no. 10 (Oct. 1924): 662; Cumming, *How Mission School Students Spend Sunday*.

13. Chen Xikang and Chen Liangheng, "Jiangyin Lishi zhongxue jianshi," p. 48.

14. Egbert Smith, *Essential Facts*, p. 24.

15. *James Sprunt*, pp. 74–76; Chen Xikang and Chen Liangheng, "Jiangyin Lishi zhongxue jianshi," p. 49.

16. Lu, "Anti-Christian Thoughts," p. 118; Lutz, "Students," pp. 293–94.

17. Hobart, *Long Sand*, pp. 306–8; Greene, *Hsiang-Ya*, pp. 34–35.

18. Emma Worth letter, 25 Aug. 1925, CL; Lacy Little letter, 19 June 1925, in *Monthly Messenger* 16, no. 6 (June 1925): 1703. On troubles at other schools, see Lutz, *Chinese Politics*, chap. 6.

19. Jane Lee letter, 10–17 Nov. 1925, and William Cumming letter, 22 Jan. 1926, CL.

20. Emma Worth letter, 26 Jan. 1926, and Virginia Lee letter, 9 Nov. 1926, CL.

21. Latourette, *Christian Missions*, p. 811; Varg, *Missionaries*, pp. 195–97; Wu, *International Aspect*, pp. 257–58. For an extended discussion of missionary views, see Borg, *American Policy*, chap. 5.

22. William Cumming letter, 11 Dec. 1925, in *Monthly Messenger* 16, no. 10 (Dec. 1925): 1749.

23. Andrew Allison letter, 18 Nov. 1926, in *Monthly Messenger* 17, no. 9 (Nov. 1926): 1851.

24. William Cumming letter, 26 Dec. 1926, CL.

25. *FRUS*, 1927, 2:254, 257; Lacy Little, "Rays of Light," p. 304; *Monthly Messenger* 18, no. 2 (Feb. 1927): 1886; George Worth letter, 7 Feb. 1927, Histories of Churches and Woman's Work in Wilmington Presbytery, FPCW; Jane Lee letter, Shanghai, Jan. 1928, CL.

26. George Worth letter, 7 Feb. 1927, Histories of Churches and Woman's Work in Wilmington Presbytery, FPCW.

27. Lacy Little, *Rivershade*, pp. 60–61; Andrew Allison letter, 14 Mar. 1927, and Jane Lee letter, Jan. 1928, CL.

28. George Worth letter, in Bulletin, 17, 24 Apr. 1927, FPCW.

29. The occupation of missionary schools and hospitals for use as headquarters and barracks by the National Revolutionary Army was reported to be a deliberate policy inspired by left-wing elements in the movement (Varg, *Missionaries*, p. 191).

30. George Worth letter, Shanghai, 6 Oct. 1927, in Wilmington Presbyterial Auxiliary, *Worth Memorial Booklet*, p. 28; William Cumming letter, 29 Mar. 1927, CL; Kiangyin Station Photographs, Presbyterian Church in the United States Missions, China, DHR.

31. Andrew Allison letters, 14 Mar. 1927, 4 Feb. 1929, CL.

32. Wilmington Presbyterial Auxiliary, *Worth Memorial Booklet*, pp. 28–29; Lacy Little, *Rivershade*, p. 31; William Cumming letter, 29 Mar. 1927, Andrew Allison letter, Shanghai, 20 June 1927, and Jane Lee letter, Shanghai, Jan. 1928, CL.

33. George Worth letter, Shanghai, 7 Feb. 1927, Histories of Churches and Woman's Work in Wilmington Presbytery, FPCW.

34. Ju I-hsiung interview by author, Lexington, Va., 15 Aug. 1980; Hu, "Wo zai Jiangyin," p. 182.

35. Andrew Allison letter, Shanghai, 20 June 1927, CL; Charles Worth, "Chinese Christian Church," p. 420.

36. *Chinese Recorder* 58, no. 4 (Apr. 1927): 227; Chapman, *Chinese Revolution*, p. 106; Wilbur, *Nationalist Revolution*, p. 92. For a brief account of the Nanjing Incident, see Borg, *American Policy*, pp. 290–95.

37. Lacy Little, *Rivershade*, p. 61; George Worth letter, Shanghai, 6 Oct. 1927, in Wilmington Presbyterial Auxiliary, *Worth Memorial Booklet*, p. 29; William Cumming letter, 29 Mar. 1927, CL; *FRUS*, 1927, 2:264. Burke, *My Father*, pp. 320–21, discusses the significance of different coded messages devised by the consul-general to warn Americans of the level of danger.

38. *FRUS*, 1927, 2:267; Corley, "Go Home," p. 14.

39. Lacy Little, *Rivershade*, pp. 61–62; George Worth letter, Shanghai, 6 Oct. 1927, in Wilmington Presbyterial Auxiliary, *Worth Memorial Booklet*, p. 29; William Cumming letter, 29 Mar. 1927, CL.

40. Latourette, *Christian Missions*, p. 820.

41. Quoted in Donald Richardson, *Church in China*, p. 209.

42. Quoted in Borg, *American Policy*, p. 363.

43. Lacy Little, *Rivershade*, pp. 62–63; Presbyterian Church in the United States, Executive Committee of Foreign Missions, *Annual Report*, 1928, p. 8, quoted in Bear, "Mission Work," 5:138.

44. Lacy Little letter, 1 June 1927, Lacy L. Little Papers, DHR; *Presbyterian Survey* 19, no. 1 (Jan. 1929): 29.

45. The following account of the 1928 Communist attacks is based on a very detailed report in George Worth, "News Letter," Shanghai, 14 Apr. 1928, Missions Folder, FPCW.

46. Government troops occupied the school property at the station off and on in 1928 and 1929 despite the protests of the missionaries (ibid.; Charles Worth letter, in Bulletin, 26 May 1929, FPCW).

47. George Worth, "News Letter," Shanghai, 14 Apr. 1928, Missions Folder, and Lacy Moffett letter, 24 Oct. 1928, in Bulletin, 16 Dec. 1928, FPCW.

48. Gregg, *Educational Autonomy*, pp. 155–56; Heininger, "Private Positions," pp. 289–91.

49. William Overholt interview, Swannanoa, N.C., 5 Sept. 1980, in North Carolina's China Connection Archive, North Carolina China Council Papers, in possession of author.

50. Ella Allison letter, *Bi-Monthly Bulletin* 7, no. 5 (Sept.–Oct. 1915): 698; George Worth letter, Shanghai, 7 Feb. 1927, Histories of Churches and Woman's Work in Wilmington Presbytery, FPCW (emphasis in original).

51. See station letters, in Bulletin, 26 Jan., 16 Nov. 1919, 6, 13 June, 5 Dec. 1920, FPCW.

52. Bulletin, 13 June 1920, 3 Apr. 1921, FPCW.

53. Bulletin, 19 Nov. 1922, FPCW; Lacy Moffett letter, 22 Nov. 1922, CL.

54. *Bi-Monthly Bulletin* 13, no. 6 (Nov.–Dec. 1923): 1537.

55. George Worth letter, 28 Mar. 1924, WPF (emphasis in original).

56. *Chinese Recorder* 58, no. 7 (June 1927): 471.

57. Andrew Allison letter, Shanghai, 20 June 1927, CL.

58. Donald Richardson, *Church in China*, p. 45.

59. Lacy Little, *Rivershade*, p. 63; Charles Worth, "Recollections of a Happy Life," p. 49, CWP; Andrew Allison letter, 14 Mar. 1928, and Jane Lee letter, 26 May 1928, CL.

60. Heininger, "Private Positions," pp. 288, 292; Varg, *Missionaries*, pp. 100–103; Ch'en, *China and the West*, pp. 114–15; Donald Richardson, *Church in China*, pp. 141–42; Garrett, "Why They Stayed," p. 299.

61. T. Z. Koo, "The Future of Christianity in China," in Stauffer, *China Her Own Interpreter*, p. 147.

62. George Worth to Wilmington Presbyterial Auxiliary, 10 Feb. 1935, WPF.

63. Ernest Thompson, *Presbyterians in the South*, 3:125; G. Thompson Brown, "Overseas Mission Program," pp. 158–60.

64. Bear, "Mission Work," 5:435–38.

65. Bulletin, 1 Dec. 1907, FPCW; *Bi-Monthly Bulletin* 3, no. 8 (May–June 1909): 235; *Missionary* 42, no. 8 (Aug. 1909): 398.

66. Lacy Little, *Rivershade*, p. 42. The workings of the Jiangyin Presbytery are presented in Charles Worth letter, 9 Nov. 1931, CL.

67. Donald Richardson, *Church in China*, p. 36.

68. Heininger, "Private Positions," pp. 294–95; Rabe, "Evangelical Logistics," pp. 72–73; Latourette, *Christian Missions*, p. 801.

69. Bear, "Mission Work," 3:281.

70. Lacy Little, "Two Unusual Boys," p. 483; Bulletin, 10 Feb. 1918, FPCW.

71. Latourette, *Christian Missions*, p. 806.

72. Donald Richardson, *Church in China*, p. 42 (emphasis in original).

73. Bear, "Mission Work," 3:303–5; Carrie Lena Moffett letter, 24 Feb. 1930, CL.

74. Gregg, *Educational Autonomy*, p. 53; Peake, *Nationalism and Education*, pp. 147–48.

75. Kiang, *Student Movement*, p. 92; Yamamoto and Yamamoto, "Anti-Christian Movement," p. 140; Peake, *Nationalism and Education*, p. 150; Yip, *Religion*, p. 34; Sec, "Recent Developments," p. 239.

76. Peake, *Nationalism and Education*, p. 149. See also Kiang, *Student Movement*, pp. 88–89; Yamamoto and Yamamoto, "Anti-Christian Movement," p. 140; and Lutz, "Students," pp. 300–301.

77. Kiang, *Student Movement*, pp. 92–93; Peake, *Nationalism and Education*, p. 151; Lutz, "Chinese Nationalism," pp. 413–14.

78. Lutz, "Students," p. 296; Yamamoto and Yamamoto, "Anti-Christian Movement," p. 141; Peake, *Nationalism and Education*, p. 150.

79. Donald Richardson, *Church in China*, pp. 97, 104–5; Yip, *Religion*, pp. 41–42; Lutz, "Chinese Nationalism," pp. 408–13; Jonathan Chao, "Indigenous Church Movement," pp. 183–87; *China Christian Year Book*, 1926, pp. 480–83.

80. Wilbur, *Nationalist Revolution*, pp. 70–71; Yip, *Religion*, pp. 37–43, 62–67; Kiang, *Student Movement*, pp. 143–44; Lutz, "Chinese Nationalism," pp. 409–10; Jonathan Chao, "Indigenous Church Movement," pp. 172, 193–94.

81. Lew, "Christian Education," pp. 3–10. For an extended discussion of the Chinese Christian response to the anti-imperialist and anti-Christian movements of 1924–27, see Jonathan Chao, "Indigenous Church Movement," pp. 196–221.

82. Gregg, *Educational Autonomy*, pp. 139–40, 172; Peake, *Nationalism and Education*, pp. 151–52; Lutz, "Students," p. 292; Yip, *Religion*, pp. 56, 74; Wu, *International Aspect*, pp. 60, 64.

83. Gregg, *Educational Autonomy*, pp. 136–40, 172–76; Jonathan Chao, "Indigenous Church Movement," p. 216; Wallace, "Christian Education," pp. 227–30.

84. *FRUS*, 1929, 2:569–73, and 1930, 2:538–40.

85. Wu, *International Aspect*, p. vii.

86. Gregg, *Educational Autonomy*, pp. 170–71.

87. Bear, "Mission Work," 5:426, 428–32; George Worth letter, 14, 23 Apr. 1928, Missions Folder, FPCW.

88. Andrew Allison letter, Shanghai, 20 June 1927, CL.

89. Carrie Lena Moffett letter, in Bulletin, 17 Nov. 1929, FPCW.

90. Andrew Allison letter, 14 Mar. 1928, CL (emphasis in original).

91. Jane Lee letter, Shanghai, Jan. 1928, and Carrie Lena Moffett letter, 12 Nov. 1929, CL.

92. Andrew Allison letter, 9 Apr. 1930, CL.

93. Ibid.

94. Jane Lee letters, 8 Aug., 12 Nov. 1931, CL; Jane Lee report, *Presbyterian Survey* 21, no. 12 (Dec. 1931): 741–42.

95. Yip, *Religion*, p. 76.

96. Ella Allison report, *Presbyterian Survey* 21, no. 5 (May 1931): 304. See also Presbyterian Church in the United States, Executive Committee of Foreign Missions, *Annual Report*, 1931, pp. 35–36, quoted in Bear, "Mission Work," 5:148.

97. Carrie Lena Moffett letter, 18 Feb. 1931, Andrew Allison letter, 5 Mar. 1931, Katheryne Thompson letter, 21 Sept. 1932, Marion Wilcox letter, 22 Sept. 1933, and Jane Lee letter, 2 Dec. 1933, CL.

98. Carrie Lena Moffett letter, 5 Mar. 1933, and Jane Lee letter, Aug. 1935, CL.

99. Ruth Worth, Personal Report, 1937, RWP.

100. Susan E. Hall, "History of the Woman's Auxiliary of Wilmington Presbytery, Synod of North Carolina, 1922–1938," pp. 2–3, George Worth, "A Message to Wilmington Presbyterial," [1929], and George Worth to Wilmington Presbyterial Auxiliary, 10 Feb. 1935, WPF.

101. Alex Moffett to C. Darby Fulton, 12 July 1937, and C. Darby Fulton to Charles Worth, 26 Aug. 1937, AMP.

102. Carrie Lena Moffett letter, [Shanghai, 8 Jan. 1938], CL.

103. Minutes of Joint Committee, 8 July 1937, AMP.

104. Jiangyin School Board Notes, 10 July 1937, and Alex Moffett to C. Darby Fulton, 12 July 1937, AMP.

105. Carrie Lena Moffett letter, [Shanghai, 8 Jan. 1938], CL; Chen Xikang and Chen Liangheng, "Jiangyin Lishi zhongxue jianshi," pp. 48–49.

106. Israel, *Student Nationalism*, p. 32; Lutz, "Students," pp. 313–14.

107. Masland, "Missionary Influence," p. 287.

CHAPTER SIX

1. Lacy Little, "Rays of Light," p. 303.

2. See, for example, Ruth Hemenway's experience in Fujian (Hemenway, *Memoir*, pp. 80–81).

3. Alex Moffett interview by author, Taylorsville, N.C., 10 June 1978; Lacy Little, *River-shade*, p. 18; Bulletin, 3 Feb. 1918, FPCW; Katheryne Thompson letter, 15 Dec. 1922, in *Bi-Monthly Bulletin* 13, no. 3 (Mar.–Apr. 1923): 1462; Andrew Allison letter, 18 Nov. 1928, CL.

4. Lacy Little, "Rays of Light," p. 304.

5. Bulletin, 25 Apr., 9 May 1915, FPCW.

6. Bulletin, 24 Feb. 1924, FPCW; Murphy, *Kiangyin Hospital*, pp. 7–8; Alex Moffett interview by author, Taylorsville, N.C., 10 June 1978.

7. George Worth to Wilmington Presbyterial Auxiliary, 28 Mar. 1924, WPF; Lacy Little, "Hospital Evangelism," pp. 376–77.

8. Bulletin, 26 May, 1 Dec. 1918, FPCW; *Bi-Monthly Bulletin* 11, no. 2 (Mar.–Apr. 1919): 1185.

9. Lacy Little, "Christian Propaganda," p. 393.

10. Ibid.

11. George Worth to Dr. Wells, 5 Apr. 1904, in First Presbyterian Church, Wilmington, *Manual, 1904*, p. 28.

12. *Chinese Recorder* 44, no. 4 (Apr. 1913): 255–57; *Bi-Monthly Bulletin* 6, no. 1 (Jan.–Feb. 1914): 398, and 7, no. 2 (Mar.–Apr. 1915): 617–18.

13. Bulletin, 16, 23 Mar., 23 Nov. 1919, FPCW.

14. *Bi-Monthly Bulletin* 10, no. 2 (Mar.–Apr. 1918): 1043; Bulletin, 4 May 1919, FPCW.

15. *Bi-Monthly Bulletin* 10, no. 2 (Mar.–Apr. 1918): 1042.

16. *Bi-Monthly Bulletin* 13, no. 6 (Nov.–Dec. 1923): 1537.

17. P. Frank Price, *Our China Investment*, p. 152; Ruth Worth interview by author, Wilmington, N.C., 8 Jan. 1980, in North Carolina's China Connection Archive, North Carolina China Council Papers, in possession of author.

18. Bear, "Mission Work," 3:162.

19. Bulletin, 6 June 1915, 6 June 1920, FPCW; Lacy Little, *Rivershade*, pp. 40–41; Charles Worth letter, 11 May 1929, CL.

20. *Bi-Monthly Bulletin* 11, no. 5 (Nov.–Dec. 1919): 1260–61.

21. Buck, *American Science*, pp. 106–7.

22. Frank W. Price, *Rural Church*, p. 20.

23. Lacy Moffett's journal is a 138-page pocket-size notebook that details his visits to a dozen or so market towns and nearby villages in the Jiangyin field from October 1930 to April 1941, with some gaps due to the Japanese invasion. The journal was kindly loaned to the author by his son, Alex Moffett of New York City. Charles Worth's materials include *Pioneering in China*, a four-page pamphlet printed in 1936; a 114-page manuscript, "Recollections of a Happy Life"; and some notes of country trips in the period 1930–37. His papers are in possession of his widow, Hilda Worth of Wilmington, North Carolina.

24. Lacy Moffett, Itinerating Notes, pp. 7–8, LMP.

25. Carrie Lena Moffett letter, 3 Mar. 1935, CL.

26. Marion Wilcox letter, 8 Oct. 1936, CL, reprinted in *Presbyterian Survey* 27, no. 1 (Jan. 1937): 20–21.

27. Carrie Lena Moffett letter, 3 Mar. 1935, CL.

28. Bear, "Mission Work," 2:528; *Bi-Monthly Bulletin*, o.s., 1, no. 3 (1899): 13–14; *Missionary* 37, no. 2 (Feb. 1904): 80–81; Presbyterian Church in the United States, Executive Committee of Foreign Missions, *Annual Report*, 1906, p. 27. See Wu, *International Aspect*, pp. 194–96, for several accounts of missionary skepticism about lawsuits.

29. Lacy Moffett, Itinerating Notes, pp. 13–16, LMP.

30. Wu, *International Aspect*, pp. 55–56.

31. Donald Richardson, *Church in China*, pp. 155–56.

32. Greenawalt, "Missionary Intelligence," pp. 23–24.

33. Latourette, *Christian Missions*, p. 420; Varg, *Missionaries*, p. 19.

34. Lacy Moffett letter, in Bulletin, 13 May 1923, FPCW; Emma Worth letter, 31 Mar. 1924, CL.

35. Andrew Allison letter, 15 Nov. 1946, CL.

36. Eugenie Haden, "Happy Day," p. 470.

37. Charles Worth, "Chinese Christian Church," pp. 419–20.

38. Emma Worth letter, 31 Mar. 1924, CL.

39. Lacy Moffett, Itinerating Notes, pp. 59–65, LMP; Charles Worth, "Recollections of a Happy Life," p. 32, CWP.

40. Station letters, in Bulletin, 27 Feb. 1910, 23 Apr. 1911, 29 Dec. 1912, 19 Jan. 1913, 10 Jan. 1915, 10, 17 Feb. 1918, 6 Feb. 1921, 8 Apr., 30 Dec. 1923, 26 June 1926, FPCW; Lacy Little letter, 29 May 1925, in *Monthly Messenger* 16, no. 6 (June 1925): 1709; Charles Worth letter, 18 Dec. 1930, CL.

41. Charles Worth, "Chinese Christian Church," p. 420; Lacy Moffett, Itinerating Notes, pp. 40, 41, 104, LMP.

42. Frank W. Price, *Rural Church*, p. 110.

43. Lacy Moffett, Itinerating Notes, LMP; Charles Worth, Notes Used for Sermons, CWP.

44. Latourette, *Christian Missions*, p. 414.

45. Chiang, *Tides from the West*, p. 255.

46. Emma Worth letter, in *Missionary Survey* 8, no. 2 (Feb. 1918): 99.

47. Katheryne Thompson letter, 27 July 1939, CL.

48. Andrew Allison letter, 7 Feb. 1941, CL. For similar accounts, see Andrew Allison letter, 6 Nov. 1936, and Katheryne Thompson letter, 11 Feb. 1936, CL.

49. Katheryne Thompson letter, 19 Dec. 1949, CL.

50. Lutz, *Christian Missions*, p. 15; Bi-Monthly Bulletin 3, no. 9 (July–Aug. 1909): 271.

51. Latourette, *Christian Missions*, pp. 420–21.

52. Lacy Moffett, Itinerating Notes, pp. 40, 89, LMP. See also Charles Worth letter, 11 May 1929, CL.

53. Latourette, *Christian Missions*, p. 832.

54. Andrew Allison, *How Prayer Works*, pp. 3–4.

55. Andrew Allison letters, 29 Mar., 10 Nov. 1938, and Katheryne Thompson letter, 3 Mar. 1938, CL.

56. Lacy Moffett, Itinerating Notes, p. 3, LMP.

57. Anna Sykes letter, *Bi-Monthly Bulletin* 6, no. 1 (Jan.–Mar. 1914): 402–3.

58. See, for instance, Lacy Moffett, Itinerating Notes, pp. 2, 4, 21, LMP.

59. Ibid., pp. 115–27. The 1932 total (16) was low because he stayed for an extended period in Hangzhou during the winter and spent about four summer months in the mountains.

60. Charles Worth, "Recollections of a Happy Life," p. 33, CWP.

61. Ibid.; Charles Worth letter, 11 May 1925, CL.

62. Charles Worth, "Recollections of a Happy Life," p. 55, CWP.

63. Ibid., p. 27; Charles Worth, *Pioneering in China*.

64. Charles Worth, Notes of Country Trips, 10–14 Jan. 1933, CWP.

65. *Bi-Monthly Bulletin* 7, no. 2 (Mar.–Apr. 1915): 617–18; Charles Worth, Notes of Country Trips, CWP.

66. Andrew Allison letter, 10 Nov. 1931, CL.

67. Andrew Allison letter, 8 Feb. 1940, CL.

68. Virginia Lee letter, in Bulletin, 10 Feb. 1918, FPCW.

69. Lacy Moffett, Itinerating Notes, pp. 16, 28, 72–73, LMP.

70. Ibid., pp. 15–16, 92.

71. Ibid., pp. 53–56.

72. Ibid., p. 58.

73. Donald Richardson, *Church in China*, p. 42.

74. *Bi-Monthly Bulletin* 13, no. 5 (Sept.–Oct. 1923): 1511; *Monthly Messenger* 17, no. 7 (Sept. 1926): 1828; Charles Worth letter, 21 Aug. 1930, CL.

75. Rida Jourolman letter, Feb. 1919, Scrapbook of Church History, FPCW.

76. George Worth letter, Dec. 1922, in Bulletin, 8 Apr. 1923, FPCW.

77. Marion Wilcox letter, 28 Nov. 1931, and Jane Lee letter, 27 Nov. 1932, CL.

78. Lacy Moffett, Itinerating Notes, pp. 77–78, LMP.

79. Bear, "Mission Work," 4:166–67, 5:140–41; George Worth letter, 12 Oct. 1936, in Wilmington Presbyterial Auxiliary, *Worth Memorial Booklet*, p. 14.

80. Lacy Moffett, Memoranda-Notes, LMP.

81. *Chinese Recorder* 39, no. 10 (Apr. 1908): 222–23.

CHAPTER SEVEN

1. Israel, *Student Nationalism*, chap. 3.

2. Andrew Allison letter, 10 Nov. 1931, and Jane Lee letters, 12 Nov. 1931, Shanghai, 27 Feb. 1932, CL; Lacy Moffett, Itinerating Notes, p. 57, LMP. This attitude apparently was widespread (see Varg, *Missionaries*, p. 253).

3. George Worth to Jule and Walter Sprunt, 13 Oct. 1931, Bagley Family Papers, SHC.

4. Charles Worth letter, 21 Aug. 1930, and Carrie Lena Moffett letter, 18 Feb. 1931, CL.

5. George Worth to Jule and Walter Sprunt, 13 Oct. 1931, Bagley Family Papers, SHC.

6. Jane Lee letter, 19 July 1932, CL.

7. George Worth to Wilmington Presbyterial Auxiliary, 9 Mar. 1932, WPF; George Worth to Kinfolk, 3 Apr. 1932, Bagley Family Papers, SHC.

8. Thorne, *Limits*, pp. 206–10, 274; Crowley, *Japan's Quest*, pp. 159–68.

9. George Worth to Wilmington Presbyterial Auxiliary, 9 Mar. 1932, WPF; George Worth to Kinfolk, 3 Apr. 1932, Bagley Family Papers, SHC.

10. George Worth to Kinfolk, 3 Apr. 1932, Bagley Family Papers, SHC; Jane Lee letter, Shanghai, 27 Feb. 1932, and Charles Worth letter, 11 Mar. 1932, CL; *FRUS*, 1932, 3:331–32; George Worth to Wilmington Presbyterial Auxiliary, 9 Mar. 1932, WPF.

11. George Worth to Kinfolk, 3 Apr. 1932, Bagley Family Papers, SHC.

12. Lacy Little, "Group of Chinese Martyrs."

13. Greenawalt, "Missionary Intelligence," pp. 79–84.

14. George Worth to Jule and Walter Sprunt, 13 Oct. 1931, George Worth to Belle Bagley, 29 Feb. 1932, and George Worth to Kinfolk, 3 Apr. 1932, Bagley Family Papers, SHC; Charles Worth letter, 11 Mar. 1932, CL.

15. Masland, "Missionary Influence," pp. 287, 291.

16. "The Sino-Japanese Conflict As It Looks to Us," Moganshan, 1937, AMP (emphasis in original).

17. "A Message from China to Southern Presbyterians," Shanghai, 24 Oct. 1937, AMP.

18. Andrew Allison letter, Shanghai, 29 Mar. 1938, CL.

19. Ruth Worth to Julia Worth Sprunt, Shanghai, 30 Jan. 1938, RWP.

20. Charles Worth to Dr. Gilmour, Shanghai, 7 Jan. 1938, Histories of Churches and Woman's Work in Wilmington Presbytery, FPCW.

21. Katheryne Thompson letter, 11 Feb. 1936, CL; George Worth letter, 12 Oct. 1936, in Wilmington Presbyterial Auxiliary, *Worth Memorial Booklet*, p. 15.

22. Hsu and Chang, *Sino-Japanese War*, pp. 254–56; Andrew Allison letter, 2 Oct. 1937, CL.

23. Andrew Allison letter, 2 Oct. 1937, CL; George Worth letter, 12 Oct. 1936, in Wilmington Presbyterial Auxiliary, *Worth Memorial Booklet*, p. 15.

24. Hsu and Chang, *Sino-Japanese War*, p. 211.

25. Greene, *Hsiang-Ya*, p. 96.

26. Carrie Lena Moffett letter, Shanghai, 8 Jan. 1938, CL; Alex Moffett to Jiangsu Tax Office, Moganshan, 3 Aug. 1937, AMP.

27. Marion Wilcox letter, Zhangjiacun, 22 Feb. 1938, CL. A transcript of the entire article, entitled "Christian Loyalty" and published in the *China Press* on 27 Sept. 1937, is found in the China Materials Folder, FPCW.

28. Andrew Allison letter, Jiaodian, 10 Nov. 1938, CL; Minutes of Joint Committee, RWP.

29. Marion Wilcox letter, Zhangjiacun, 22 Feb. 1938, and Andrew Allison letters, Shanghai, 29 Mar., Jiaodian, 10 Nov. 1938, CL.

30. Marion Wilcox letter, Zhangjiacun, 22 Feb. 1938, Katheryne Thompson letter, Zhangjiacun, 3 Mar. 1938, and Andrew Allison letters, Shanghai, 29 Mar., Jiaodian, 10 Nov. 1938, CL.

31. Charles Worth to Dr. Gilmour, Shanghai, 7 Jan. 1938, Histories of Churches and Woman's Work in Wilmington Presbytery, FPCW; Marion Wilcox letter, Zhangjiacun, 22 Feb. 1938, and Charles Worth letter, Shanghai, 11 Apr. 1938, CL; Ruth Worth interview, Wilmington, N.C., 8 Jan. 1980, in North Carolina's China Connection Archive, North Carolina China Council Papers, in possession of author. The estimate of damage is taken from hand-drawn maps of the station in the Lacy I. Moffett Papers, copies in possession of author.

32. Charles Worth letter, Shanghai, 11 Apr. 1938, CL.

33. Carrie Lena Moffett letter, Shanghai, 8 Jan. 1938, and Andrew Allison letter, Jiaodian, 10 Nov. 1938, CL.

34. *China Missions News Letter*, no. 95 (Feb. 1938); Ruth Worth letter, Shanghai, 30 Jan. 1938, RWP.

35. Katheryne Thompson letter, Zhangjiacun, 3 Mar. 1938, and Andrew Allison letter, Shanghai, 29 Mar. 1938, CL.

36. *China Missions News Letter*, no. 98 (May 1938).

37. Charles Worth letter, Shanghai, 11 Apr. 1938, CL; Charles Worth, "Recollections of a Happy Life," pp. 60–62, CWP; Xie, "Huaerde ho Jiangyin Fuyin yiyuan," p. 120.

38. Katheryne Thompson letter, Zhangjiacun, 15 Jan. 1938, quoted in *China Missions News Letter*, no. 95 (Feb. 1938).

39. Hsu Ts-Jing to Lacy Little, Shanghai, 15 Feb. 1939, in Susan E. Hall, "Sketch of the Woman's Auxiliary of the First Presbyterian Church, Wilmington, N.C., 1817–1934," Histories of Churches and Woman's Work in Wilmington Presbytery, FPCW; Andrew Allison letter, Jiaodian, 10 Nov. 1938, CL.

40. Katheryne Thompson letter, Jiaodian, 12 Aug. 1938, Marion Wilcox letter, Jiaodian, 12 Aug. 1938, and Andrew Allison letter, Jiaodian, 10 Nov. 1938, CL.

41. Andrew Allison letter, Jiaodian, 10 Nov. 1938, CL.

42. *Chinese Recorder* 70, no. 3 (Mar. 1939): 150, and no. 8 (Aug. 1939): 455.

43. William Chen et al. to Alex Moffett, Jiaodian, 30 May 1938, AMP; *China Missions News Letter*, no. 101 (Sept. 1939), no. 102 (Oct. 1938), and no. 104 (Dec. 1938).

44. Andrew Allison letter, Jiaodian, 10 Nov. 1938, CL.

45. Katheryne Thompson letter, Jiaodian, 12 Aug. 1938, Marion Wilcox letter, Jiaodian, 12 Aug. 1938, and Andrew Allison letter, Jiaodian, 10 Nov. 1938, CL.

46. Andrew Allison letter, Jiaodian, 10 Nov. 1938, CL.

47. Ju I-hsiung interview by author, Lexington, Va., 15 Aug. 1980.

48. Andrew Allison letters, Jiaodian, 5 July, 10 Nov. 1938, CL.

49. Katheryne Thompson letter, Jiaodian, 12 Aug. 1938, and Andrew Allison letters, Shanghai, 29 Mar., Jiaodian, 10 Nov. 1938, 6 Feb. 1939, CL.

50. Andrew Allison letter, Jiaodian, 17 Dec. 1938, and Kate and Lacy Moffett letter, Shanghai, 25 Feb. 1939, CL; *China Missions News Letter*, no. 105 (Jan. 1939).

51. Andrew Allison letters, Jiaodian, 17 Dec. 1938, 6 Feb. 1939, CL.

52. *China Missions News Letter*, no. 102 (Oct. 1938); Presbyterian Church in the United States, Executive Committee of Foreign Missions, *Minutes of the Mid-China Mission* 8, no. 3 (1938–40): 2, 4.

53. Katheryne Thompson letter, 27 July 1939, CL.

54. Kate and Lacy Moffett letter, 10 Nov. 1939, CL; Chen Xikang and Chen Liangheng, "Jiangyin Lishi zhongxue jianshi," p. 49.

55. *Circle of Prayer*.

56. Andrew Allison letters, 7 Nov. 1940, 7 Feb. 1941, CL; *China Missions News Letter*, no. 125 (Nov. 1940); Charles Worth, "Kiangyin Transformation," pp. 3–4, CWP; Presbyterian Church in the United States, Executive Committee of Foreign Missions, *Minutes of the Mid-China Mission* 8, no. 4 (1940–41): 28. The lab technician, Chen Liangheng, makes a brief reference to the attack in his article, coauthored with Yang Jinxiu, "Jiangyin xian Fuyin yiyuan jianshi," p. 61.

57. Presbyterian Church in the United States, Executive Committee of Foreign Missions, *Minutes of the Mid-China Mission* 8, no. 4 (1940–41): 5.

58. Elberton, Ga., *Observer*, 6 Sept. 1942, clipping in China Materials Folder, FPCW; Marion Wilcox circular letter, Elberton, Ga., 26 Oct. 1942, RWP; Marion Wilcox letter, 8 Jan. 1947, CL; Charles Worth, "Recollections of a Happy Life," p. 91, CWP.

59. Charles Worth, "Recollections of a Happy Life," pp. 91–92, CWP.

60. Marion Wilcox letter, 8 Jan. 1947, CL; *Presbyterian Survey* 37, no. 8 (Aug. 1947): 397–98.

61. C. Darby Fulton circular letter, Nashville, 21 May, 4 June 1946, AMP.

62. Lewis Lancaster to C. Darby Fulton, Shanghai, 8 July 1946, C. Darby Fulton circular letter, Nashville, 18 July 1946, and C. Darby Fulton to Alex Moffett, Nashville, 4 Oct. 1946, AMP.

63. Varg, *Missionaries*, p. 278.

64. Marion Wilcox letters, 24 June 1946, 8 Jan. 1947, CL.

65. Charles Worth, "Recollections of a Happy Life," p. 89, CWP; Andrew Allison letter, 16 Sept. 1946, Marion Wilcox letter, 19 Oct. 1946, and Katheryne Thompson letter, 8 May 1947, CL; Varg, *Missionaries*, p. 281; Andrew Allison to Sue [Hall], 26 Feb. 1947, China Materials Folder, FPCW; Chen Xikang and Chen Liangheng, "Jiangyin Lishi zhongxue jianshi," p. 50.

66. Marion Wilcox letter, 8 Jan. 1947, CL.

67. Katheryne Thompson letter, 19 Nov. 1948, and Marion Wilcox letter, 11 Dec. 1948, CL.

68. Marion Wilcox letters, 24 June 1946, 22 Oct. 1947, CL.

69. Marion Wilcox letters, 19, 22 Oct. 1947, and Katheryne Thompson letter, 19 Nov. 1948, CL.

70. Andrew Allison letters, 21, 29 May 1946, 13 May 1947, CL.

71. Marion Wilcox letters, 22 Oct. 1947, 31 May, 11 Dec. 1948, CL.

72. Correspondence between Alex Moffett and Mid-China Mission, 21 July, 8 Aug. 1937, AMP; Marion Wilcox letters, 31 May 1948, 20 Sept., 19 Dec. 1949, 4 Apr. 1950, CL; "News Bulletin, Sept. 1948," First Presbyterian Church, Wilmington, File, DHR.

73. Andrew Allison letter, 13 Mar. 1946, Katheryne Thompson letter, 8 May 1947, and Marion Wilcox letters, 22 Oct. 1947, 31 May 1948, CL; Andrew Allison to First Presbyterian Church, Wilmington, 13 Aug. 1948, Missions Folder, FPCW. For an overview of postwar inflation in China, see Spence, *Search for Modern China*, pp. 498–504.

74. Marion Wilcox letters, 8 Jan. 1947, 11 Dec. 1948, CL.

75. Nancy Tucker, "Unlikely Peace," pp. 99, 102–4; Bush, *Religion*, pp. 41–42.

76. Bush, *Religion*, pp. 40–41; "Message," reprinted in MacInnis, *Religious Policy*, pp. 151–56.

77. Lacy, "Missionary Exodus," p. 301; Nancy Tucker, "Unlikely Peace," pp. 109–11.

78. John Cabot Lodge memorandum, 16 Nov. 1948, Report of Sub-Committee on Fields of the Executive Committee of Foreign Missions, 14 Dec. 1948, and Minutes of Ad-Interim Committee, 18 Nov. 1948, AMP.

79. Marion Wilcox letter, 11 Dec. 1948, CL; Report of Sub-Committee on Fields of Executive Committee of Foreign Missions, 14 Dec. 1948, AMP.

80. Marion Wilcox letters, 20 Sept. 1949, 24 Nov. 1950, and Katheryne Thompson letter, 29 Dec. 1950, CL.

81. Katheryne Thompson letter, 19 Sept. 1949, and Marion Wilcox letter, 20 Sept. 1949, CL; Nancy Tucker, "Unlikely Peace," p. 107; Katheryne Thompson to Creighton Lacy, Sioux Falls, 20 Dec. 1951, in possession of Creighton Lacy.

82. Katheryne Thompson letters, 19 Sept. 1949, 4 May 1950, Marion Wilcox letter, 4 Apr. 1950, and Andrew Allison letter, Ellisville, Miss., 22 Mar. 1950, translating letter of a former student at Jiangyin, CL.

83. Katheryne Thompson letters, 19 Dec. 1949, 4 May 1950, and Marion Wilcox letter, 4 Apr. 1950, CL.

84. Reprinted in MacInnis, *Religious Policy*, pp. 27–28. See also Bush, *Religion*, pp. 77–79.

85. Yang and Chen, "Jiangyin xian Fuyin yiyuan jianshi," p. 62; Chen Xikang and Chen Liangheng, "Jiangyin Lishi zhongxue jianshi," p. 50.

86. Lacy, "Missionary Exodus," p. 302; Bush, *Religion*, pp. 44–45; MacInnis, *Religious Policy*, pp. 97–100; Jonathan Chao, "Indigenous Church Movement," p. 284.

87. Bush, *Religion*, pp. 45–46; Lacy, "Missionary Exodus," p. 302.

88. Marion Wilcox letter, 24 Nov. 1950, CL.

89. Marion Wilcox letter, 1 Jan. 1951, and Katheryne Thompson letter, 29 Dec. 1950–1 Jan. 1951, CL. On the Christmas celebrations, see also Katheryne Thompson, "Christmas Carols," p. 20.

90. Katheryne Thompson to Creighton Lacy, Sioux Falls, 20 Dec. 1951, in possession of Creighton Lacy. The two women arrived back in the United States on 20 June (*Presbyterian Survey* 41, no. 8 [Aug. 1951]: 60).

CHAPTER EIGHT

1. Chester, *Behind the Scenes*, p. 39; Ernest Thompson, *Presbyterians in the South*, 3: 126–27; Stuart, *Fifty Years*, pp. 30–33; Shaw, *American Missionary*, pp. 18–19.

2. Lacy Little, *Rivershade*, p. 33; First Presbyterian Church, Wilmington, *Handbook, 1892–1913*, pp. 14, 17–18; Mrs. J. A. Brown, *Wilmington Presbyterial Auxiliary*, p. 73; Bulletin, 4 Oct. 1908, 30 May 1909, 23 Apr. 1911, FPCW.

3. Julia Sprunt to Reverend Crowe, Wilmington, 22 Aug. 1947, Histories of Churches and Woman's Work in Wilmington Presbytery, FPCW.

4. Bulletin, 17 Apr. 1921, FPCW.

5. See explanation in Bulletin, 2 Oct. 1910, FPCW.

6. *North Carolina Presbyterian*, 2 Apr. 1896; "Testimonial to Dr. Worth," Histories of Churches and Woman's Work in Wilmington Presbytery, FPCW.

7. See correspondence between Reverend Crowe of the First Presbyterian Church and the Executive Committee of Foreign Missions, 28 Apr., 5 May 1943, 25 Feb., 11 Mar. 1946, Sessional Records, FPCW; Alex Moffett interview by author, Taylorsville, N.C., 10 June 1978.

8. Wilmington *Morning Star*, [10 July 1924], quoted in *James Sprunt*, p. 109.

9. *James Sprunt*, pp. 35, 39–40; James Sprunt to Fred Olds, Wilmington, 12 Feb. 1910, ASSP. For an account of the firm's business operations, see Killick, "Transformation of Cotton Marketing."

10. George Rountree to James Sprunt, 10 Apr. 1909, ASSP.

11. While Taft was in Wilmington, Sprunt also loaned his car, reputedly the grandest in the city, to the president's party (see correspondence between James Sprunt and James Chadbourn, Wilmington, 29 Sept., 1 Oct. 1909, ASSP).

12. *James Sprunt*, pp. 27–28; Hall, *She Was All Love*, p. 16.

13. First Presbyterian Church, Wilmington, *Handbook, 1892–1913*, p. 17; J. Campbell White to James Sprunt, Greensboro, 19 May 1908, ASSP.

14. See Robert Speer to Reverend McClure, 23 May 1908, D. L. Pierson to Reverend McClure, 25 May 1908, and J. Campbell White to James Sprunt, 27 May 1908, 1 Mar. 1909, ASSP.

15. James Sprunt to Mrs. J. Campbell White, Wilmington, 1 Mar. 1920, ASSP.

16. James Sprunt to Edwin Willis, Wilmington, 10 Dec. 1919, ASSP.

17. Bulletin, 16 Nov. 1919, FPCW. See also Bulletin, 26 Jan. 1919, 6, 13 June, 5 Dec. 1920, FPCW.

18. William Sprunt, Jr., letter, 23 Jan. 1921, quoted in Bulletin, 27 Feb. 1921, FPCW and in Wilmington Presbyterial Auxiliary, *Minutes*, 1921, pp. 18–19; James Sprunt to Dr. Wells, Wilmington, 28 Feb. 1921, and William Sprunt, Jr., to James Sprunt, Suzhou, 4 Mar. 1921, ASSP. Worth bought his X-ray machine in 1922, as previously noted, while in the United States on furlough with funds provided by the Jiangyin gentry (Katheryne Thompson letter, 15 Dec. 1922, in *Bi-Monthly Bulletin* 13, no. 3 [Mar.–Apr. 1923]: 1462).

19. Balme, *China and Modern Medicine*, pp. 104–5.

20. George Worth to James Sprunt, 6 Apr. 1921, and James Sprunt to George Worth, Wilmington, 9 May 1921, ASSP.

21. Bulletin, 2 Mar. 1913, FPCW.

22. James Sprunt to Mrs. J. Campbell White, Wilmington, 1 Mar. 1920, ASSP.

23. In 1910 and 1911, he contributed $3,000 a year (Private Ledgers, ASSP), but by the end of the decade, the annual amount was $5,000 (James Sprunt to Edwin Willis, Wilmington, 10 Dec. 1919, J. C. Williams to James Sprunt, Wilmington, 21 Oct. 1920, 4 Oct. 1921, and Private Ledger, 1922, ASSP).

24. Bulletin, 10 Mar. 1912, 25 Jan. 1914, FPCW; Lacy Little, *Our Kiangyin Schools*, p. 3; Bear, "Mission Work," 5:142; Virginia Lee letter, 10 July 1923, CL.

25. James Sprunt to Alexander Sprunt, Wilmington, 14 July 1919, ASSP.

26. Charles Worth, "Recollections of a Happy Life," p. 24, CWP.

27. *James Sprunt*, pp. 63–64.

28. W. H. Sprunt to Dr. Gilmour, Wilmington, 12 Sept. 1924, Sessional Records, FPCW; "Sessional Letter" to First Presbyterian Church congregation, 8 Mar. 1925, Dr. James Sprunt Folder, FPCW.

29. Correspondence between Walter Sprunt and Reverend Gilmour, Wilmington, 1, 7, 31 Dec. 1937, 14 Jan., 1 Feb. 1938, Sessional Records, FPCW.

30. Greenawalt, "Missionary Intelligence," pp. 4–5. This study is based on thousands of circular letters written by missionaries of six denominations and one interdenominational board that together sent about 70 percent of all American Protestant missionaries to China in the 1930s and 1940s.

31. Virginia Lee letter, "White and Gold," received at Nashville, Apr. 1920, CL.

32. Charles Worth letter, 26 Nov. 1936, in Wilmington Presbyterial Auxiliary, *Worth Memorial Booklet*, p. 10. For an assessment of missionaries' interpretive abilities, see Greenawalt, "Missionary Intelligence," pp. 12–13.

33. First Presbyterian Church, Wilmington, *Manual*, 1904, pp. 24–30.

34. See, for example, Bulletin, 25 Oct. 1908, FPCW.

35. The First Presbyterian Church has nearly complete sets of bulletins from eighteen years of this twenty-three-year period. The exceptions are 1916 and 1917 bulletins, of which only one or two are available, and 1927, 1928, and 1930 bulletins, of which only about half have been preserved. The average figure given in the text is based on the eighteen years from which all or nearly all bulletins are available.

36. For instance, see Bulletin, 29 Dec. 1912, FPCW.

37. Bulletin, 14 Feb. 1926, FPCW.

38. Lacy Moffett letter, 5 Oct. 1922, in Bulletin, 19 Nov. 1922, FPCW.

39. Bulletin, 29 Nov. 1908 (curios), 16 Jan. 1910 (map), 5 Mar. 1911 (banner), 19 Jan. 1913 (photographs), FPCW.

40. Alexander Sprunt to James Sprunt, Charleston, 21 Nov. 1921, ASSP. John Rawlinson has given a detailed account of the activities of his father on home leave in "Frank Raw-

linson." See also Reed, *Missionary Mind*, pp. 24–26, for a comment on the role of furloughs in mission work.

41. Bulletin, 5 Feb. 1911, FPCW.

42. Wilmington Presbyterial Auxiliary, *Worth Memorial Booklet*, p. 18; George Worth to Wilmington Presbyterial Auxiliary, 10 Feb. 1935, WPF.

43. A copy of this film, made in 1939–40, was given to the author by Ruth Worth.

44. Bulletin, 26 Apr. 1936, Scrapbook of Church History, FPCW.

45. Lacy Little, *Rivershade*, pp. 33–34; Bulletin, 1 Dec. 1929, FPCW.

46. See, for example, Andrew Allison to James Sprunt, 19 Sept. 1917, ASSP.

47. First Presbyterian Church, Wilmington, *Record and Manual*, 1895–1896, pp. 15–16.

48. Andrew Howell, *First Presbyterian Church*, p. 12.

49. Centennial Anniversary Program, 1–8 Apr. 1917, First Presbyterian Church, Wilmington, File, DHR.

50. Kate and Lacy Moffett letter, 1 Apr. 1922, CL.

51. George Worth to Julia Worth Sprunt, Oct. 1931, Bagley Family Papers, SHC.

52. Bulletin, 13 June 1909, FPCW.

53. Bulletin, 3 Feb. 1918, FPCW.

54. Beaver, *American Protestant Women*, pp. 25, 87–88; Keller, "Lay Women," pp. 242–43.

55. Keller, "Lay Women," p. 264 (emphasis in original).

56. Beaver, *American Protestant Women*, p. 54; Montgomery, *Western Women*, pp. 243–44.

57. Keller, "Lay Women," p. 245.

58. Ernest Thompson, *Presbyterians in the South*, 3:384–88; Winsborough, *Woman's Auxiliary*, pp. 18–19; Boyd and Brackenridge, *Presbyterian Women*, pp. 217–18.

59. Ernest Thompson, *Presbyterians in the South*, 3:389–91; Winsborough, *Woman's Auxiliary*, pp. 19–26; Boyd and Brackenridge, *Presbyterian Women*, pp. 218–21. The 1913 figures are taken from the Presbyterian Church in the United States, *Minutes of General Assembly*, 1913, p. 70e.

60. Jennie Hanna to Margaret Sprunt Hall, Kansas City, 28 Dec. 1887, 18 Jan. 1888, MSHP.

61. Mrs. J. A. Brown, *Wilmington Presbyterial Auxiliary*, pp. 16–19; Margaret Sprunt Hall, "Sketch of Woman's Foreign Missionary Union of Wilmington Presbytery," 1911, p. 1, WPF.

62. Minutes of Woman's Foreign Missionary Committee, 1890, MSHP; Mrs. J. A. Brown, *Wilmington Presbyterial Auxiliary*, pp. 22–23, 47.

63. Wilmington Presbyterial Auxiliary, *Minutes*, 1912, pp. 3–9.

64. Ibid., 1926, p. 13.

65. Jourolman, *Little Golden Sister*.

66. Mrs. J. A. Brown, *Wilmington Presbyterial Auxiliary*, p. 70.

67. Wilmington Presbyterial Auxiliary, *Minutes*, 1925, p. 21. Fees paid directly by patients offset about 70–75 percent of the hospital's total expenses in the 1920s (Wilmington Presbyterial Auxiliary, *Minutes*, 1922, p. 2; George Worth to Wilmington Presbyterial Auxiliary, 28 Mar. 1924, WPF; Murphy, *Kiangyin Hospital*, p. 8).

68. Copy of article in China Materials Folder, FPCW.

69. Wilmington Presbyterial Auxiliary, *Minutes*, 1907, pp. 19–20; Bulletin, 13 Oct. 1907, 30 Apr. 1922, FPCW.

70. George Worth to Mrs. Howell, 26 Apr. 1934, George Worth Memorials and Letters Folder, FPCW.

71. George Worth to Wilmington Presbyterial Auxiliary, 7 Aug. 1936, in Wilmington Presbyterial Auxiliary, *Worth Memorial Booklet*, p. 6.

72. Susan Hall, "Memorial Paper," in Wilmington Presbyterial Auxiliary, *Worth Memorial Booklet*, p. 33.

73. Wilmington Presbyterial Auxiliary, *Minutes*, 1935, p. 13; George Worth to Wilmington Presbyterial Auxiliary, 10 Feb. 1935, WPF.

74. Wilmington Presbyterial Auxiliary, *Minutes*, 1937, p. 18.

75. Ibid., 1913, p. 17.

76. Julia Worth Sprunt to C. Darby Fulton, Wilmington, 7 Mar. 1953, LMP.

77. Wilmington Presbyterial Auxiliary, *Minutes*, 1911, p. 5.

78. Mrs. J. A. Brown, *Wilmington Presbyterial Auxiliary*, p. 55.

79. George Worth to Mrs. W. P. M. Currie, 9 June 1932, George Worth Memorials and Letters Folder, FPCW.

80. Wilmington Presbyterial Auxiliary, *Minutes*, 1933, p. 13.

81. Rabe, *Home Base*, pp. 144–45.

82. William Chen and H. Chang to Wilmington Presbyterial Auxiliary, 25 Feb. 1929, in Wilmington Presbyterial Auxiliary, *Minutes*, 1929, p. 25.

83. Ibid., 1938, p. 16; Minutes of Executive Committee of Wilmington Presbyterial Auxiliary, 4 Feb. 1936, RWP.

84. Wilmington Presbyterial Auxiliary, *Minutes*, 1927, p. 24.

85. *Chinese Recorder* 58, nos. 5–6 (May–June 1927): 335.

86. Lobenstine, "Mission and Church," p. 194.

87. Julia Worth Sprunt letter, Wilmington, 16 Feb. 1942, China Materials Folder, FPCW; Wilmington Presbyterial Auxiliary, *Minutes*, 1942, p. 21, and 1948, pp. 20–21.

88. Yang and Chen, "Jiangyin xian Fuyin yiyuan jianshi," p. 62.

89. Ruth Worth to Julia Worth Sprunt, Bulape, Congo, 20 Feb. 1953, and Julia Worth Sprunt to C. Darby Fulton, Wilmington, 7 Mar. 1953, LMP; Wilmington Presbyterial Auxiliary, *Minutes*, 1954, pp. 24–26.

90. George Worth to Wilmington Presbyterial Auxiliary, 10 Feb. 1935, WPF; Minutes of Executive Committee of Wilmington Presbyterial Auxiliary, 4 Feb. 1936, RWP.

CHAPTER NINE

1. David Z. T. Yui, "The Needs of the Christian Movement," in Chao Tzu-ch'en et al., *China Today*, p. 148.

2. A. R. Kepler, "The Need for a Changed Approach to the People in Our Missionary Enterprise," *Chinese Recorder* 51, no. 1 (Jan. 1920), quoted in Lutz, *Christian Missions*, p. 19.

3. Hopkins, *Social Gospel*, p. 140.

4. Schlesinger, "Missionary Enterprise," pp. 350–55; Hutchison, *Errand to the World*, pp. 80–82.

5. Hyatt, "Protestant Missions," p. 94.

6. Feuerwerker, *Foreign Establishment*, p. 43; Hunter, *Gospel of Gentility*, pp. 9–10.

7. Balme, *China and Modern Medicine*, p. 32.

8. Hutchison, *Errand to the World*, p. 101.

9. This point was brought to my attention by Daniel Bays, who developed it in an unpublished paper on American Pentecostal missionaries to China presented at a conference at Fuller Theological Seminary in March 1994.

10. See Schlesinger, "Missionary Enterprise."

11. Buck, *American Science*, pp. 13–21.

12. China Educational Commission, *Christian Education*, p. 36.

BIBLIOGRAPHY

MANUSCRIPT SOURCES

Chapel Hill, North Carolina

North Carolina's China Connection Archive, North Carolina China Council Papers, in
  possession of author
Southern Historical Collection, Wilson Library, University of North Carolina
  Bagley Family Papers

Durham, North Carolina

Manuscript Collection, Perkins Library, Duke University
  Alexander Sprunt and Son Papers

Montreat, North Carolina

Department of History and Records, Presbyterian Church (U.S.A.)
  China Letters, 1919–51, Missionary Correspondence Department, Board of World
    Missions, Presbyterian Church in the United States
  First Presbyterian Church, Wilmington, File
  Margaret T. Sprunt Hall Papers
  Kiangyin Station Photographs, Presbyterian Church in the United States Missions,
    China
  Lacy L. Little Papers
  Wilmington Presbyterial Files, Women of the Church Synodical and Presbyterial
    Collection

Wilmington, North Carolina

First Presbyterian Church
  Bulletin, 1906–15, 1918–30, 1950
  China Materials Folder
  Church History Folder
  Histories of Churches and Woman's Work in Wilmington Presbytery
  Minutes of the Woman's Auxiliary, 1919–34
  Missions Folder
  Scrapbook of Church History, 1886–1938
  Sessional Records, 1914–51
  Dr. James Sprunt Folder
  Mrs. George C. Worth Folder
  George Worth Memorials and Letters Folder

Private Papers

Alex Moffett Papers. Copies in possession of author.
Lacy I. Moffett Papers. Copies in possession of author.
Charles W. Worth Papers. In possession of Mrs. Charles W. Worth, Wilmington, N.C.
Ruth Worth Papers. Copies in possession of author.

INTERVIEWS

Ju I-hsiung. Interview by author. Lexington, Va., 15 August 1980.
Moffett, Alex. Interview by author. Taylorsville, N.C., 10 June 1978.
Worth, Ruth. Interviews by author. Wilmington, N.C., 12 August 1977, 10 December 1982.

PERIODICALS

Bi-Monthly Bulletin, 1898–99, 1905–24 (*Monthly Messenger*, 1925–27)
China Mission Year Book, 1910–25 (*China Christian Year Book*, 1926–40)
China Missions News Letter, 1930–41
Chinese Recorder, 1868–1941
Far Eastern Bulletin, 1941–43
Jiangsu wenxian (Historical materials of Jiangsu province), 1977–88
Jiangyin wenshi ziliao (Jiangyin historical materials), 1983–88
Journal of Presbyterian History, 1962–84 (*American Presbyterians*, 1984–89)
Missionary, 1868–1911 (*Missionary Survey*, 1911–24; *Presbyterian Survey*, 1924–51)

BOOKS, PAMPHLETS, ARTICLES, AND DISSERTATIONS

Abend, Hallett. *Treaty Ports*. Garden City, N.Y.: Doubleday, Doran, and Company, 1944.
Allison, Andrew. "An Entertainment for the Famine Fund: A Remarkable Evening at Kiangyin, China." *Missionary* 44, no. 7 (July 1911): 343–44.
———. *How Prayer Works in Mid-China*. Nashville: Presbyterian Church in the United States, Executive Committee of Foreign Missions, n.d.
———. "President Yuan Shih-k'ai's Message to the Nation Regarding the Sacrifice to Confucius." *Missionary Survey* 5, no. 3 (March 1915): 195.
———. "Strike! for Your Native Land." *Missionary Survey* 10, no. 8 (October 1920): 633–35.
———. "War Experiences at Kiangyin, China." *Presbyterian Survey* 15, no. 6 (June 1925): 374–76, 15, no. 7 (July 1925): 417–18.
———. "A Young Timothy — Kiangyin." *Monthly Messenger* 17, no. 10 (December 1926): 1867–68.
[Allison, Ella Ward]. "Opening of the Woman's Hospital." *Missionary Survey* 6, no. 5 (May 1916): 335–39.
Arnold, Julean. "China's Economic Problems and Christian Missionary Effort." *Chinese Recorder* 50, no. 8 (August 1919): 515–24.

Austin, Alvyn J. *Saving China: Canadian Missionaries in the Middle Kingdom, 1888–1959.* Toronto: University of Toronto Press, 1986.

Ballou, Earle H. *Dangerous Opportunity: The Christian Mission in China Today.* New York: Friendship Press, 1940.

Balme, Harold. *The Awakening of China in Relation to the Modern Missionary Program.* London: Baptist Laymen's Missionary Movement, [1921].

———. *China and Modern Medicine: A Study in Medical Missionary Development.* London: United Council for Missionary Education, 1921.

———. *What Is Happening in China?* London: Edinburgh House Press, 1925.

Barnett, Eugene E. "As I Look Back: Recollections of Growing Up in America's Southland and of Twenty-six Years in Pre-Communist China, 1888–1936." Unpublished manuscript, n.d.

Barnett, Suzanne W. "Protestant Expansion and Chinese Views of the West." *Modern Asian Studies* 6, no. 2 (April 1972): 129–49.

Bastid, Marianne. *Educational Reform in Early Twentieth-Century China.* Translated by Paul J. Bailey. Ann Arbor: University of Michigan Center for Chinese Studies, 1988.

Bays, Daniel. "Christianity and Chinese Sects: Religious Tracts in the Late Nineteenth Century." In *Christianity in China: Early Protestant Missionary Writings,* edited by Suzanne W. Barnett and John K. Fairbank, pp. 121–34. Cambridge: Harvard University Committee on American–East Asian Relations, 1985.

———. "Christianity and the Chinese Sectarian Tradition." *Ch'ing-shih wen-t'i* 4, no. 7 (June 1982): 33–55.

Beahan, Charlotte L. "Missionaries and Social Change in China, 1874–1905." Unpublished manuscript, 1980.

Bear, James E. "The Mission Work of the Presbyterian Church in the United States in China, 1867–1952." 5 vols. Unpublished manuscript, 1963–73.

Beaver, R. Pierce, ed. *American Missions in Bicentennial Perspective.* South Pasadena, Calif.: William Carey Library, 1977.

———. *American Protestant Women in World Mission: History of the First Feminist Movement in North America.* Grand Rapids, Mich.: William B. Eerdmans, 1980.

Bell, Richard M. "Southern Presbyterian Missionaries to China, 1867–1952: An Historical Assessment." Master's thesis, University of Tennessee, 1970.

Bennett, Adrian A., and Kwang-ching Liu. "Christianity in the Chinese Idiom: Young J. Allen and the Early Chiao-hui hsin-pao, 1868–1870." In *The Missionary Enterprise in China and America,* edited by John K. Fairbank, pp. 159–96. Cambridge: Harvard University Press, 1974.

Blair, J. Mercer. "A Year in the Mid-China Mission." *Missionary* 35, no. 2 (February 1902): 71–79.

Blair, Karen. *The Clubwoman as Feminist: True Womanhood Redefined, 1868–1914.* New York: Holmes and Meier, 1980.

Borg, Dorothy. *American Policy and the Chinese Revolution, 1925–1928.* New York: American Institute of Pacific Relations, 1947.

Borthwick, Sally. *Education and Social Change in China.* Stanford, Calif.: Hoover Institution Press, 1983.

Boyd, Lois A., and R. Douglas Brackenridge. *Presbyterian Women in America.* Westport, Conn.: Greenwood Press for the Presbyterian Historical Society, 1983.

Breslin, Thomas A. *China, American Catholicism, and the Missionary*. University Park: Pennsylvania State University Press, 1980.

Brown, G. Thompson. "Overseas Mission Program and Policies of the Presbyterian Church in the U.S., 1861–1983." *American Presbyterians* 65, no. 2 (Summer 1987): 157–70.

Brown, Mrs. J. A. *History of Wilmington Presbyterial Auxiliary, 1888–1922*. Raleigh: Edwards and Broughton, 1923.

Brown, William A. "The Protestant Movement in China (1920–1937)." In *American Missionaries in China: Papers from Harvard Seminars*, edited by Kwang-ching Liu, pp. 217–48. Cambridge: Harvard University East Asian Research Center, 1966.

Brumberg, Joan Jacobs. *Mission for Life: The Story of the Family of Adoniram Judson*. New York: Free Press, 1980.

Buck, Peter. *American Science and Modern China, 1876–1936*. Cambridge: Cambridge University Press, 1980.

Burke, James. *My Father in China*. New York: Farrar and Rinehart, 1942.

Burns, Richard D. *Guide to American Foreign Relations since 1700*. Santa Barbara, Calif.: ABC-Clio for Society of Historians of American Foreign Policy, 1983.

Bush, Richard C. *Religion in Communist China*. Nashville: Abingdon Press, 1970.

Butterfield, Fox. "A Missionary View of the Chinese Communists (1936–1939)." In *American Missionaries in China: Papers from Harvard Seminars*, edited by Kwang-ching Liu, pp. 249–301. Cambridge: Harvard University East Asian Research Center, 1966.

The Cambridge History of China. Vol. 12, *Republican China, 1912–1949*, part 1, edited by John K. Fairbank. Cambridge: Cambridge University Press, 1983.

Carpenter, Joel A., and Wilbert R. Shenk, eds. *Earthen Vessels: American Evangelicals and Foreign Missions, 1880–1980*. Grand Rapids, Mich.: William B. Eerdmans, 1990.

Carter, Paul A. *The Decline and Revival of the Social Gospel: Social and Political Liberalism in American Protestant Churches, 1920–1940*. Ithaca: Cornell University Press, 1954.

Chan, F. Gilbert, and Thomas H. Etzold, eds. *China in the 1920s: Nationalism and Revolution*. New York: New Viewpoints, 1976.

Chang, C. S. "The Anti-Religion Movement." *Chinese Recorder* 54, no. 4 (April 1923): 459–67.

Chao, Jonathan. *A Bibliography of the History of Christianity in China*. Waltham, Mass.: China Graduate School of Theology, 1970.

———. "The Chinese Indigenous Church Movement, 1919–1927: A Protestant Response to the Anti-Christian Movements in Modern China." Ph.D. dissertation, University of Pennsylvania, 1986.

Chao Tzu-ch'en et al. *China Today through Chinese Eyes*. 2d ser. London: Student Christian Movement, 1926.

Chapman, Herbert Owen. *The Chinese Revolution, 1926–1927*. London: Constable, 1928.

Ch'en, Jerome. *China and the West: Society and Culture, 1815–1937*. Bloomington: Indiana University Press, 1979.

———. *The Military-Gentry Coalition: China under the Warlords*. Toronto: University of Toronto–York University Joint Center on Modern East Asia, 1979.

Chen Liangheng. "Jiangyin xian Jidujiao shilue" (Historical sketch of Christianity in Jiangyin County). *Jiangyin wenshi ziliao*, no. 4 (1983): 103–5.

Chen Xikang and Chen Liangheng. "Jiangyin Lishi zhongxue jianshi" (Brief history of Jiangyin's James Sprunt Academy). *Jiangyin wenshi ziliao*, no. 5 (1984): 46–50.

Chester, Samuel H. *Behind the Scenes: An Administrative History of the Foreign Mission Work of the Presbyterian Church in the United States*. Austin: Von Boeckmann–Jones Press, 1928.

———. *Lights and Shadows of Mission Work in the Far East*. Richmond: Presbyterian Committee of Publication, 1899.

———. *Medical Missions in China*. Nashville: Presbyterian Church in the United States, Executive Committee of Foreign Missions, n.d.

Cheung, Yuet-Wah. *Missionary Medicine in China: A Study of Two Canadian Protestant Missions in China before 1937*. Lanham, Md.: University Press of America, 1988.

Cheung, Yuet-Wah, and Peter Kong-ming New. "Toward a Typology of Missionary Medicine." *Culture* 3, no. 2 (1983): 31–45.

Ch'i, Hsi-sheng. *Warlord Politics in China, 1916–1928*. Stanford, Calif.: Stanford University Press, 1976.

Chiang Monlin. *Tides from the West: A Chinese Autobiography*. New Haven: Yale University Press, 1947.

China Educational Commission. *Christian Education in China*. New York: Foreign Missions Conference of North America, 1922.

"China Missions in History." Special issue of *Journal of Presbyterian History* 49, no. 4 (1971).

Chinese National Association for the Advancement of Education. *Bulletin*, vol. 2. Peking, 1923.

Choa, G. H. *"Heal the Sick" Was Their Motto: The Protestant Medical Missionaries in China*. Hong Kong: Chinese University Press, 1990.

Chong, Key Ray. *American and Chinese Reform and Revolution, 1898–1922: The Role of Private Citizens in Diplomacy*. Lanham, Md.: University Press of America, 1984.

Circle of Prayer, for the Blessing of Church of Kiangyin, China. Shanghai: Committee for Restoring Kiangyin Church, 1940.

Clifford, Nicholas R. *Shanghai, 1925: Urban Nationalism and the Defense of Foreign Privilege*. Ann Arbor: University of Michigan Center for Chinese Studies, 1979.

Cohen, Warren I. *The Chinese Connection: Roger S. Greene, Thomas W. Lamont, George E. Sokolsky, and American–East Asian Relations*. New York: Columbia University Press, 1978.

———, ed. *New Frontiers in American–East Asian Relations*. New York: Columbia University Press, 1983.

Coleman, Michael C. "Presbyterian Missionary Attitudes toward China and the Chinese, 1837–1900." *Journal of Presbyterian History* 56, no. 3 (Fall 1978): 185–200.

Corley, Florence F. "Go Home, Foreign Devils!: Christian Missionary Activity and the Anti-Christian Movement in Twentieth Century China." Unpublished manuscript, 1984.

Correll, Emily Clare Newby. "Woman's Work for Woman: The Methodist and Baptist Woman's Missionary Societies in North Carolina, 1878–1930." Master's thesis, University of North Carolina, 1977.

Crabtree, Loren W. "Christianity and Revolution: J. Harry Giffin, an American Baptist in South China, 1904–1934." Western Conference of the Association for Asian Studies, *Selected Papers in Asian Studies*, no. 15 (1984): 15–27.

Crane, Sophie M. "A Century of PCUS Medical Mission, 1881–1983." *American Presbyterians* 65, no. 2 (Summer 1987): 135–46.

Crowley, James B. *Japan's Quest for Autonomy.* Princeton, N.J.: Princeton University
Press, 1966.

Cumming, W. C. *How Mission School Students Spend Sunday.* Nashville: Presbyterian
Church in the United States, Executive Committee of Foreign Missions, 1925.

Daggett, Mrs. L. H., ed. *Historical Sketches of Woman's Missionary Societies in America
and England.* Boston, 1879.

"Data Respecting the Christian Schools and Colleges of China: Kiangyin High School
for Boys." Typescript, 1909.

Davids, Jules, ed. *American Diplomatic and Public Papers: The United States and China:
The Sino-Japanese War to the Russo-Japanese War, 1894–1905.* Vol. 2, *Missionary Affairs and Anti-Foreign Riots.* Wilmington, Del.: Scholarly Resources, 1982.

Dean, Britten. "Sino-American Relations in the Late Nineteenth Century: The View
from the Tsungli Yamen Archive." *Ch'ing-shih wen-t'i* 4, no. 5 (June 1981): 77–107.

Djung, Lu-dzai. *A History of Democratic Education in Modern China.* Shanghai: Commercial Press, 1934.

DuBose, Hampden C. *Preaching in Sinim; or the Gospel to the Gentiles.* Richmond:
Presbyterian Committee of Publication, 1893.

Duiker, William J. *Cultures in Collision: The Boxer Rebellion.* San Rafael, Calif.: Pre-
sidio Press, 1978.

Fairbank, John K. "Assignment for the '70's." *American Historical Review* 74, no. 3 (February 1969): 861–79.

———. *Chinese-American Interactions: A Historical Summary.* New Brunswick, N.J.:
Rutgers University Press, 1975.

———, ed. *The Missionary Enterprise in China and America.* Cambridge: Harvard University Press, 1974.

Feuerwerker, Albert. *The Foreign Establishment in China in the Early Twentieth Century.* Ann Arbor: University of Michigan Center for Chinese Studies, 1976.

Field, James E., Jr. "Near East Notes and Far East Queries." In *The Missionary Enterprise in China and America,* edited by John K. Fairbank, pp. 23–55. Cambridge: Harvard University Press, 1974.

First Presbyterian Church, Wilmington. *Handbook, 1892–1913.* N.p., [1913].

———. *Manual, 1904.* N.p., [1904].

———. *Memorial of the First Presbyterian Church, Wilmington, N.C.: Seventy-fifth Anniversary, 1817–1892.* Richmond: Whittet and Shepperson, 1893.

———. *Record and Manual, 1895–1896.* N.p., 1896.

Fitch, George. *My 80 Years in China.* Taipei, 1967.

Flemming, Leslie A., ed. *Women's Work for Women: Missionaries and Social Change in
Asia.* Boulder, Colo.: Westview Press, 1989.

Forman, Charles W. "A History of Foreign Mission Theory." In *American Missions in Bicentennial Perspective,* edited by R. Pierce Beaver, pp. 69–140. South Pasadena, Calif.:
William Carey Library, 1977.

Forsythe, Sidney A. *An American Missionary Community in China, 1895–1905.* Cambridge: Harvard University East Asian Research Center, 1971.

Garrett, Shirley. *Social Reformers in Urban China: The Chinese YMCA, 1895–1926.*
Cambridge: Harvard University Press, 1970.

———. "Why They Stayed: American Church Politics and Chinese Nationalism in the Twenties." In *The Missionary Enterprise in China and America*, edited by John K. Fairbank, pp. 283–310. Cambridge: Harvard University Press, 1974.

Gewurtz, Margo S. "Do Numbers Count?: A Report on a Preliminary Study of the Christian Converts of the North Henan Mission, 1890–1925." *Republican China* 10, no. 3 (June 1985): 18–26.

Greenawalt, Bruce S. "Missionary Intelligence from China: American Protestant Reports, 1930–1950." Ph.D. dissertation, University of North Carolina, 1974.

Greene, Ruth Altman. *Hsiang-Ya Journal*. Hamden, Conn.: Shoe String Press for Yale China Association, 1977.

Gregg, Alice H. *China and Educational Autonomy: The Changing Role of the Protestant Educational Missionary in China, 1807–1937*. Syracuse: Syracuse University Press, 1946.

Haden, Eugenie H. "Glimpses of the Work in Kiangyin." *Missionary* 30, no. 8 (August 1897): 361–62.

———. "A Happy Day at Chen San Church." *Missionary* 39, no. 10 (October 1906): 468–70.

Haden, R. A. "Encouragements at Kiangyin." *Missionary* 31, no. 6 (June 1898): 264–65.

———. "Kiangyin Station: Organization and Subsequent History." *Missionary* 40, no. 4 (April 1907): 177–79.

Hall, Susan E. *She Was All Love*. Wilmington, N.C.: James L. Sprunt, 1961.

Hanna, Jennie, comp. *A Brief Statement of the Work Which Resulted in the Organization of the Woman's Auxiliary of the Presbyterian Church, U.S.* N.p., 1912.

Heininger, Janet E. "Private Positions versus Public Policy: Chinese Devolution and the American Experience in East Asia." *Diplomatic History* 6, no. 3 (Summer 1982): 287–302.

Hemenway, Ruth V. *A Memoir of Revolutionary China, 1924–1941*. Amherst: University of Massachusetts Press, 1977.

Hersey, John. *The Call*. New York: Penguin Books, 1986.

Hill, Patricia R. *The World Their Household: The American Woman's Foreign Mission Movement and Cultural Transformation, 1870–1920*. Ann Arbor: University of Michigan Press, 1985.

Hobart, Alice Tisdale. *By the City of the Long Sand: A Tale of New China*. New York: Macmillan, 1926.

Hogg, W. Richie. "The Role of American Protestantism in World Mission." In *American Missions in Bicentennial Perspective*, edited by R. Pierce Beaver, pp. 354–402. South Pasadena, Calif.: William Carey Library, 1977.

Hopkins, Charles H. *The Rise of the Social Gospel in American Protestantism, 1865–1915*. New Haven: Yale University Press, 1940.

Howell, Andrew J. *First Presbyterian Church, Wilmington, North Carolina: History*. Wilmington, N.C.: First Presbyterian Church History Committee, 1951.

Howell, Gertrude J. *The Woman's Auxiliary of the Synod of North Carolina, 1912–1937*. Wilmington, N.C.: Executive Board of the [North Carolina] Synod, [1938].

Hoyt, Frederick B. "Protection Implies Intervention: The U.S. Catholic Mission at Kanchow." *Historian* 38, no. 4 (1976): 709–27.

Hsu Long-hsuen and Chang Ming-kai, comps. *History of the Sino-Japanese War*. Taipei: Chung Wu Publishing Company, 1971.

Hudson, George A. "The Southern Presbyterian Church in China (1867–1942)." Ph.D. dissertation, Union Theological Seminary, 1946.

Hume, Edward H. *Doctors East, Doctors West: An American Physician's Life in China.* New York: W. W. Norton, 1946.

Hunt, Michael H. *The Making of a Special Relationship: The United States and China to 1914.* New York: Columbia University Press, 1983.

———. "New Insights but No New Vistas: Recent Work on Nineteenth-Century American–East Asian Relations." In *New Frontiers in American–East Asian Relations,* edited by Warren I. Cohen, pp. 17–43. New York: Columbia University Press, 1983.

Hunter, Jane. *The Gospel of Gentility: American Women in Turn-of-the-Century China.* New Haven: Yale University Press, 1984.

Huntley, Martha. *Caring, Growing, Changing: A History of the Protestant Mission in Korea.* New York: Friendship Press, 1984.

Hu Shanyuan. "Wo zai Jiangyin Lishi xuetang" (My years at Jiangyin's James Sprunt Academy). *Jiangsu wenshi ziliao xuanji* 18 (August 1986): 174–92.

Hutcheson, Paul. *China's Real Revolution.* New York: Missionary Education Movement of the United States and Canada, 1924.

Hutchison, William R. *Errand to the World: American Protestant Thought and Foreign Missions.* Chicago: University of Chicago Press, 1987.

Hyatt, Irwin T. *Our Ordered Lives Confess: Three Nineteenth-Century American Missionaries in East Shantung.* Cambridge: Harvard University Press, 1976.

———. "Protestant Missions in China, 1877–1890: The Institutionalization of Good Works." In *American Missionaries in China: Papers from Harvard Seminars,* edited by Kwang-ching Liu, pp. 93–126. Cambridge: Harvard University East Asian Research Center, 1966.

Israel, John. *Student Nationalism in China, 1927–1937.* Stanford, Calif.: Stanford University Press, 1966.

James Sprunt: A Tribute from the City of Wilmington. Raleigh: Edwards and Broughton, 1925.

Jiangyin Shengdao nuxiao jianzhang (Pamphlet on Jiangyin Christian Girls School). N.p., n.d.

Jiangyin xianzhi (Jiangyin gazetteers). Reprints of 1878 and 1920 editions. Taipei: World Publishing Company, 1968.

Jiaowu jiao'an dang (Archives on missionary affairs and cases). 7 vols. Taipei: Zhongyang yanjiuyuan, jindai lishisuo, 1974–82.

Jordan, Donald A. *The Northern Expedition: China's National Revolution of 1926–1928.* Honolulu: University Press of Hawaii, 1976.

Jourolman, Rida. *Little Golden Sister.* [Nashville: Presbyterian Church in the United States, Executive Committee of Foreign Missions], n.d.

———. "Visitors and Visiting in China." *Missionary* 40, no. 9 (September 1907): 441–42.

Junkin, Nettie DuBose, comp. *For the Glory of God: Memoirs of Dr. and Mrs. H. C. DuBose of Soochow, China.* Lewisburg, W.Va., n.d.

Keller, Rosemary Skinner. "Lay Women in the Protestant Tradition." In *Women and Religion in America,* vol. 1, *The Nineteenth Century,* edited by Rosemary Radford Reuther and Rosemary Skinner Keller, pp. 242–93. San Francisco: Harper and Row, 1981.

Kiang, Wen-han. *The Chinese Student Movement.* New York: King's Crown Press, 1948.

The Kiangyin Hospital, China. N.p., [1911].

"The Kiangyin Riot." *Missionary* 29, no. 8 (August 1896): 349–50.

Killick, J. R. "The Transformation of Cotton Marketing in the Late Nineteenth Century: Alexander Sprunt and Son of Wilmington, N.C., 1884–1956." *Business History Review* 55, no. 2 (Summer 1981): 143–69.

Kuhn, Philip. "Local Self-Government under the Republic: Problems of Control, Autonomy, and Mobilization." In *Conflict and Control in Late Imperial China*, edited by Frederic Wakeman, Jr., and Carolyn Grant, pp. 257–98. Berkeley: University of California Press, 1975.

Lacy, Creighton. "The Missionary Exodus from China." *Pacific Affairs* 28, no. 4 (December 1955): 301–14.

———. "Protestant Missions in Communist China." Ph.D. dissertation, Yale University, 1953.

Latimer, James V. *Let's Go Campin.* Shanghai, 1926.

Latourette, Kenneth Scott. *Christianity in a Revolutionary Age,* vol. 5, *The Twentieth Century outside Europe.* New York: Harper and Row, 1962.

———. *A History of Christian Missions in China.* New York: Macmillan, 1929.

Lee, Frank. "Communism and the Anti-Christian Movement." *Chinese Recorder* 56, no. 4 (April 1925): 232–35.

Lee, Jane. *Kiangyin Girls' School.* Nashville: Presbyterian Church in the United States, Executive Committee of Foreign Missions, 1925.

Lee, Virginia. "A Litany for China." *Chinese Recorder* 51, no. 9 (September 1920): 602.

———. *Little Wives of China.* Nashville: Presbyterian Church in the United States, Executive Committee of Foreign Missions, n.d.

———. *Smiles.* Nashville: Presbyterian Church in the United States, Executive Committee of Foreign Missions, 1929.

Lee, Y. L. "The Anti-Christian Movement in Canton." *Chinese Recorder* 56, no. 4 (April 1925): 220–26.

Leonard, Charles Alexander. *Repaid a Hundredfold.* Grand Rapids, Mich.: William B. Eerdmans, 1969.

Leung Yuen-sang. *The Shanghai Taotai: Linkage Man in a Changing Society, 1843–1890.* Singapore: Singapore University Press, 1990.

Lew, Timothy Tingfang. "Christian Education in China." In *Education in China,* edited by T. Y. Teng and T. T. Lew. Peking: Society for the Study of International Education, 1923.

Lin Zhiping. *Jidujiao ruhua baiqishinien jinianji* (Commemorative volume on the 170th anniversary of Christianity in China). Taipei: Yuzhouguang, 1977.

Lipphard, William B. *Out of the Storm in China: A Review of Recent Developments in Baptist Mission Fields.* Philadelphia: Judson Press, 1932.

Little, Ella Davidson. "Resuming Work at Kiangyin." *Missionary* 34, no. 5 (May 1901): 213–15.

———. "A Trip from Kiangyin." *Missionary* 36, no. 2 (February 1903): 74–76.

Little, Lacy L. *China's Call to Christendom.* Nashville: Presbyterian Church in the United States, Executive Committee of Foreign Missions, [1922].

———. "China's Famine." *Missionary* 32, no. 8 (August 1899): 361–63.

———. "Christianity and Socialism in Kiangyin." *Chinese Recorder* 44, no. 4 (April 1913): 255–57.

———. "Christian Propaganda." *Chinese Recorder* 59, no. 6 (June 1928): 391–93.
———. "'Flower Mountain,' Kiangyin." *Missionary* 32, no. 5 (May 1899): 221–22.
———. "A Group of Chinese Martyrs." *Presbyterian Survey* 22, no. 6 (June 1932): 374–76.
———. "Hospital Evangelism." *Presbyterian Survey* 15, no. 6 (June 1925): 376–77.
———. "In Satan's Stronghold." *Chinese Recorder* 48, no. 3 (March 1917): 204–5.
———. "Notes from Kiangyin." *Missionary* 34, no. 2 (February 1901): 72–73.
———. *Our Kiangyin Schools*. Nashville: Presbyterian Church in the United States, Executive Committee of Foreign Missions, 1916.
———. "Rays of Light in China's Darkness." *Presbyterian Survey* 17, no. 5 (May 1927): 303–34.
———. "Riots and Consular Assistance." *Missionary* 30, no. 6 (June 1897): 263–65.
———. *"Rivershade": A Historical Sketch of Kiangyin Station, China*. N.p., [1928].
———. "Silent Sermons in Sinim." *Presbyterian Survey* 30, no. 2 (February 1940): 71.
———. "Times of Refreshing at Kiangyin." *Missionary* 42, no. 8 (August 1909): 398–99.
———. "Two Unusual Boys of Kiangyin, China." *Presbyterian Survey* 17, no. 8 (August 1927): 483.
———. "A Visit to a Chinese Prison." *Chinese Recorder* 30, no. 8 (August 1899): 406–7.
———. "A Year at Kiangyin." *Missionary* 43, no. 12 (December 1910): 596–98.
Liu, Judith. "Contested Terrain: The Curriculum at St. Hilda's School for Girls." Unpublished manuscript, 1993.
Liu, Kwang-ching, ed. *American Missionaries in China: Papers from Harvard Seminars*. Cambridge: Harvard University East Asian Research Center, 1966.
———. *Americans and Chinese: A Historical Essay and a Bibliography*. Cambridge: Harvard University Press, 1963.
Lobenstine, E. C. "The Relation of Mission and Church." *China Christian Year Book*, no. 14 (1926): 178–95.
Lodwick, Kathleen, comp. *The Chinese Recorder Index: A Guide to Christian Missions in Asia, 1867–1941*. Wilmington, Del.: Scholarly Resources, 1986.
Luo Rongqu and Jiang Xiangze. "Research in Sino-American Relations in the People's Republic of China." In *New Frontiers in American–East Asian Relations*, edited by Warren I. Cohen, pp. 1–16. New York: Columbia University Press, 1983.
Lu Shih-chiang. "An Analysis of the Anti-Christian Thoughts of Chinese Intellectuals in the Early Republican Period." In *Symposium on the History of the Republic of China*, 2:116–45. Taipei, 1981.
Lutz, Jessie G. *China and the Christian Colleges*. Ithaca: Cornell University Press, 1971.
———. "Chinese Nationalism and the Anti-Christian Campaigns of the 1920s." *Modern Asian Studies* 10, no. 3 (1976): 395–416.
———. *Chinese Politics and Christian Missions: The Anti-Christian Movements of 1920–1928*. Notre Dame: Cross Cultural Publications, 1988.
———, ed. *Christian Missions in China: Evangelists of What?* Boston: D. C. Heath, 1965.
———. "December 9, 1935: Student Nationalism and the China Christian Colleges." *Journal of Asian Studies* 26, no. 4 (August 1967): 627–48.
———. "Students and Political Parties in the Educational Rights Movement, 1924–1928." In *Symposium on the History of the Republic of China*, 3:292–324. Taipei, 1981.

McClellan, Robert F. "Missionary Influence on American Attitudes toward China at the Turn of This Century." *Church History* 38, no. 4 (December 1969): 475–85.

McCutcheon, James M., comp. *China and America: A Bibliography of Interactions, Foreign and Domestic.* Honolulu: University of Hawaii Press, 1973.

MacGillivray, Donald, ed. *A Century of Protestant Missions in China (1807–1907).* Shanghai: American Presbyterian Mission Press, 1907.

MacInnis, Donald. *Religious Policy and Practice in Communist China: A Documentary History.* New York: Macmillan, 1972.

"Manifesto of Chinese Presbyterians at Kiangyin, Kiangsu." *Chinese Recorder* 58, no. 7 (July 1927): 471.

Masland, John W. "Missionary Influence upon American Far Eastern Policy." *Pacific Historical Review* 10, no. 3 (September 1941): 279–96.

Metallo, Michael V. "Presbyterian Missionaries and the 1911 Chinese Revolution." *Journal of Presbyterian History* 62, no. 2 (Summer 1984): 153–68.

Miao, Chester, and Frank W. Price. *Religion and Character in Christian Middle Schools.* Shanghai: Chinese Christian Education Association, 1929.

Miao Quansun, comp. *Jiangyin jinshi lu* (Account of recent events in Jiangyin). Reprint of supplement to 1920 Jiangyin gazetteer. Taipei: Chengwen, 1970.

"Minwu Jiangyin fan Yuan duli jingguo" (The 1916 anti-Yuan independence movement). *Jiangsu wenxian*, no. 15 (15 August 1980): 16.

Moffett, Carrie Lena. "Women's Conference at Kiangyin." *Missionary* 41, no. 9 (September 1908): 449–50.

Montgomery, Helen B. *Western Women in Eastern Lands: An Outline Sketch of Fifty Years of Woman's Work in Foreign Missions.* New York: Macmillan, 1910.

Murphey, Rhoads. *The Outsiders: The Western Experience in India and China.* Ann Arbor: University of Michigan Press, 1977.

Murphy, Eliza Wright. *The Story of the Kiangyin Hospital, China.* Wilmington, N.C.: Wilmington Presbyterial Auxiliary, [1930].

Neils, Patricia, ed. *United States Attitudes and Policies toward China: The Impact of American Missionaries.* Armonk, N.Y.: M. E. Sharpe, 1990.

New, Peter Kong-ming, and Yuet-Wah Cheung. "The People's Republic of China: A Socio-Historical Examination of Its Health Care Delivery." In *Third World Medicine and Social Change*, edited by John H. Morgan, pp. 173–86. Washington, D.C.: University Press of America, 1983.

Paterno, Roberto. "Devello Z. Sheffield and the Founding of the North China College." In *American Missionaries in China: Papers from Harvard Seminars*, edited by Kwang-ching Liu, pp. 42–92. Cambridge: Harvard University East Asian Research Center, 1966.

Paulsen, George E. "The Szechwan Riots of 1845 and American 'Missionary Diplomacy.'" *Journal of Asian Studies* 28, no. 2 (February 1969): 285–98.

Peake, Cyrus H. *Nationalism and Education in Modern China.* New York: Columbia University Press, 1932.

Polachek, James M. "The Moral Economy of the Kiangsi Soviet (1928–1934)." *Journal of Asian Studies* 42, no. 4 (August 1983): 805–29.

Porter, Lucius C. *China's Challenge to Christianity.* New York: Missionary Education Movement of the United States and Canada, 1924.

Presbyterian Church in the United States. *Minutes of General Assembly.* Richmond, 1913.

Presbyterian Church in the United States, Board of World Missions. *In Memory of Missionaries of the Presbyterian Church, U.S., Who Have Entered into Rest in the Years 1960–1961.* Vol. 6. Nashville, n.d.

Presbyterian Church in the United States, Executive Committee of Foreign Missions. *Annual Report.* Nashville, 1862–1911.

———. *Minutes of the China Mission.* N.p., 1894–99. .

———. *Minutes of the Mid-China Mission.* Shanghai: Presbyterian Mission Press, 1899–1941.

Presbyterian Church in the United States, Woman's Auxiliary. *How Can a Woman Help in the Million and a Half Campaign?* Kansas City, Mo., [1913].

———. *An Outline of the Woman's Auxiliary of the Presbyterian Church in the United States.* Richmond, n.d.

Price, Frank W. *The Rural Church in China.* New York: Agricultural Missions, 1948.

Price, P. Frank. "The China Conference." *Missionary* 33, no. 7 (July 1900): 309–11.

———, ed. *Our China Investment: Sixty Years of the Southern Presbyterian Church in China.* Nashville: Presbyterian Church in the United States, Executive Committee of Foreign Missions, 1927.

Rabe, Valentin H. "Evangelical Logistics: Mission Support and Resources to 1920." In *The Missionary Enterprise in China and America,* edited by John K. Fairbank, pp. 56–90. Cambridge: Harvard University Press, 1974.

———. *The Home Base of American China Missions, 1880–1920.* Cambridge: Harvard University Press, 1977.

Rawlinson, John. "Frank Rawlinson, China Missionary, 1902–1937: Veteran Deputationist." In *United States Attitudes and Policies toward China: The Impact of American Missionaries,* edited by Patricia Neils, pp. 111–32. Armonk, N.Y.: M. E. Sharpe, 1990.

Rawski, Evelyn S. "Elementary Education in the Mission Enterprise." In *Christianity in China: Early Protestant Missionary Writings,* edited by Suzanne W. Barnett and John K. Fairbank, pp. 135–51. Cambridge: Harvard University Committee on American–East Asian Relations, 1985.

Reed, James. *The Missionary Mind and American East Asia Policy, 1911–1915.* Cambridge: Harvard University Council on East Asian Studies, 1983.

Reeves, William, Jr. "Sino-American Cooperation in Medicine: The Origins of Hsiang-Ya (1902–1914)." In *American Missionaries in China: Papers from Harvard Seminars,* edited by Kwang-ching Liu, pp. 129–82. Cambridge: Harvard University East Asian Research Center, 1966.

Remer, C. F. *A Study of Chinese Boycotts.* Baltimore: John Hopkins University Press, 1933.

Reuther, Rosemary Radford, and Rosemary Skinner Keller. *Women and Religion in America.* Vol. 1, *The Nineteenth Century*; Vol. 3, 1900–1968. San Francisco: Harper and Row, 1981, 1986.

Rhoads, Edward J. "Lingnan's Response to Chinese Nationalism: The Shakee Incident (1925)." In *American Missionaries in China: Papers from Harvard Seminars,* edited by Kwang-ching Liu, pp. 183–214. Cambridge: Harvard University East Asian Research Center, 1966.

Richardson, Agnes R. *The Claimed Blessing: The Story of the Lives of the Richardsons in China, 1923–1951.* Cincinnati: C. J. Krehbiel, 1970.

Richardson, Donald W. *The Church in China*. Richmond: Presbyterian Committee of
    Publication, 1929.
Rubinstein, Murray A. "Witness to the Chinese Millennium: Southern Baptist Percep-
    tions of the Chinese Revolution, 1911–1921." In *United States Attitudes and Policies to-
    ward China: The Impact of American Missionaries*, edited by Patricia Neils, pp. 149–
    70. Armonk, N.Y.: M. E. Sharpe, 1990.
Schlesinger, Arthur, Jr. "The Missionary Enterprise and Theories of Imperialism." In
    The Missionary Enterprise in China and America, edited by John K. Fairbank, pp. 336–
    73. Cambridge: Harvard University Press, 1974.
Scott, Anne Firor. *The Southern Lady: From Pedestal to Politics, 1830–1930*. Chicago:
    University of Chicago Press, 1970.
Scott, E. C., ed. *Ministerial Directory of the Presbyterian Church in the United States,
    1861–1941*. Austin: Von Boeckmann–Jones Press, 1942.
Sec, Fong F. "Recent Developments in Chinese Government Education." *China Chris-
    tian Year Book*, no. 14 (1926): 236–41.
Shaw, Yu-ming. *An American Missionary in China: John Leighton Stuart and Chinese-
    American Relations*. Cambridge: Harvard University Council on East Asian Studies,
    1992.
———. "The Reaction of Chinese Intellectuals toward Religion and Christianity in the
    Early Twentieth Century." In *China and Christianity: Historical and Future Encoun-
    ters*, edited by James Whitehead et al., pp. 154–82. Notre Dame: University of Notre
    Dame Center for Pastoral and Social Ministry, 1979.
Shen, T. L. "A Study of the Anti-Christian Movement." *Chinese Recorder* 56, no. 4
    (April 1925): 227–31.
Shen Songshou. "Jiangyin nao jiao'an" (Jiangyin's antimissionary disturbance). *Jiangyin
    wenshi ziliao*, no. 1 (1983): 99–100.
Sims, Anastatia. "Feminism and Femininity in the New South: White Women's Organi-
    zations in North Carolina, 1883–1930." Ph.D. dissertation, University of North Car-
    olina, 1985.
Smith, Arthur H. *China in Convulsion*. New York: Fleming H. Revell, 1901.
Smith, Egbert W. *Essential Facts about Our Mission Work in China*. Nashville: Presby-
    terian Church in the United States, Executive Committee of Foreign Missions, 1925.
Song Changzhi. "Jiangyin tuwei yilun" (Recollection of breaking a siege at Jiangyin).
    Jiangsu wenxian, no. 8 (15 November 1978): 55–57.
Spence, Jonathan D. *The Search for Modern China*. New York: W. W. Norton, 1990.
Stamps, Elizabeth B. *To China with Love*. Ormond Beach, Fla., 1972.
Stauffer, Milton, ed. *China Her Own Interpreter*. New York: Student Volunteer Move-
    ment for Foreign Missions, 1927.
———. *The Christian Occupation of China*. Shanghai: China Continuation Commit-
    tee, 1922.
Street, T. Watson. *The Story of Southern Presbyterians*. Richmond: John Knox Press,
    1960.
Strother, Edgar E. *A Bolshevized China: The World's Greatest Peril*. 11th ed. Shanghai:
    North China Daily News and Herald, 1927.
Stuart, John Leighton. "Changes of Emphasis in Missionary Work." *China Mission Year
    Book*, no. 10 (1919): 65–73.

————. *Fifty Years in China*. New York: Random House, 1954.

Sweeten, Alan Richard. "The Ti-pao's Role in Local Government as Seen in Fukien Christian 'Cases,' 1863–1869." *Ch'ing-shih wen-t'i* 3, no. 6 (December 1976): 1–27.

Teng, T. Y., and T. T. Lew, eds. *Education in China*. Peking: Society for the Study of International Education, 1923.

Thompson, Ernest T. *Presbyterians in the South*. 3 vols. Richmond: John Knox Press, 1963–73.

Thompson, Katheryne. "Christmas Carols Still Ring in China." *Presbyterian Survey* 41, no. 12 (December 1951): 20.

Thomson, James C., Jr. *While China Faced West: American Reformers in Nationalist China, 1928–1937*. Cambridge: Harvard University Press, 1969.

Thomson, James C., Jr., Peter Stanley, and John Curtis Perry. *Sentimental Imperialists: The American Experience in East Asia*. New York: Harper and Row, 1981.

Thorne, Christopher. *The Limits of Foreign Policy: The West, the League, and the Far Eastern Crisis of 1931–1933*. New York: Capricorn Books, 1973.

Timmons, Sarah L. *Glorious Living: Informal Sketches of Seven Missionaries of the Presbyterian Church in the United States*. Atlanta: Presbyterian Church in the United States, Committee on Women's Work, 1937.

Tolley, Kemp. *Yangtze Patrol: The U.S. Navy in China*. Annapolis: Naval Institute Press, 1971.

Trani, Eugene. "Woodrow Wilson, China, and the Missionaries, 1913–1921." *Journal of Presbyterian History* 49, no. 4 (1971): 328–51.

Tucker, Nancy. "An Unlikely Peace: American Missionaries and the Chinese Communists, 1948–1950." *Pacific Historical Review* 45, no. 1 (1976): 97–116.

Tucker, Ruth A. *Guardians of the Great Commission: The Story of Women in Modern Missions*. Grand Rapids, Mich.: Zondervan Publishing House, 1988.

U.S. Department of State. *Papers Relating to the Foreign Relations of the United States*. Washington, D.C.: Government Printing Office, 1861–1932.

Varg, Paul A. *Missionaries, Chinese, and Diplomats: The American Protestant Missionary Movement in China, 1890–1952*. Princeton, N.J.: Princeton University Press, 1958.

————. "The Missionary Response to the Nationalist Revolution." In *The Missionary Enterprise in China and America*, edited by John K. Fairbank, pp. 311–35. Cambridge: Harvard University Press, 1974.

Wakeman, Frederic, Jr. "Localism and Loyalism during the Ch'ing Conquest of Kiangnan: The Tragedy of Chiang-yin." In *Conflict and Control in Late Imperial China*, edited by Frederic Wakeman, Jr., and Carolyn Grant, pp. 43–85. Berkeley: University of California Press, 1975.

Wallace, Edward W. "Christian Education in 1925." *China Christian Year Book*, no. 14 (1926): 224–35.

Walters, Laura. "Mid-China Mission: Kiangyin Station (1895–1951), An Annotated Bibliography." Unpublished manuscript, 1979.

Webster, James B. *Christian Education and the National Consciousness in China*. New York: E. P. Dutton, 1923.

Webster, John C. B. "American Presbyterian Global Mission Policy: An Overview of 150 Years." *American Presbyterians* 65, no. 2 (Summer 1987): 71–84.

Wehrle, Edmund S. *Britain, China, and the Antimissionary Riots, 1891–1900*. Minneapolis: University of Minnesota Press, 1966.

Welter, Barbara. "She Hath Done What She Could: Protestant Women's Missionary Careers in Nineteenth Century America." *American Quarterly* 30, no. 5 (Winter 1978): 624–38.

West, Philip. *Yenching University and Sino-Western Relations, 1916–1952*. Cambridge: Harvard University Press, 1976.

White, Hugh V. *Southern Presbyterians under Fire*. Richmond: Presbyterian Committee of Publication, [1927].

Whitehead, James, et al., eds. *China and Christianity: Historical and Future Encounters*. Notre Dame: University of Notre Dame Center for Pastoral and Social Ministry, 1979.

Wiest, Jean-Paul. "Lineage and Patterns of Conversion in Guangdong." *Ch'ing-shih wen-t'i* 4, no. 7 (June 1982): 1–32.

———. *Maryknoll in China: A History, 1918–1955*. Armonk, N.Y.: M. E. Sharpe, 1988.

Wilbur, C. Martin. *The Nationalist Revolution in China, 1923–1928*. Cambridge: Cambridge University Press, 1984.

Wilcox, Marion. *Chinese Witnesses for Christ*. Nashville: Presbyterian Church in the United States, Executive Committee of Foreign Missions, n.d.

———. *Vi Wo's Favorite Game*. Nashville: Presbyterian Church in the United States, Executive Committee of Foreign Missions, 1936.

Williams, Henry F. *In China: A Sketch of the Foreign Missions of the Presbyterian Church, U.S., in China*. Nashville: Presbyterian Church in the United States, Executive Committee of Foreign Missions, [1923].

———. *In Four Continents: A Sketch of the Foreign Missions of the Presbyterian Church, U.S., in China*. Richmond: Presbyterian Committee of Publication, 1910.

———. *Medical Missions in China*. Nashville: Presbyterian Church in the United States, Executive Committee of Foreign Missions, [1928].

Wilmington Presbyterial Auxiliary. *George C. Worth Memorial Booklet*. Wilmington, N.C., [1937].

———. *Memorial Appreciations of Mrs. George C. (Emma Chadbourn) Worth*. Wilmington, N.C., 1926.

———. *Minutes of Annual Meeting*. Wilmington, N.C., 1901–54.

Winsborough, Hallie P. *The Woman's Auxiliary, Presbyterian Church, U.S.* Richmond: Presbyterian Committee of Publication, 1927.

Woodbridge, Samuel I. *Fifty Years in China*. Richmond: Presbyterian Committee of Publication, 1918.

Woollcott, Philip. "Fifty-four Years of the Y.M.C.A." *The University [of North Carolina] Magazine*, April 1914, pp. 285–94.

Worth, Charles W. "A Chinese Christian Church." *Presbyterian Survey* 19, no. 7 (July 1929): 419–20.

———. "The Eternal Struggle." *Chinese Recorder* 72, no. 10 (October 1944): 532–37.

———. "Memorial to Charles William Worth." In *Minutes, the Presbytery of Wilmington*, Spring 1973, appendix, p. A.

———. *Mr. King of "In Statu Quo."* Nashville: Presbyterian Church in the United States, Executive Committee of Foreign Missions, 1925.

———. *Pioneering in China*. Nashville: Presbyterian Church in the United States, Executive Committee of Foreign Missions, 1936.

Worth, Emma C. "The First Christian Wedding in Kiangyin." *Missionary* 37, no. 8 (August 1904): 388–89.

———. *Woman's Ward, Kiangyin Hospital.* N.p., n.d.

Worth, George C. *Hospital Work in Kiangyin, China.* Nashville: Presbyterian Church in the United States, Executive Committee of Foreign Missions, 1925.

———. "Wearing Chinese Dress and Queue." *Missionary* 30, no. 1 (January 1897): 22–23.

Worth, George C., Ruth Worth, and Charles Worth. *Messages from a Missionary Family.* N.p., [1936].

Wu, Chao-kwang. *The International Aspect of the Missionary Movement in China.* Baltimore: Johns Hopkins University Press, 1930.

Xie Jili. "Huaerde ho Jiangyin Fuyin yiyuan" (George Worth and the Jiangyin Gospel Hospital). *Jiangyin wenshi ziliao,* no. 9 (1988): 120–21.

Yamamoto, Tatsuro, and Sumiko Yamamoto. "The Anti-Christian Movement in China, 1922–1927." *Far Eastern Quarterly* 12, no. 2 (February 1953): 133–47.

Yang Jinxiu and Chen Liangheng. "Jiangyin xian Fuyin yiyuan jianshi" (A brief history of Jiangyin County's Gospel Hospital). *Jiangyin wenshi ziliao,* no. 5 (1984): 58–62.

Yip, Ka-che. *Religion, Nationalism, and Chinese Students: The Anti-Christian Movement of 1922–1927.* Bellingham: Western Washington University Center for East Asian Studies, 1980.

Young, Marilyn. *The Rhetoric of Empire: American China Policy, 1895–1901.* Cambridge: Harvard University Press, 1968.

Zhao Fusan. "The Chinese Revolution and Foreign Missions Seen through the May Fourth Movement." *Far East Reporter,* June 1980, pp. 3–19.

INDEX

Guling resort, 104, 117
Guomindang. *See* Nationalist Party

Haden, R. A., 20, 22–23, 28, 81, 94, 96, 133;
    founder of Jiangyin Station, 10–12; and
    Jiangyin riot, 13–18; 1900 evacuation, 26;
    transferred to Suzhou, 27; death of, 64,
    172 (n. 79); letters home, 141
Hall, Margaret Sprunt, 146
Hangzhou: mission station at, 26, 28, 86,
    142; as refuge, 114
Hangzhou Christian College, 81
Hanna, Jennie, 145–46
Hospital: patient fees at, 31, 36, 57, 185
    (n. 67); patients at, 33, 36; opening of,
    35; women's ward, 35, 36, 46; fire at, 36;
    personnel, 36, 46, 57, 123; and school
    registration, 88–89; evangelical work at,
    92–93; under government control, 130,
    155
Houcheng (outstation), 98, 101; Commu-
    nist activity at, 76
Huan Chi-yao, 11–12, 13–14, 17
Huashu (outstation), 103, 110; during
    Japanese occupation, 124–25
Hudson, George, 10, 110
Hudson, W. H., 146, 148
Hu Shi, 82

Idol destruction, 101–2
Idol money, 96, 101, 102
Imperialism in China, 4–5; and missions,
    3, 10, 70, 128, 130, 158. *See also* Cultural
    imperialism
Indigenous church. *See* Three-self
    movement
Inflation: in postwar period, 127
Itinerating work, 22, 27, 94, 95, 103–8,
    126–27; means of travel in, 105–6, 126;
    curtailed after 1949, 129

James Sprunt Male Academy, 44, 47; brass
    band, 25, 46, 63, 93; founding of, 39;
    charitable work, 48–49; student unrest,
    48–49, 71, 72; student union, 67–68;
    military drills, 68; graduates of, 70. *See
    also* Boys school

Japanese-American relations, 123–24
Japanese invasion, 6, 89–90, 115–17; stu-
    dent protest over, 112; preparations for
    in Jiangyin, 112–13, 114; missionary state-
    ments on, 115–16; and Jiangyin, 116–19
Jernigan, T. R. (U.S. consul-general,
    Shanghai), 14, 17–18
Jiang Jieshi. *See* Chiang Kai-shek
Jiangsu province, 50, 95; Communist
    movement in, 73
Jiangyin: as seat of county government, 6;
    geographic setting, 6–8; strategic impor-
    tance, 7–8; captured by Qing armies, 8;
    captured by Japanese, 116–19, 155; "lib-
    erated" by Red Army, 129
Jiangyin anti-Christian riot (1896), 13–19
Jiangyin Board of Education, 87
Jiangyin Chamber of Commerce, 51
Jiangyin County: population, 6; geo-
    graphic setting, 6–7
Jiangyin Educational Association, 62
Jiangyin forts, 8, 14, 25, 41, 45, 51–52, 58,
    61; soldiers' uprising at, 44–45; strength-
    ening of, 112, 116; seized by Japanese, 117
Jiangyin gentry: initial opposition to mis-
    sionaries, 10, 12; support of missionaries,
    53–55, 62–64, 72, 93, 167 (n. 32); and
    Christianity, 54
Jiangyin magistrate, 35, 36, 41, 72; relations
    with missionaries, 10, 20, 45, 55, 63, 93,
    148. *See also* Liu Yan Kwang
Jiangyin missionaries: monthly gatherings,
    28, 95; peacekeeping efforts, 51–52; daily
    prayer meetings, 92
Jiangyin mission field, 22, 91, 94; statistics
    on, 110
Jiangyin Presbytery, 81
Jiangyin Station: thirtieth anniversary
    celebration (1925), 1, 62–64; layout,
    8–9; establishment of, 10–11; reputation
    among Chinese Christians, 19; as
    refuge, 45, 53, 59–60, 113, 114; mission
    staff, 65, 77, 94; 1927 evacuation, 71–72,
    74–75, 79; National Revolutionary
    Army occupation of, 72–73, 75; in exile
    during Japanese invasion, 118; destroyed
    by Japanese, 118–19; 1939 reopening of,

Made in the USA
Lexington, KY
26 January 2015